FASHION IN HISTORY

MARYBELLE S. BIGELOW
San Diego State College

Apparel in the Western World

BURGESS PUBLISHING COMPANY • Minneapolis, Minnesota

To Mary—the dearest of friends, a silent driver—whose expectations of the author have been a continuing inspiration.

FOREWORDS

This volume draws together a voluminous treasury of information regarding the garments of men throughout time. Professor Bigelow develops through untiring research highly exciting descriptions and illustrations of costumes, their construction and function. The author further elaborates on the most important concept of why the clothing needs are in constant flux and how this reflects the tempo of the era. This rich omnibus of costume study will serve as a guide and resource to all areas touched by the garb of mankind. Arenas of study such as art, theater, fashion, textiles and history will benefit immeasurably by this compilation.

The illustrative continuum enriches the text by unfolding visually expressive aspects of man as he appeared in the garments discussed. As the author skillfully handles the study of each era, we are encouraged to look beyond the surface into why this particular fabric or design developed at that time.

The other two important areas covered in this book, costume design and fashion illustration, bring practical application to the present day. Although these sections are covered as useful ways of interpreting costume, they never descend to simplified "how-to-do-it" adaptations but rather as ways of seeing into the mode of the moment and going on from there.

Jo Ann L. Tanzer
Professor of Art
San Diego State College

The role of fashion in history is that of a reflector. It mirrors through evolving styles of personal adornment, sociological and political concepts of a given time period. In this text, *Fashion in History*, the three interacting aspects of fashion are explored, history of costume, costume design, and fashion illustration. The author relates the changing esthetics that dominate clothing forms and accessories as these in turn are influenced by social attitudes of a parallel time span. Thus the concept of the importance of costume as a social record is developed.

The impact of this concept on the total understanding of the many specialists concerned with personal, individual expression through fashion—be they costume historians, costume designers, fashion reporters, visual fashion reporters or recorders, or designers for the theater—establishes the sociological relevance of apparel. The creative costume designer may study his area of specialization under varying curricular circumstances, but the motivation for his contemporary innovations is often given impetus by researching past clothing forms.

Long ago great artists were also fashion designers and fashion illustrators who had apprenticed in the studios of masters or an atelier of an art academy. Today art schools and universities or college departments of art or home economics introduce the basics of the designing field to student designers. Mastery of the three-dimensional sculptural esthetic nature of clothing combines with the technical skills of the construction of wearing apparel.

History of clothing offers these students resources for contemporary adaptations. Their research is expanded by visual records left by fashion illustrations, past and present, which express through drawing the social attitudes of a given time. The fashion illustration of the past communicates the importance of social attitudes just as the designers who create fashion incorporate social and political concepts current at the time of the creation of a particular fashion into gowns, coats, and suits.

Thus, *Fashion in History* becomes an omnibus exploring the three facets of fashion to expand students' understanding of the relevance of clothing forms, which in turn will broaden the students' creative potential. No costumes constructed—be they body coverings of a pharoah of Egypt or the personal adornments of the *beautiful people* —has worth because of their construction alone. They must be esthetically of their time, functional for their time, and skillfully made to establish their integrity as a product of creative activity. Professor Bigelow deftly relates the recorded historical facts with a perceptive artist's understanding of the effect on the life style of a specific period of the esthetic concepts of that time.

Janice Yount
Assistant Professor of Home Economics
San Diego State College

PREFACE

Fashion has three facets: history of costume, costume design, and fashion illustration. Contemporary forms and styles are dependent on and indebted to past costume forms and fancies. The record of these forms and styles has been left by master painters and sculptors. Through this legacy we can put together patterns of past civilizations. These resources often give rise to inventive contemporary adaptations. The student of fashion design must be aware of these modes of his antecedents. Thus, historic costume is one of the significant contributors to present-day costume design. The young designer gives form to a design concept for a costume in a number of ways—draping, pattern drafting, and drawing or sketching. The last is most readily mastered and clearly bridges the content development of this text. Fashion drawing and illustration report current vogues and record fashions of a specific period. These reports and records are dependent on sensitive and skillful drawing. By combining these three facets of fashion—the history of costume, the procedures of designing, and the qualities of drawing required in creating a reporting record—a comprehensive and unified approach to the total area of personal adornment develops.

ACKNOWLEDGMENTS

I wish to thank the following whose great help has assisted in abstract and concrete ways in putting together this book: Conde Nast Publications, Inc., for allowing the reproduction of several illustrations in this text listed specifically in the credits; the Metropolitan Museum of Art, New York City; the British Museum, London; the Brooklyn Museum, Brooklyn; Victoria and Albert Museum, London; Museo Archeologico, Florence; Museo Nuevo Capitolino, Rome; the Tannhauser Foundation, Inc., New York; Museo Nazionale della Terme, Rome; the Pierre Matisse Gallery, New York; the Costume Institute, Metropolitan Museum of Art, New York, specifically Paul Stone, Librarian, for his help and memory when mine momentarily lapsed; Mr. and Mrs. Walter C. Baker; Paul H. Bonner, Jr.; and most particularly Jeanne Dillman for too many reasons to list here; Kenneth G. Kingrey, Professor of Art, University of Hawaii, a former instructor of mine whose past guidance and motivation have been invaluable; the late Louise P. Sooy, Professor Emeritus, University of California, Los Angeles, who first introduced me to the many facets of fashion; George Sorenson, Associate Dean and Professor of Art, San Diego State College, for his encouragement and understanding; JoAnn L. Tanzer, Professor of Art, San Diego State College, colleague, for her wise criticism of the illustrations prepared for this text and for her kind words in the foreword; Janice Yount, Assistant Professor of Home Economics, San Diego State College, for her helpful comments and her foreword; Dr. Harriet Haskell, Professor of English, San Diego State College, for her discerning editorial review; the production staff of Burgess Publishing Company for their work on the design of the book; and last but by no means least, Olive Whaley Schmidt, without whose patience, wisdom, encouragement and help the manuscript would never have been.

M.S.B.

CONTENTS

PART I—HISTORY OF COSTUME

PART II—FASHION DESIGN

PART III—FASHION ILLUSTRATION

PART 1

HISTORY OF COSTUME

INTRODUCTION

Necessity, convenience, and ego have combined in determining the manner in which man clothes his person. The pocket and belt were invented to meet the needs of the hunter. They were utilitarian devices rather than articles of clothing, appearing long before there were tunics to girdle. When man found that his search for food was hindered by carrying in his hands the tools he had fashioned for hunting, he freed one hand by making a pouch from an animal's skin. Into this he put the weapons of the hunt. Then he freed both hands by inventing a belt to hold the pouch about his body. Need and convenience also gave rise to devising crude items of apparel to be worn on the body. Warmth and protection from the elements motivated the selection of animal skins as the first body coverings. But primitive man felt other more complex needs connected with his ego and his relation to other men and supernatural forces. For these reasons he stained his face with vegetable juices, in garish designs. He also used powdered chalk and colored earth for early cosmetic decorations. In time, the patterns painted on his person came to have specific meanings and defended him in battle and protected him from evil. Slashes on his skin served as a means of individual decoration or tribal identity in a way not unlike the dueling scars of university students of Austria and Germany not so long ago. These scars indicated personal prowess and established a peer group identity, simultaneously functioning as a type of personal adornment. Seed, stone, and shell beads worn by prehistoric males attested to the affluence of the wearer. But when they proved hampering to the more masculine pursuits of the hunt and war, women donned these success symbols of that age. Then as now, women were decorated according to their own or their husbands' degree of wealth. Those in less fortunate circumstances wore inexpensive imitations, but the imitations were meant to represent wealth. Necklaces for men again became a fashion after the mid-twentieth century. Young men denying the affluent society of this period affected single strand necklaces as a symbol of the rejection of the establishment. The fashions introduced by the Hippies in the late 1960s brought costumes full circle. Since this group wished to return to a simple, almost primitive society, the garb they wore reflected this desire. The stone and shell beads of these "flower children" reminded one of the ornaments of various primitive cultures, however different the needs fulfilled in wearing them.

One garment form, the tunic, was common to all early cultures regardless of the contact between them. Each kingdom, tribe, or country adapted and refined this early garment to meet the needs of the established social order. The loincloth was also a basic form devised by early man as a simple body covering. Both of these simple garments and the square or rectangular cape were logical forms. The tunic, made of a length of woven material or animal skin, folded in half, sewn up the sides, with a slit for a neck opening, was a direct design. The cape, which was the obvious refinement of the rhino or animal skin, was also an evolutionary apparel item. It is not surprising that these types of clothing appeared in many different geographical locations as the earliest means of covering, protecting, and

3

decorating the person. As each culture developed weaving techniques and refined them, the decorative aspects of clothing received greater attention. As the trade between areas expanded, one culture adopted and improved the refinements of another. Improvisation of garment forms to meet the needs of the people were made in direct proportion to the level of cultural sophistication.

As clothing forms and fashions of each age changed, figure emphasis areas and pose patterns developed. There has been a direct relationship between the part of the figure receiving the focus of attention and the resulting posturing, pose pattern, or movement. During the Egyptian period the head and shoulders received emphasis and were elaborately decorated with wigs and large collars of beads or jewels. In more modern times, when the posterior was given silhouette importance, the bustle and train were added to the costume. The Greeks emphasized the body as a whole and swathed it in the draped chiton. This demanded that the wearer learn to walk with a graceful, gliding step, a walk which in turn brought attention to the emphasis area, the entire body. Ancient cultures of Egypt, Greece, and Rome treated the human figure "in puris naturalibus" but without the sexual considerations or implications of the plastic garb of the 1960s which was apparently devised to deny the Puritan ethic. The body, thus clothed, however, had none of the grace or dignity of the figure seen beneath the gossamer gala gown of the Egyptian era. The many different costume details that evolved also controlled the posturing and activity patterns of the wearer. For example, the maneuvering of the beruffled train of the late nineteenth century required activity skills and demanded specific pose patterns. The Spanish ruffs of the sixteenth century, the paniers of the eighteenth century, the hoop skirts of the nineteenth century, and the fringed chemises of the early twentieth century are other illustrations. Ruffs doubtless limited the gesturing movements of the head. Paniers caused ladies to use a swaying step, leading first with one side and then the other to avoid colliding with nearby objects. The geometric construction of the fashions of the late twentieth century demanded posturing that defied the hinge and ball construction of the human body. Details like coiffures, eyebrows, and lips; fans, gloves, and walking sticks; capes, skirts, and bodices combined to direct attention to parts of the figure considered most significant during a particular fashion period.

Forms of personal adornment appear, fade, and then reappear centuries later. As a rule, the first stage of a style development is simple, a direct form. Each following phase becomes more and more exaggerated. When the elaboration and exaggeration become too cumbersome or grotesque, the style disappears to be supplanted by another that will move through the same cycle. Up to a certain point the slave of fashion has willingly accepted the limitations imposed by the exaggerations of a style. In each age he has excitedly awaited these limiting innovations and accepted them with only minor personal adaptations. The human being is marvelously adaptive, and this is abundantly clear when we review the way he has decorated his person. Such a review is possible because each change has been recorded in stone or with paint or by photograph. To follow these changes constitutes the intriguing study of the history of costume.

Gown and shendot, male; kalasiris and necklace, female (Egypt: XIX Dynasty, permission The Metropolitan Museum of Art, Rogers Fund, 1915)

Chapter 1

COSTUMES OF ANCIENT EGYPT

*W*HILE *the Paleolithic peoples of Western Europe were still coping with the Ice Age, those of Northern Africa had settled into a basic but comfortable existence. The ancient culture of Egypt began along the banks of the Nile River. Egyptians of this early period benefited from heavy rains and luxurious vegetation. But their simple yet abundant life was forced into different living patterns as the climate changed, turning the area into a desert region. With the changes in climate, groups of people banded together forming small communities around the many desert oases and along the banks of the Nile. Slowly these sparsely populated desert communities developed a social order evolving into independent states. In time, these states united, forming two*

5

kingdoms, Upper and Lower Egypt. It is believed that the two kingdoms were joined about 3700 B.C. by a king called Menes, though some authorities set the date of unification at 2900 B.C. under the leadership of King Namar. The political and social system that developed was dominated by a supreme ruler, or pharoah. He had complete control of all land, power to establish the nobility, and total direction of the masses of the population who lived at the level of slaves. The economic base of this culture was agricultural, although lesser industries such as stone cutting, metal working, goldsmithing, and pottery making made contributions to the financial status of the country. These industries, though somewhat limited in productive capacity, were based on highly refined techniques. A system of commerce using the products of Egyptian agriculture and industry was carried on between the Bedouins of Sinai and the inhabitants of the Aegean region. By 3000 B.C. the Egyptians had invented a pictorial method of writing and a calendar. As this ancient culture become more sophisticated, the Egyptians tamed animals, learned to use metal, and developed a unique system of irrigation. The Nile river, thus harnessed, contributed to the economic stability of Egypt. During the early developmental stages, the powerful pharoahs and their appointed nobles established a feudalistic form of government. The pharoah's power was eventually eroded away as the strength of the noble class increased. The stronger nobility expanded the leisure class activities and engaged in boating on the Nile, hunting fowl and hippopotamus in the papyrus, and in general enjoying the pleasures of outdoor living. Houses of this class were well built and the utilitarian objects in them well designed and well constructed of wood, glazed pottery, ivory, and metal. Utensils and furniture were decorated with carved images of the animal and plant life of the region, for the Egyptians were aware of the powers of nature and honored these forces by such carvings.

Sun and river were important to the formal religion of Egypt, based on the belief that the warmth of the sun, the waters of the river, the trees, grass, birds, flowers and grains were the gifts of nature. The sun became the mighty god Ra (Re or Amen-Ra) who sailed through the sky each day from east to west. The religion of Ra was worldly; he was thought to be a dynamic masculine deity. In contrast to the sun-god, the Osirian religion was based on a belief in afterlife and the creative power of the river. It was part of the cult of Isis and fundamentally a maternalistic religion. The river was thought to be the resurrected Osiris, consort of the goddess Isis. He became the god of death and king of the Dark Nile, the river of the world after death. The rebirth of Osiris was symbolized by the rising each year of the river by which the Egyptians lived and which nourished the crops that supplied their food. These ancient people identified with the annual life cycle and believed that after death, rebirth to a new life was possible. The strength of this belief contributed much to the total development of the Egyptian civilization.

The ancient Egyptian temperament, dominated by religion rich in symbolic imagery, influenced the rigid concepts inherent in their art and architecture. Symbols of formal worship became design motifs not only for their architecture but for their clothing as well. The lotus, the water plant growing on the banks of the inner waterways of the Nile, became identified with the Upper Kingdom. Modified lotus designs were used to decorate the capitals of the massive columns of tombs and temples of that region. The papyrus, the dominant growth of the delta area, was stylized and employed as a design element characteristic of the Lower Kingdom.

During the early Egyptian periods, women were not given a high social position. A queen portrayed in sculpture with her husband would be depicted as a small subordinate figure by his feet. Later, women were held in high esteem and were awarded a portion of their husbands' wealth as part of marriage contracts. Another sign of female importance in Egypt was the number of women who became supreme rulers. Hatshepsut, Nefertiti, and Cleopatra were three such queenly rulers who have been remembered down through the ages for differing reasons. Queens often wore false beards symbolizing their authority and establishing a masculine identity.

Much remains of this civilization because Egyptians built their tombs and temples of permanent materials. The information available for a time span covering thousands of years presents an enduring picture of their cultural development. The Old Kingdom, especially between the years 2800-2400 B.C., was a period of state organization, refinement of the arts, and economic prosperity. This period of tranquility and stability was reflected in the costumes. Linen fabrics and cloth made of ramie fiber were used to make the simple gown and skirt forms worn by both men and women. The constancy of elegant simplicity in all forms of personal adornment persisted until about 1500 B.C. Invasions, followed by economic expansion, contributed to the introduction of more sumptuous garments and accessories. Under the New Kingdom a wider range of colors was introduced as well as the fashion of wearing garments designed after the patterns of those used in previous periods. The practice of covering the figure completely had been introduced through contacts with Semitic people. This had great influence on costume forms. Large and elaborate wigs, elegant jewelry forms, and intricate pleating accented the emphasis areas of the body which included the head, the shoulders, and the waist. Though the accessories became more sumptuous the basic garment forms retained a simplicity revealing the nude bodies beneath gossamer gowns.

Kilt with goffered front panel (Egypt: V Dynasty, permission The Metropolitan Museum of Art, Rogers Fund, 1926)

BASIC GARMENTS OF ANCIENT EGYPT (3700 B.C.—525 B.C.)

LOINCLOTH
(3400 B.C.-525 B.C.)
Men and Women

The loincloth was the basic garment of both men and women in Egypt. In its earliest form it was a simple length of fabric, rectangular in shape, taken directly from the loom on which it was woven. The original manner of donning this one-piece body covering was to wrap the fabric around the figure beginning at the left front, across the back, and then to the center front. The loincloth was held in place by a belt that was tied or knotted in front.

This wound and belted garment was usually thigh length. Egyptian men also wore a shaped loincloth. This was a T-form and worn between the legs with the horizontal section covering the back of the figure as well as the front just below the waist. It was tied by tapes in front, holding the section that was passed between the legs in place.

shenti

The *shenti*, a version of the loincloth, was put about the figure in the same manner as the earliest style with the exception that the first left corner protruded above the waist. The fabric was then wound one and three-quarter times around the figure, ending in the back. The outer end was brought over the left shoulder and tied to the first or protruding end. This style was belted with a long sash that was tied in back, the ends trailing to the level of the ankles. A decorative series of woven tassels was suspended from the front of the sash belt. A simpler fabric arrangement without the shoulder strap but with a pleated or goffered front panel was called the

kilt

kilt. The length of the shenti and kilt varied throughout the centuries. During the Old Kingdom the general wearing length covered the figure from waist to mid-thigh, but later the hemline dropped in the male style, falling first to the calf length and then to the ankle. The female wearing fashion of this basic garment was the same as that of the male, but the garment covered the figure from just under the bust and extended to just above the ankle bone. Women wore the belts just under the breasts. Men wore the longer versions belted at the waist with long decorative sashes.

PROCARDIUM
(2000 B.C.)
Men and Women

The *procardium* was also a wrapped garment and worn by both men and women. A rectangular length of material was wound around the body in the same manner as the loincloth; however one (often decorative) shoulder strap was added. In the female version, this strap was attached to the upper edge of the bust-to-ankle procardium at a point between the breasts. The waist-to-calf or waist-to-ankle length male procardium positioned the shoulder strap off center and secured it in back on the opposite side. Later versions were made with two straps which were very decorative. These V-shaped straps were fastened in the center of the top edge of the bust-revealing garment. As this garment was refined in styling, both men and women wore the bust-to-ankle variation. There is no visual record of the rear arrangement of the double strap version. It was worn with or without a belt. If belted, the belt was worn just below the bust. The design of the procardium belt varied,

Double strap male procardium

Kalasiris (Egypt: V Dynasty, permission The Metropolitan Museum of Art, Rogers Fund, 1926)

Gala gown

but one style consisted of a long band about five inches wide. This was tied in front with the trailing ends reaching to the hem. The front tabs were often decorated with small metal shapes and semiprecious stones. These belts added elegance to an otherwise basic body covering.

KALASIRIS
(1000 B.C.)
Men and Women

The *kalasiris* was a simple garment made from a rectangular length of material. The piece of fabric used in making this tunic was twice the height of the wearer from shoulder to ankle. It was folded in half with a slit cut on the fold to create the neckline. The side seams of the sleeveless kalasiris were sewn together, tapering from hem to armhole. The version with sleeves had straight side seams, slit or round neckline, and elbow-length sleeves. They were wider or flared at the open end. The latter style was worn with a belt or girdle tied at the normal waistline. Depicted as a close fitting garment by the artists of the period, the kalasiris was actually amply cut, allowing for ease of movement.

GOWN
(800-600 B.C.)
Men and Women

The gown, simple in construction, was a garment worn for festive occasions and often referred to as the *gala* gown. It was made of very fine linen that was often heavily starched. The rectangular length of fabric was twice the height of the wearer and the width was that of the wearer's outstretched arms. The fabric was folded in half covering the figure front and back, from shoulder to ankle. A small round hole was cut on the fold forming the neckline. This versatile garment was revealing, often worn as the only body covering. It was worn either loose or belted. Because of the sheer quality of the fabric and the heavy starching, elaborate pleated effects were possible. These pleats were concentrated in the center front, created by creasing the front section in vertical accordian folds and by bringing the back forward and pleating the front edges in the same manner. A slight side drape was thus created over the hips, and pleated sleeves were formed when the gala gown was tightly girdled. The center pleating radiated upward over the arms, adding breadth to the shoulder line. This festival garment of royalty was decorated with large, jeweled collars and elaborately designed belts and shendots. Egyptian women often wore huge circular collars about their necks and decorative braided belts about their waists beneath the gown. Men, on occasion, wore the loose gala gowns over kilts but generally as the only body covering.

GALA SKIRT
(2000 B.C.)
Men

The gala skirt was a wrap-around garment worn in much the same manner as the loincloth. It was wound around the figure one and one-half times and was held in place by a girdle. The gala skirt varied in length from waist to mid-thigh or waist to mid-calf. The curved front panel, often goffered (pleated), was the distinguishing design detail of this male skirt. If the skirt had a smooth front panel, the large truncated triangular tab, the *shendot*, was worn as a decorative device. This decoration took many different forms. It was either flat and encrusted with jewels and metal shapes or a stiff three-dimensional projection. This was usually goffered or pleated with vertical accordian pleats that radiated from the center to the wide hemline. This style might have been created by gathering the skirt in the front, creasing it into pleats, and securing it with a belt. The flat triangular versions varied in size and shape from long, thin, ankle-length tabs to wide forms that extended to the knees. These styles were attached to belts which encircled the figure at the waist. The shendot was introduced as a decorative male accessory some time after 2500 B.C. When the gala skirt was worn without the shendot it was girdled with a variety of belts. The belts were frequently elaborately patterned and trimmed with fringe. The gala skirt, like the gala gown, was a royal garment.

shendot

TUNIC
Women

The tunic worn by Egyptian women was a slender garment with deep bat-wing sleeves and a long center slit from waist to hem. The finest linen was used for women's clothing, designed to expose the body. The tunic was such a garment, made of transparent fabric, revealing the nude figure beneath the tight fitting blouse section and through the deep skirt slit. Several important queens, including Nefertiti, preferred transparent fashions, and the tunic was said to be this handsome queen's favorite style. In the Egyptian culture interest in the nude figure was a dominant factor in all clothing design. Nobles and servants often went without clothes, and in the case of court dancers they seldom wore more than decorative belts. These enhanced their supple bodies and the movements of the dances they performed.

Man's Nemes head-dress, kilt, shendot (2060-1788 B.C.)

CAPES
Men and Women
rectangular cape

While wraps worn for warmth were not necessary in the warm climate of Egypt, thin outer garments or capes were often used. Two basic styles persisted for many centuries. The earliest cape form was rectangular. It was made from a length of fabric slightly longer than twice the height of the wearer and was about thirty inches wide. It was

oval cape

fur and animal skin wraps

HAIR STYLES
(300-500 B.C.)
Men and Women wigs

Goffered gala skirt and wig

placed across the back, brought forward over the shoulders, and arranged over the upper arms. The rectangular cape was fastened in the front with a pin or clasp. The clasp was positioned either at the level of the breastbone or just above the waistline. This cape was never belted, and the ends hung loosely to the ground. The oval style was made of sheer fabric cut in the form of a circle or an oval. The diameter was equal to the width of the wearer's outstretched arms. A round or eliptical hole was cut in the center for the neck opening. If the neckline was small, a slit was made in the back. It is possible that in some variations of the oval cape the slit extended from the neckline to the hem. A pin was used at the back of the neck to hold this wrap snugly about the throat.

Tanned animal skins, usually leopard, were worn by warriors. These furs or skins were never cut or sewn together but were left in the shape of the animal. The skins of the legs were loosely knotted in the front with the main body of the animal covering the shoulders and the upper arms.

It was customary for both men and women of the nobility or high economic station to shave their heads. This practice was dictated by the attention these people gave cleanliness. In place of their natural hair they wore wigs made of natural hair, wool, flax, palmfiber, felt, or other substitute materials. Wigs were generally black; however, deep blue and gilded wigs were also worn. The wig was constructed over a close fitting skull cap made of fiber netting. The method used in attaching the natural hair or substitute materials to the net cap created a large wig with the hair standing out from the skull. This kind of construction formed a type of insulation and protected the wearer's head from the hot rays of the sun. The wigs were intricately arranged and very decorative. Wig styles ranged from simple closely cropped head-hugging designs, during the Old Kingdom, to complicated styles of later periods. Early wigs had curls arranged in rows from the crown of the head to just below the ears. The larger versions were made of human hair with lambs' wool added to create the full bouffant size desired, falling straight from the crown to the shoulders. Wig styles favored by men were imitated by women during the early centuries. Generally the closely cropped style worn over a completely bald head was preferred by both. Later women reversed this preference, wearing wigs of great bulk over their natural hair. Their own hair was allowed to show beneath the wig.

gala wigs
(1000 B.C.)

Gala wigs of festive design with golden decorations and colorful braid or bead trimmings were worn much as hats are today. By this time the fetish of cleanliness had been abandoned. A "crown cap" of golden pendant discs, linked closely together, was often worn over the wig all but obscuring the hair. Gold circlettes and colorful braid headbands were worn low on the forehead. Hair and wigs were an important part of the total Egyptian costume. Great care was taken in arranging both wig and real hair. Throughout most of the periods shaved heads remained the sign of nobility and were always covered. The famous bust of Nefertiti indicates she wore her crown without a wig, at times. She was noted, however, for her large, deep blue wigs.

head pad

During one period, beginning about 1400 B.C., a shaved, artificially elongated head was the fashion. The distortion of the head was achieved by wearing a padded form at the nape of the neck. This strange vogue was originated by the daughters of Nefertiti, whose heads had been deformed at birth and whose appearance was copied by the women of the court. Early hair and wig styles were short, with small curls arranged in horizontal rows. Wigs were worn by adults while children's hair was cut, shaved, and styled in a number of unique coifs. Young girls' heads were often shaved except for two locks in front of each ear. These were then either curled into long corkscrew curls or braided. At other periods the head was shaved except for the top or crown of the head. The hair that was left was then braided and allowed to fall down the back or over one shoulder. Young boys had their heads shaved except for the "youth lock," a small curl originating in front of one ear. In time the short, round adult wig fashions were discarded and during the Middle Kingdom shoulder length, braided wigs were worn. As wig forms continued to change, they were lengthened; and by the Eighteenth Dynasty the hair in back was long enough to cover the shoulder blades. The hair in front was shorter, pulled forward, and it framed the face. The dominant fashion for centuries was the balloon-shaped wig. This wig style was made up of many tiny braids or pencil thin curls. Creams, dyes, oils, and fixatives were used in caring for the hair or wig. Intricately made crowns and hat forms, symbolically indicating rank, were worn over the wigs.

youth lock

balloon wig

slave hair styles

The slaves and servants of Egypt were not allowed to wear wigs or to shave their heads; however, they fashioned their own hair in elaborate styles mimicking the wigs of the nobility. Mud and clay were used by these classes of the masses to set their hair into large bouffant shapes. Black felt caps shaped like the wigs of royalty were also worn by slaves. Warriors wore heavy fiber wigs as head protection, for Egyptians never devised helmets of metal.

ACCESSORIES
Men and
Women
headwear

crowns

Headgear, symbolic of royal rank, and crowns in a variety of shapes were worn throughout the many periods of this ancient civilization. The tall flared cylinder, the tall crown with a knob on top, the high, round tube, and the falcon crown are only a few of the many crowns worn by the kings and queens of Egypt.

kerchief

Nemes
headdress

The characteristic Egyptian head covering, the kerchief, was made of stiff heavy fabric, often shot with gold thread if worn by nobility. It was worn low over the forehead, fastened in back, with the side pieces arranged in a pyramidal form reaching the shoulders. The *Nemes* headdress, a kerchief variation of royalty, had two elongated tabs that fell in front of the shoulders and covered the chest. The more simple form was generally worn by men and women of low status. More decorative, and perhaps in the classification of jewelry,

Headdress of a lady of the court (Egypt: XVIII Dynasty, permission The Metropolitan Museum of Art, purchased with funds given by Harry Walters and Edward S. Harkness, 1926)

"golden veils"

hairpins

were the golden disc head coverings. These discs, often delicately chased, measured about five-eighths of an inch in diameter and were attached to each other with small gold links. Such elaborate "golden veils" were made in a number of intricate patterns. Some fell from the crown of the head, while others were suspended from a band that encircled the forehead. The crowns and headcovering devices, as well as the wigs, were often held in position with long hairpins, made of thorn, bone, bronze, and gold. The metal pins were designed with large, decoratively carved heads.

footwear
sandals

Simple sandals made of woven palm leaves or papyrus and a single plaited fiber thong were worn out of doors. The thong slipped between the first and second toes and attached to the sole at either side. A sturdy leather sandal with a closed heel and several thong straps arranged over the toes and instep developed during the later period. The sole of this style was made of woven papyrus. Delicate golden duplicates of the single-thong sandal, the funeral sandal, were placed on the feet of mummies.

jewelry
collars

rings

Massive jewelry was an important element of Egyptian costume. Beaded collars were fashioned of semiprecious stones, glass, pottery, and hollow gold beads. Beads ornamented this familiar Egyptian accessory in rows; often each row varied in size, shape and type of bead. Generally it went about the neck and tied with thin cords in back, forming a circular collar that covered the shoulders and chest. Signet rings were an important finger accessory, for they were used as official signatures on documents. The engraved stone set of a ring pivoted on the shank, for often each side was decorated with an intaglio image such as the scarab on one side and a signature hieroglyph on the other. Other simple band rings were also worn, sometimes made of twisted wires of gold.

bracelets

Wide, gold bracelets, made in two parts, hinged on one side and fastened on the other with an invisible clasp. Egyptians used a number of decoration techniques, including designs created by an enamel-like surface. Large segmented bracelets were also hinged together and fastened with hidden latches. This style was set with small sphinx or lion motifs carved from alabaster or other types of colorful stones.

necklaces

Single strand necklaces were made of pottery beads of many shapes, hollow, round gold beads and beads of "stone that melts" (glass). Flat gold segments made in the shapes of highly stylized plants, animals and insects provided other forms of neckwear. The fly design appeared repeatedly as one of the motifs for both necklaces and bracelets. Each segment was a copy of the first but not an exact duplicate and such design variations gave these pieces an interesting and vital quality.

earrings

Long, dangling earrings made of gold or "white metal" (silver) formed rather large, elegant pieces of jewelry that added interest to the emphasis areas of head and shoulders. Large gold loops, pottery beads arranged in alternating colors and shapes and a basic pendant style became characteristic earring forms.

hand held accessories umbrella fan

The large feather fan, or umbrella fan, was a symbol of importance. In its manufacture, feathers arranged in a half circle fit into a decorative holder that was attached to a long handle. Others made in the shapes of large leaves mounted golden staffs. This type, carried by a slave, served several purposes; protection from the sun, for creating slight breezes, adding pomp to festivals and for driving away insects. When used indoors, groups of slaves (each slave with a fan moving gently) kept the air circulating.

fan

Individuals used single feather fans, also mounted on long handles. Both types were made of multicolored feathers set in handles decorated with stylized plant or animal head forms. So much attention given to grooming made the mirror an important personal accessory. The Egyptian mirror was made in a variety of shapes but was usually one of three; oval, pear, or round. Copper or mixed metals polished to a high luster supplied the reflective section, set into a handle which was eight or ten inches long. The materials used in making handles included ivory, wood, and faïence, beautifully decorated with carved images of birds, flowers, or animals. All women, even women slaves, possessed mirrors.

mirror

cosmetic aids

The Egyptian toilette included numerous cosmetics. Oils and perfumes were used extensively. During one period, the custom developed of placing a scented cake of congealed fat under the wig or head covering. As it melted, the oils trickled down the face and body, giving off a sweet or spicy aroma. Dyes were used on both wigs and hair as well as on eyebrows and lashes. Lip rouge and eye liner added to the beauty of these appearance conscious people.

beards

While the custom of being clean shaven at all times, except when in mourning, prevailed, pharoahs and queens affected false beards. These were ceremonial accessories, primarily, symbolizing masculine authority. Made of hair, the beards were of a rectangular shape about four inches long and two inches wide. Two thin cords with loop ends that were slipped over the ears held each beard in place at the tip of the chin. This false beard was known as a *postiche*.

postiche

GARMENT DETAILING
buttons
embroidery

Immigrants introduced bone and bronze buttons into this ancient culture some time between 2500 B.C. and 1200 B.C. They were used as decorations rather than fastening devices. Elaborate embroidery typified Egyptian costumes. One style, worked with a needle, combined linen thread and tufted woolen loops. The motifs used often derived from religious origins and included the lotus and papyrus designs as well as geometric patterns. In many cases the entire kalasiris was embroidered. Gold and silver beaten out with a hammer and cut into thin strips were used as embroidery thread as well as the more common dyed linen thread. There are indications that the silver and gold thread was worked into a "network of gold," possibly the earliest form of lace made. However, this golden network was not made with the refined pattern usually associated with lace, created for the first time as a uniformly designed trim about the sixteenth century A.D.

lace

fringe

tassels

Fringe, as a garment decoration, resulted from tying off the extra lengths of thread of the warp of the material. Tassels evolved from this practice and developed into more complex forms by braiding, twisting, and tying the ends. Both fringe and tassels were shot with gold thread when gold thread was used in weaving the basic length of garment fabric. Mention of fringe appeared in an antique record listing gifts brought to a pharoah of the Eighteenth Dynasty. Ribbons were decorative woven bands. They were sewn on just above the fringe to prevent raveling. Braid, woven or plaited from bits of handsome fabric, formed belts, girdles, and head, neck, and arm ornaments. All colors were used except red, which was considered the color of violence. During the later dynasties, white was the color used for the major garment, accented by green, yellow, blue, and magenta.

ribbons

braid

Additional pictorial resources:

1. wall painting—women spinning and weaving—(shenti, loincloth, kerchief, and long wig) 2000-1788 B.C., Metropolitan Museum of Art, New York

2. bas-relief—King Seti I—(gala gown, girdle with shendot—male figure; procardium, beaded collar—female figure) 1313-1292 B.C., Archeological Museum, Florence

3. sculpture—Temple-tomb of Ramses II—(gala skirt, Nemes headdress) c. 1330 B.C., Abu-Simbel, Egypt

4. wall painting—Sandal Makers—(loincloth, sandals) c. 2000 B.C., Metropolitan Museum of Art, New York

5. wall painting—Neb-Amon tomb—(gala gown, beaded collar, wide enameled bracelet, elongating head pad, pencil curl long wig—female group; belt, small short wig—dancers; falcon headdress—seated figures) Eighteenth Dynasty, British Museum, London

6. actual garment—loincloth,—1580-1350 B.C., Museum of Art, Boston

7. sculpture—Akhenaton and Nefertiti—(flared cylinder crown, gala gown, braid girdle, single-thong sandal, large ankle bracelets—female; horizontal or sunburst pleated loincloth, shendot, beaded collar—male) Eighteenth Dynasty, Louvre, Paris

Bodice and bell skirt; owl crown (late Minoan)

Chapter 2

THE DRESS OF CRETE

*B*EHIND *the cultural development of Greece lay the influences of several prehistoric peoples and early civilizations. One of the more dominant influences was that of Crete. Information relating to the origins of the Cretans and the nature of their social order is sketchy. Their identifiable civilization lasted from 2000 B.C. to 1100 B.C. This society developed contemporaneously with the predynastic Egyptians. The Aegean and Cycladic island cultures (7000-2000 B.C.) had been the forerunner societies of the area. The Cretans, through trade with the kingdoms of North Africa, Asia Minor and those bordering the Aegean, assimilated much from these peoples. Originally the population of Crete was composed of the Grimaldi Negroid peoples of Southern Europe and* the Celto-Germanic races. At a very early date this latter group had penetrated the Greek peninsula and the Aegean islands, which had been populated since the Neolithic period. The Cretan civilization, at its zenith, embraced the island of Crete and areas of the mainland including Mycenae, Tiryns, and Troy. The governmental system was a basic form of democracy. They were not a united people, however, but rather a group of city states, some of which were Knossos, Phaestus, and Gournia.

The geographic position of Crete directed the broad and varied economic base upon which the society evolved. Agriculture flourished in the mild climate of the Aegean islands and peninsula. The expansion of marine trade routes was natural. The Cretans became expert seafarers and traveled the Aegean Sea and the Mediterranean as far as Sicily. One of their most important exports was pottery which was highly refined and beautifully decorated. By the year 2000 B.C., they had invented a system of written communication and later a form of script. They were expert metal workers, using both the repousse and damascening techniques.

These pre-Hellenic peoples loved comfort and luxury, as illustrated by the palace at Knossos with its vast high ceilings, broad stairways, paved floors, and tinted, oiled parchment windows. The wealthy classes had homes of equal elegance, equipped with a central heating system. The Cretans had developed a drainage system and their plumbing included hot and cold running water in bathrooms. Gold and silver taps controlled the flow of water into solid silver basins and bathtubs. Other luxury items included gold and silver cups with repoussé decorations, pottery vessels of eggshell thinness, and gaming boards of gold, silver, or ivory elaborately inlaid and engraved.

As a people, the Cretans were alert, gay, and adventuresome, with lithe, athletic bodies. Their agility played an important part in their religious observances. Their chief deities were female—mother or fertility goddesses. Snakes and bulls also played important roles in the observance of some cults. Festivals in honor of the bull-god involved intricate gymnastic displays on the backs of bulls. Participants tumbled over these animals, defying the dangers of horn and hoof. The bulls were then offered as a sacrifice to Cretan gods residing in the labyrinthian cave shrines beneath the earth's surface. A love of nature also played an important part in the religion of Crete. Tenderness toward all flora and fauna was represented visually in ceramic decorations, sculpture, and wall painting.

Imagination, vigor, gaiety, grace, and rhythm, all part of the attitudes of the Cretans, can be seen throughout their art and costume forms. The Cretans exercised an extensive influence on the costumes of the Mediterranean areas. The originality of their clothing design spread via the trade routes from the shores of the Black Sea to the eastern limits of the Mediterranean. Cretan costume had become much more elaborate by 1580 B.C. Trade with the Phoenicians had resulted in the distribution of these garment design concepts to neighboring kingdoms. Availability of raw materials, design ideas, and decorative motifs as well as highly refined clothing construction techniques determined the fashions of the Aegean people. Theirs was a unique dress fashion, particularly the costumes of the women. This influence was strong in Cyprus, the Syrian coast, and even in Egypt, persisting until the rise of the Myceneans in

1400 B.C. After the Dorian conquests in 1200 B.C. the Cretans retreated. Some of them immigrated into Asia Minor. During this period cultural aspects borrowed from the Near East were superimposed on the Cretans, leading to a modification of their clothing. The short trousers and sleeved chiton worn by the male figures in a fresco at Thebes (1600-1400 B.C.) on the Cadmean illustrate the extent of Cretan acceptance of apparel design with origins outside their own culture. The vast textile trade established early in the Minoan period had the greatest impact on costume forms. Changes included the use of fabrics decorated with designs of real or imaginary animals and floral patterns. These were more dynamic and possibly more angular than the flowing, rhythmic designs characteristic of most Cretan art forms. A proud people with an intense interest in the grace of the human body, they lived in a region with a mild climate where garments were not needed for warmth. This, coupled with their interest in athletics, motivated their development of figure-revealing garments.

BASIC GARMENTS OF CRETE
(200 B.C. — 1100 B.C.)

LOINCLOTH or SHENTI
(1700-1550 B.C.)
Men
   phallustache
   wraparound
   skirt
   sheath and
   short skirt
   apron
   loincloth

Cretan men wore four basic styles of loincloth or *shenti*. The most simple was a thigh-length skirt or *phallustache*, worn in much the same manner as the Egyptian version of this garment. As a rule it covered the figure from waist to mid-thigh. Another basic style was the wraparound skirt, which generally was ankle length. More complex designs included the short skirt with frontal sheath, and the apron loincloth. The former consisted of a back panel that barely covered the gluteus maximus, and a rigidly constructed leather form for the protection of the male organs. The panel had curved edges that came forward, just covering the loins. The apron loincloth style was made of a triangular piece of fabric with the point worn in the back. This point was often greatly exaggerated and turned upward, held thus by some type of stiffening, to create a taillike appendage in the rear. Double apron loincloths were fashioned with points front and back. Multiskirt arrangements of this same style created a tiered skirt variation of this basic male garment.

colors
fabric
trim

Polychrome loincloths were introduced about the fifteenth century B.C. Some styles, both elegant and costly, were decorated with fringe. It is believed that such materials as heavy woolen fabric, fine linen and leather were used in making these male garments. The design of the loincloth depended on the plastic qualities of the material

Male loincloth with leather frontal sheath and metal girdle; decorative headdress (Crete)

Phallustache (female phallustache took same form)

Double apron loincloth of late Minoan period with dipthera (cape wrap) and half boots

leather and metal cinch belts

used. To emphasize the small waists so characteristic of all Cretans, cinch belts of leather or metal were worn with the loincloths. The metal belts had rolled edges and were studded with copper, silver, or gold rosettes. Spiral and stylized floral patterns were also used as decorative devices. These belts were often soldered about the waists of children at the age of six or seven to ensure that as adults they would have the desired waist girth of not more than twelve inches. This was a practice begun about 1700 B.C., lasting until 1550 B.C. The narrowness of the waist made the shoulder and chest areas of the figure seem more robust by comparison.

double apron loincloth (early Minoan) Women

The apron or double apron loincloth was preferred by women when engaged in athletic events. It was not the normal everyday female costume. It was made of patterned fabrics with geometrically ordered borders and fringe trim and was worn with the decorative metal belt.

SHORTS (late Minoan) Men

A form of extremely brief pants or shorts was worn by men. These garments were introduced as articles of male apparel very late in the period. The general acceptance of this garment form is questionable, for they were referred to in ancient records as "garments of demons" or as "garments of foreigners."

TUNIC Men

The males of Crete wore snug fitting tunics with the brief shorts. This simple garment was made by folding a length of fabric in half and sewing up the side seams. A modest space was left just below the fold on either side seam for the armholes. A slit or round hole cut on the fold acted as a neck opening. A basic *chiton* made by pinning two rectangular pieces of material together on the shoulders was an alternate upper body covering, worn with the shorts. The simple chiton was worn hanging free or tucked into the cinch belt.

chiton

SKIRT (2000 B.C.) Women bell skirt tiered skirt

Women wore bell or tiered skirts, perhaps creating the tiered effect, in earliest times, by wearing several skirts of varying lengths one on top of the other. During later periods the skirt assumed a conical shape as a result of the rather complex method used in creating the garment. This particular Cretan skirt indicated that the sewing techniques and dressmaking processes were highly refined. The bell skirt was made of long bands of fabric, gathered on one edge to make a ruffle or volant. The ruffles were sewn onto a simple skirt in tiers. The flounces creating the tiers were some-

volant flounce

times of equal size and sometimes were of graduated size, the smaller being at the waist. Each row of volants was separated by elaborate ornamentation. At one time in Cretan fashion the skirt fitted the figure snugly from waist to hips, where flounced ruffles were attached to cascade to the floor in ever-widening circles about the legs. Later bell skirt styles were designed with pleated rather than gathered volants. This costume was in existence for many centuries, appearing on women represented on seals as early as 2400 B.C. This first visual record showed the multilayer style.

There is no complete record of these people and it is not known whether Cretan women wore the first hoop skirts to hold the tiered or bell skirts in the desired shape. All visual records indicate they were very stiff rigid skirts. If there were hoops under the skirts they would have been made of bone and braid or other available materials, such as reeds. A series of underaprons of graduated size would also have served as a functional skirt support. Starches, known and used by the Egyptians to set the horizontal and radiating pleats of their kilts, gala skirts, and gala gowns, may also have been used to hold the tiered skirt in the bell or conical shapes. By 1700 B.C. the female skirt became much slimmer and fitted tightly over the hips and thighs.

The skirt was usually belted or double-girdled with a braid-trimmed tab sash. The double girdle was arranged by placing the sash about the waist, crossing it in the back, and bringing it to the front, where it was tied. The metal belt, with its rolled edges, was also worn with the skirt. If neither belt nor sash was used, a corset made of a series of hinged metal plates, each about two inches by three inches, was worn.

The bell and tiered skirts were made of linen or wool, depending on the season of the year. Wool was the earliest fabric used, regardless of the climate, until textile trade developed. The finely pleated volants possibly were made of linen. Unfortunately no actual remnants of the materials used by these peoples exist because of the destructive effects of the hot dry climate of the region.

Small snake goddess figurines of the period indicate that the colors ranged from white through beige to deep, rich browns. Blues and reds were chosen as accent colors. There is some evidence that more brilliant shades of yellow, red, orange,

reed skirt
supports
underapron
supports

belts
girdles

metal belt

fabrics

colors

Cretan tiered skirt with padded roll support

and bright purple were used. Often the skirt tiers were made of fabric in alternating colors and arranged to form a checkerboard patterned skirt.

skirt trim

The decorative bands between each flounce were made of braid. The design motifs for this trim included geometric forms, leaf shapes, trellis patterns and stylized wave borders. Oval and lozenge shapes were popular decorative elements of the late Cretan period.

BLOUSE
(2000 B.C.)
Women

The blouses worn with the skirt were snug fitting. The breast-exposing, plunging necklines may well have been sophisticated adaptations of the forms created when untanned hides were worn to cover the upper body. The neckline was usually band-trimmed. The body of the garment was laced together in the front at the waist. Cretan blouses were made with three different types of sleeves: tight sleeves, cap sleeves, and puffed sleeves. The latter were held in the desired puffed form by braids or ribbons criss-crossed in back.

shift

The shifts, or undergarments worn by women were made of transparent fabric with a round or oval neckline. All women except priestesses wore this garment, which, though transparent, did fill in the front of the blouse, functioning as part of its overall design.

collar

In the late Minoan period the blouse was designed with a high standing collar which framed the back of the head. Two styles of the blouse dominated throughout the period, one with side panels that curved snugly under the bust with a triangular shape beneath the lacings separating the breasts, and the other with sides curving counter to the bustline, the two blouse halves separated by about three inches between the lacings.

CLOAK
(2000-1000 B.C.)
Men and Women

A simple though ample rectangle of woolen cloth formed the protective cloak worn by the Cretan people. It was often trimmed with fringe. Worn by both men and women exclusively when going about in their high speed form of transportation, the chariot, it was a very simple outer garment form. For other occasions a brief cape or *diphtera* was worn as a light wrap. The diphtera was first made of animal skins but later was fashioned of heavy woolen material and still later of linen. The vase drawings and wall paintings of the period illustrate that a shawl form of rather stiff fabric was also worn. This shawl may easily have been the diphtera. It was worn wrapped quite high behind the

cape
diphtera

head, drawn over the shoulders and held in the center front by one hand. This shawl form did not extend below the elbows.

BOLERO JACKET
Women

A small bolero jacket with short curved cuffs on the sleeves was a decorative as well as functional light wrap for women. It was designed in the same manner as the female blouse, snug fitting and with a plunging neckline. It was made of the same fabric (linen and wool) as other Cretan apparel in bright colors including yellow, red, blue, and purple, and was trimmed with braid using traditional design motifs of the culture or with embroidered bands.

GOWN
Men and Women

The one-piece gown, used primarily for ceremonial purposes, was worn at festivals by both men and women. Dating this garment is difficult but judging from the simplicity of design, it was a remnant of an early period elevated to ceremonial status out of deference to its antiquity. This gown was a simple sleeved tunic which clung to the figure rather snugly, with a slight flare at the hem. Bands of contrasting colors—reds, deep blues, ochres, and blue greens—trimmed neckline and sleeve cuffs. The decorative bands about the neck extended down the center front to the hem.

CASSOCK
Men

The cassock was a ceremonial outer garment, which also protected the wearer against the elements. It is described as having large hinged segments similar to those used in the construction of protective battle apparel, the cuirass. These hinged segments were arranged to give maximum coverage to the arms. It may be assumed that the cassock was used during military spectaculars.

ACCESSORIES
(200-1100 B.C.)

For some time the Cretan society was believed to be a rather poor society. The remains of this civilization are so scant that an accurate picture of the true economic condition or social order is vague. However, recent archeological finds indicate that this culture was rich and possessed the techniques of fine jewelry making and highly refined metalcraft. On the small figurines in existence, it is difficult to determine the exact forms of these accessories. It has been recently ascertained that the Cretan jewelry was elaborate and elegant. Heavy carved bracelets were worn by both men and women. Necklaces were worn by noble and commoner alike. The latter wore simple necklaces made from stone beads strung on a flax thread. Agate, rock crystal, cornelian, amethyst, and blue

jewelry

bracelets
necklaces

Late Minoan male gown and diphtera

steatite were the favored stones used for the necklaces of those of wealth and royal rank. Paste beads imitative of lapis lazuli were also used in creating decorative neckwear. Round beads made from a variety of stones were used alternately with pendants which took the forms of birds, animals, and small stylized human figures.

earrings

Earrings were often a combination of beads and pendants fashioned from forms similar to those used in neckwear. Twisted gold wire earrings were also worn.

hairpins

diadems

Copper and gold hairpins with floral, spiral, or semiprecious stone heads were beautifully crafted hair ornaments. Diadems of gold were constructed of hinged segments designed in the shape of leaves.

headwear
head bands

head coverings

Simple golden bands, worn encircling the forehead, were also used as a type of head and hair decoration. It is believed that the hat was introduced into Europe by the Cretans. These head coverings took many exotic shapes. Such bizarre forms as towering truncated cones with tiered effects, turbans, tricorns, and styles with tall pointed crowns are but a few of the many creative hat shapes these people devised. Decorative elements trimming these hats were equally imaginative and elaborate. Rosettes and curled plumes combined with ribbon streamers to add gay touches to Cretan headwear.

footwear

slippers
shoes
boots
Women

slippers
shoes
boots
Women

Women, while not house-bound, were depicted in Cretan wall paintings as having extremely fair complexions indicating little exposure to the sun's rays. It has been assumed that while much of the time was spent indoors, slippers or shoe forms were not worn inside dwellings. This assumption is based on the contrasting conditions of the remains of interior and exterior stairways. The latter are deeply grooved, while the former show little or no wear. Slippers, shoes with heels, and high boots, however, were worn by women when they ventured abroad. These forms of footwear were functional rather than decorative.

boots
sandals
Men

Men, who spent more time outdoors than women, chose half boots as the preferred foot coverings. The closed, calf-high boots were tied about the lower leg with thongs. These heavy boot forms were necessary because of the ruggedness of the Cretan terrain. Men wore sandals when going about the streets of the city. These were made with a leather sole and were crosslaced up the

Male loincloth with cinch waist silhouette (fourteenth century B.C.)

lower leg with thongs. Leather of red, white, and natural color was the basic boot material. Men also went barefoot indoors.

HAIR STYLES
Women

Hair styles of the early Cretan period were simple. Long curls fell from the crown of the head, cascading over the shoulders, reaching to the waist or below. Simple bands were worn as decorations and functioned to hold the hair away from the eyes and face. Later coif arrangements were influenced by the Syrian style, which included drawing the hair back off the forehead, and gathering it in a towering pug on the back of the head with two rather lank curls allowed to fall in front of the ears, framing the face. Another hair arrangement consisted of parting the hair in the center, drawing it in waves rather low over the forehead and securing it at the nape of the neck. The hair in back was shoulder length and arranged in small pencil curls or in a series of small braids. Pointed or conical hair fashions were held in place by headbands. Three flowers were often worn in the headband in the center of the forehead. Garlands of flowers and bright-colored ribbons were also entwined in the free hanging locks as decorative elements.

Men

Men wore their hair long, smoothed back from the brow and falling free about the shoulders. Curls were sometimes piled into a peak at the crown of the head. Another fashion for men included drawing the hair to the nape of the neck and forming a club-shaped pigtail in back.

Additional pictorial resources

1. bas-relief—Apollo and Herakles fighting—(sheath and skirt shenti, hat forms) c.1100-700 B.C., Olympia Museum, Olympia, Greece

2. fresco—woman with ivory chest—(bell skirt, bodice and Syrian-influenced hair style, diadem, and bracelets) c. 1500 B.C., Metropolitan Museum of Art, New York

3. painted sarcophagus—procession—(diphtera, gown, fabric patterns) c. 1400 B.C., Metropolitan Museum of Art, New York

4. amphora—Artemis, Apollo and two nymphs—(gown, diphtera, headband with flowers—women; tunic and sheath and skirt shenti—male) c. 800 B.C., Athens Museum, Athens

5. fresco—procession (loincloth) 1450-1375 B.C., Palace of Minos, Knossos

6. painting—Priest King of Knossos—(headdress and loincloth) c. 1400 B.C., Palace of Minos, Knossos

7. figurine—Snake goddess—(bodice and bell skirt) c. 1700-1550 B.C., Metropolitan Museum of Art, New York

8. vase—warriors (armor), 1375-1200 B.C., Metropolitan Museum of Art, New York

Chapter 3

GARB OF THE GREEKS

THROUGH its art, architecture, philosophy, and drama Greece made significant contributions to the cultural development of both the ancient and modern worlds. It is generally accepted that Ionian peoples from the western Adriatic immigrated to Greece some time before 1100 B.C., to be joined shortly after by Aeolians from Asia Minor. These two nomadic tribes were fused with the more militant Indo-Europeans, earlier invaders, and the Dorians. A society based on a tribal organizational system evolved, and this in turn developed into a loosely knit kingdom made of city states. At the time of the earliest penetration of the Aegean islands and the mainland of Greece, there were frequent battles between the inhabitants and the invaders. This was the

27

era of the Siege of Troy and the struggles which took place around the stronghold of Mycenae. The first rulers of these city states were kings, followed by nobles, tyrants, benevolent despots, and finally the people, in a unique experiment with total democracy. The flourishing city states constantly battled one another. The most important of them were Athens, Sparta, and Corinth. The Aegean and Mediterranean Seas offered pathways of expansion for vigorous trading and colonization. Thus the boundaries of Greece, both cultural and geographic, were extended. Contacts with older civilizations altered the Greek culture. From Egypt, Babylonia-Assyria, and Phoenicia Greece acquired a wide variety of concepts ranging from moral standards to aesthetic philosophies. In their turn the Greeks spread their cultural achievements via the Mediterranean water routes and the surrounding Aegean Sea from Asia Minor to Sicily, from southern Italy to Spain and France.

The Greek peninsula had, then as now, a diversity of topography and climate, with freedom from extremes of heat and cold. The sun in the bright sky intensified the forms of nature. It is little wonder that the ancient Greeks, made so aware of their surroundings, developed a nature-based religion. Religious involvement with nature slowly led to the personification of nature. Anthropomorphic gods were given idealized human proportions and were endowed with the properties of grace and beauty, nobility and grandeur. These man-gods were held in high esteem and became to the Greeks the measure of all things. In time individual perfection became the ideal. It is possible that the natural environment fostered individuality. This concept led to the development of significant personal roles in religious festivals. Spectacular ceremonies were offered in homage to their gods. The Olympic games, presented every four years, honored Zeus and gave individual athletes an opportunity to display their personal excellence. It was only through religion that these small city states found unity. All of them used the various shrines and temples, including those at Delphi, and participated in the Olympic Games. However, in war and invasion they did not unite in support of common causes. An event exemplifying this disunity occurred during the fierce Persian Wars (500-449 B.C.) when one city state refused aid to another although both would have benefited.

Athens fell to Sparta in the fifth century B.C. during the Peloponnesian Wars. However, the men of the Age of Pericles and the intellectual, political, philosophical, and aesthetic concepts of Athens persisted. Great contributions to Greek culture were made by such men as Sophocles, Euripides, Phidian, Socrates, Plato, and Aristotle. The ideals and principles of democracy were born in Greece. Athens, Sparta, Corinth, and Macedon, in turn, dominated this peninsula. Alexander, Philip of Macedon's son, by conquest and colonization, spread Greek culture throughout the known world, and it held sway in the Aegean and the Mediterranean areas until conquered by Rome in 146 B.C.

The citizens of Athens gathered each day in the agora (marketplace) where they lounged in the cool shaded areas, discussing philosophy and politics. After visiting the marketplace the men would proceed to the gymnasium for a period of vigorous exercise and for more discussion. Hours of leisure were possible because slaves attended to the day-to-day businesses owned by upper class freemen. Slaves had limited, though

Earrings, Ganymede and the Eagle used as a motif (Greek: 440-130 B.C., permission The Metropolitan Museum of Art, Harris Brisbane Dick Fund, 1937)

Double girdled short chiton (Greek, permission The Metropolitan Museum of Art, gift of John D. Rockefeller, Jr., 1932)

important, responsibilities in both commerce and education. The education of young boys was of paramount importance in this society.

Grecian women had very little importance in this male-oriented civilization. While boys received a thorough education, girls were given only rudimentary training. They were taught to run a household, to read, to write, and to do basic arithmetic. From mothers or nurses they learned to sing and to play the lyre. Spartan girls, however, were trained in gymnastics, as were the boys, to develop grace of movement. Adult women were given less authority than slaves. Marriages were arranged when the couples were children. The Greek wedding ceremony contributed a few traditions still observed such as the white gown and the veiled face as well as the practice of carrying the bride over the threshold. To the Greeks this latter act was part of the elaborate two-part wedding ritual begun in the bride's father's house and ending when the groom carried his bride into his father's home, signifying that the bride was now the groom's possession.

Greek arts (sculpture and architecture) and Greek crafts (pottery making and goldsmithing) combined geometric and curvilinear forms. Perfection of form was developed through proportional relationships based on the theory referred to as the "golden mean." The Parthenon is an architectural monument of perfection achieved by the application of this rule. The sculptural representations of the anthropomorphic gods were startlingly beautiful. Archaic sculpture evolved into astonishingly realistic images of idealized human forms during the Classical period. The beautifully proportioned marble figures, draped in chitons and himations, created by the master sculptors of ancient Greece are an excellent resource of the costume forms of this period.

BASIC GARMENTS OF ANCIENT GREECE
(1500 B.C. — 150 B.C.)

CHITON
(1500-150 B.C.)
Men and Women

Archaic chiton Men

Doric chiton Men

The chiton was the most characteristic Greek garment worn by both men and women. During the many periods of this civilization the male chiton had two basic forms. The most simple of these was made by pinning two rectangles of fabric together on the shoulders and girdling them around the waist. The sides were left open and the arms left bare. The pin or fibula, was a primitive fastening made of a metal wire with a point at one end, a loop in the middle, and a hook latch on the other end. In appearance it resembled a safety pin. The chiton of the Archaic period covered the figure from shoulder to thigh. The Doric style was made from one long piece of material, also rectangular in shape. The fabric was folded in half, the fold and open ends acting as side seams. The garment was created by placing the folded edge under one arm, drawing one half of the material over the

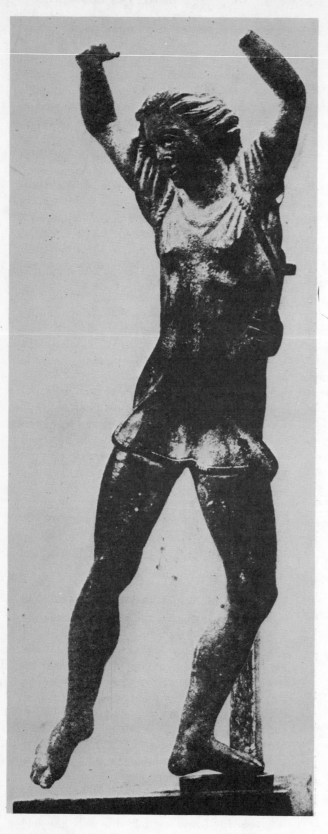

Tunic (Greek: 350 B.C., courtesy Museo
Archeologico, Florence)

Doric chiton (477 B.C.)

front of the figure, the other over the back and pinning it with a fibula on each shoulder. It was then belted and the desired draping effects arranged. It was not a full or cumbersome garment at this time, being either thigh or floor length.

Ionic chiton Men

This style differed from the long Ionic male chiton which, though placed about the figure in the same manner, used a length of fabric twice as long as the wearer's outstretched arms, from elbow to elbow. The Ionic chiton, because of the greater amount of fabric used, was much fuller, with deeper draped folds. Short sleeves were made by using the excess material that fell from the shoulders, pinning it along the outside of the upper arms.

Classical chiton Men

The Classical style for males was distinguished from the earlier versions by an overfold that extended from the shoulders to the waist. In all other aspects this garment was the same, including the fibula fastenings, the draping and the single or double girdling. During all the style phases of this costume, the girdling was arranged to please the wearer.

Archaic chiton Women

The female chiton during the Archaic period was made from two pieces of material, each slightly wider than the width of the woman's shoulders. It too, was made by pinning the fabric together on the shoulders and belting it at the waist. It covered the figure to the ankles.

Doric chiton Women

The women in Doric times wore an amply draped chiton similar to the male Ionic style. The girdling of this period was much more complex, often being double or triple windings. In the latter case, a space was left between the cords allowing the material to puff out between them. The girdling cords were also sometimes wrapped around the waist several times, then brought up from the sides to cross between the breasts and again in back, and finally tied in front. The neckline of the later chiton was V-shaped, the result of the larger amount of material used in making the garment. Sleeves were fashioned from the excess of material in the same way as in the male garment. However, women improvised full-length sleeves by using longer fabric lengths and placing the many pins used several inches apart. This created an open, looped sleeve effect.

Ionic chiton Women

The Ionic chiton was a much fuller version than the Doric style. This extra fullness was achieved by using a piece of fabric twice the length of the wearer's outstretched arms and as wide as the wearer's height plus eighteen or twenty inches. This extra width was folded, the fold becoming the shoulder line. It was placed around the figure and secured with pins and girdle. The overfold, if

Chiton and simple sandals (Greek: 455–450 B.C., permission The Metropolitan Museum of Art, Fletcher Fund, 1927)

apotygma
Classical
chiton
Women
kolpos

TUNICS
(1100-146 B.C.)
Men and
Women

Ionic chiton and peplos arrangement
achieved by double girdling

shallow, was allowed to hang free, forming the *apotygma*. In the Classical chiton the overfold was extremely long, reaching to the hip socket or below. Spaced triple girdling was wound over this longer apotygma. The bloused section above the waist was called the *kolpos*. During the Classical period the chiton covered the feet and trailed slightly on the ground.

The tunic, basic garment of all ancient people, was worn by both sexes. It was made by cutting two simple T-shaped pieces the size of the wearer and sewing them together across the shoulders, under the arms, and down the side seams. A small round hole with a slit in front formed the neckline. This garment was belted at the waist. The male version was short, covering the figure sometimes to just below the buttocks, sometimes to mid-thigh. The tunic worn by women resembled the Doric chiton, but had sewn side seams. The female tunic was ankle length and was usually worn as an undergarment. Women seldom girdled this costume.

Greek umbrella carried by a male servant (wearing tunic) to provide shade
for the lady wearing a chiton with
peplos (500 B.C.)

Peplos (Greek: late sixth century B.C., permission The Metropolitan Museum of Art, gift of John Marshall)

Deplos (Mr. and Mrs. Walter C. Baker Collection, by special permission of Mrs. Baker)

LOINCLOTH
(1100 B.C.)
Men and Women

The loincloth was worn by male and female slaves. It was a thin band worn between the legs, brought up over the lower part of the body and secured by twisting the ends together about the waist. Women of all stations of life wore the loincloth as an undergarment. Free men of early Greek times wore no clothing whatever, except the himation when the weather was chilly.

SUPER TUNIC
(1000-146 B.C.)
Men and Women

The super tunic was worn over the chiton for warmth. Like the basic tunic this garment was cut in a T-form out of two pieces of fabric, although some were made from a folded length. The fold of this variation formed the shoulder line. The female super tunic was knee length, while the male's was short or waist length.

PEPLOS
(540-146 B.C.)
Women

There were several styles of *peplos*. At first the peplos was made by girdling the overfold or apotygma of the chiton. The fabric of the overfold was pulled up, bloused, and draped over the girdling, for the most part obscuring it. The overfold creating this style of peplos was extremely long. In later periods the peplos was a separate article acting as a decorative accessory. It was made from a rectangle of fabric with ribbon ties on the ends of the top edge, which went under one arm and tied on the opposite shoulder. The peplos was made in two sizes, one waist length and one covering the entire figure. The borders were trimmed with traditional geometric patterns. Both the peplos and the female chitons were made of light weight wool or linen with overall embroidered designs. The motifs for these patterns included dots, palmettes, stylized flowers, and basic geometric shapes.

HIMATION
(1100-146 B.C.)
Men and Women

For some time men wore the figure-swathing *himation* as the only body covering. This outer wrap was made from a rectangle of woolen cloth with weights attached at each of the corners. It was placed around the figure beginning at the left shoulder, drawn across the front, under the right arm, across the back, over the left shoulder, with the wearer devising a series of graceful ways of tucking or twisting the end to secure it about the figure. Women wore the himation in much the same way, but with the chiton beneath. An alternate wearing style consisted of folding the himation in half, lengthwise, using part as a head covering.

DEPLOS
(350-146 B.C.)
Women

The *deplos* was a type of wrap developed from the doubled or folded himation. It too was made of a long wide rectangle of woolen fabric, folded in

Double girdled male chiton and
chlamys, back figure in male himation

half, lengthwise, creating an overfold. It was
wrapped about the figure with the overfold drawn
up over the head and held closely at the throat
with one hand. A style variation of the deplos was
made from a length of material narrower in width,
with a small or elbow-length overfold. When
worn, not as a protection against rainy weather,
but as a warm wrap, the overfold served as a
shoulder cape.

CHLAMYS
(1100-146 B.C.)
Men

The *chlamys* was a simple thigh-length wrap made
from a square or rectangle of heavy woolen fabric.
It was worn around the shoulders, usually with
the open side over the right arm and was pinned
with a fibula on the right shoulder. This rough,
basic outer body covering was worn primarily by
travelers and soldiers.

PALLIUM
(c. 900-146 B.C.)
Men

The *pallium* was a large circular outer garment of
the Greek male wardrobe. It was cut in a circle
with a center front opening from round neck to
hem and was worn fastened snugly about the
throat. Occasionally it was designed with an attached pointed hood. A hoodless circular cloak, a

Greek peasant; tunic and felt hat, the petasus

Tholia, himation, and chiton (Greek women, fourth to fifth century B.C.)

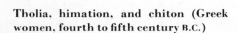

tribon

ACCESSORIES
(1100-146 B.C.)
Men and Women

petasus

pileus

tholia

variation of the pallium, made of very heavy woolen cloth, was called the *tribon*. This rude garment was an outer wrap for slaves and commoners.

An early hat form worn primarily by men of Greece was called the *petasus*. This head covering, made of felt, consisted of a round bowl-shaped crown and a rather wide brim made of two sections. A V-shaped slit was formed where the two halves of the brim met over the ears. Thin cords, tied under the chin, held this hat in place. When not on the head, the ties were loosely knotted, holding the hat on the person, but left to fall down in back. The felt *pileus* was a tall-crowned skull cap, common to all ancient peoples. It was worn by men only. Women seldom wore any hat forms, but on very sunny days donned the *tholia*, which was worn on top of the drawn-up himation or the overfold of the deplos. This small, rather amusingly shaped hat had a small brim and a tall pointed or conical shaped crown. It was placed rather precariously atop the head, possibly held in place with a long stiletto pin driven through the crown

phrygian cap and into the chignon hair arrangement. The *phrygian cap* was an oddly shaped hat made of leather or perhaps woolen cloth. It was designed rather like a hood with a rounded point that projected forward. When the cap was made of stiff material the point stood up, curving toward the front. A pair of falls covered the cheeks in front of the ears, and a veil or neck sheath covered the back of the head, extending to the shoulders. If made of softer fabric the point was worn crushed down almost disappearing into the cap section. The **sakkos** *sakkos* was a pointed cap with a tassel trim. This cap covered much of the head and had a small brim or visor in front that stood semi-erect.

veils Women covered their heads with a variety of veils made of wool or linen. Earlier versions were small, draped over the head simply, reaching no farther than the shoulders. Later versions were sheer, gossamer trims encircling the head like a misty cloud. These diaphanous veils were usually white although saffron, blue, and purple were other hues used. The **snood** snood and *sphendon scarf* were both **sphendon** head coverings and chignon supports. The latter **scarf** cradled the bun of hair in back, partially covering it, and was drawn forward over the brow where it was secured by winding the ends together and tucking them into the back section. The former was primarily a hair support. It was a loosely woven net, made of linen cords or gold wires. This coif decoration was held in place by a tiara worn rather low on the forehead.

footwear The earliest shoes worn by the Greeks were made **shoe** with felt, leather, or wooden soles bound to the foot by thongs. Later straps were attached to the sole, arranged in a variety of crisscrossed patterns, to form the traditional Grecian sandal. Boots and **boot** shoes that covered the feet were laced over the instep. These laces were tied at the ankle or at the calf of the leg. High boots worn by warriors or slaves had wooden soles and wide leather strap laces. These rugged boots had leather tops and an **crepida** enclosed heel. Boots referred to as *crepida* were made of a heavy leather sole that was somewhat larger than the foot. The excess of sole was brought up over the foot and attached over the instep by thongs laced through large slits cut into the edge of the sole. These afforded a means of securing this basic style to the foot and protecting the sides of the foot as well. By the year 400 B.C. shoe and sandal making had attained a high degree of sophisticated refinement. It was at this time that the classical sandal became an elaborate form of footwear. Men of wealth and high rank wore sandals made from soft leather of natural or gold color.

Pendant earrings (Greek: fourth century B.C., permission The Metropolitan Museum of Art, Rogers Fund, 1906)

jewelry Women

The neckwear of Greek women consisted of golden forms elaborately embossed and engraved. Repoussé and plaited gold wires were combined by the skillful goldsmith to create these ornaments. A typical necklace design consisted of small gold animal forms, blue or green enameled rosettes, and pendants in vase shapes arranged alternately. Deep fringe, made of minute chains or twisted gold wires, was often added to the vase forms of the pendant necklace. Stone cameos and small vials filled with sweet scents were worn suspended from long golden chains. Bracelets were fashioned in much the same manner as necklaces, using chased and engraved motives of gold. Rings were believed to have magical powers. Their charms were thought to insure health, love, wealth and happiness. These finger ornaments were made of precious stones, jasper, rock crystal, and chalcedony set in gold with gold shanks. Intaglio and cameo engravings were used as settings in many of these rings. The *fibula* was both a functional and decorative accessory used by men and women. Its earliest form was simply a bent wire with a sharp point on one end and a hook latch on the other. As costume ornamentation became more important the fibula (pin) became more decorative. The exposed section of the pin was mounted with round, oval, or stylized animal shapes. Earrings were given protective attributes to drive away evil spirits. They were worn by both sexes. The earliest forms were simple loops while the later designs included single ball shapes, single pearls, vase pendants, and the long fringed pendants. Figures of humans or cupids were also used as earring motifs. All of these ear ornaments were suspended from a small metal loop and worn in pierced ears. Large bodkin hairpins were used to hold the elaborate Grecian coif in place. The designs of the heads of these pins ranged from geometric shapes, to stylized floral forms, to intricate insect motifs.

necklace

cameo and vial pendants

bracelets

rings

fibula

earrings

hairpins

Two simple types of fibulae

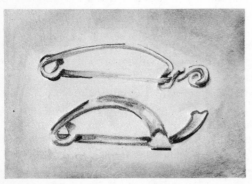

hand held accessories walking stick umbrella

The staff or walking stick was carried by the men of Greece as a sign of distinction. It was a simple form with a small crook on top. The Greeks are credited with introducing the umbrella into Europe. It, too, was a symbol of importance and was carried by a slave for the comfort of his master. It was made in several styles including a round shade section supported by reed ribs

fans

combs

perfume vials

handbags

hairnets

attached to a long handle, and the semicircular form, rib-supported, with the handle attached to the straight or back edge. An umbrella made in this design shaded only the person for whom it was carried. Fans were used by individuals or were wafted by slaves. Those used by women were small, made of linen in triangular or leaf shapes. The larger slave-manipulated fans were made of peacock feathers. Combs of boxwood and ivory were used only in a functional rather than a decorative sense. Metal and ebony combs came into use later. The comb usually had two functional sides, one fine-tooth and the other coarse. Both men and women used perfume profusely. Elaborately designed vials of alabaster, set into three-legged stands when not in use, were an important toilette accessory. White glass with glass inlay was another material frequently used in making these cosmetic accessories. Greek women carried small linen handbags made from either a gathered circle or a square of cloth. The drawstring may have acted as a handle. These purses were often decorated with embroidery. Hairnets made of a lacy golden network, strung with beads or laced with enameled figures, were worn covering the chignon.

girdles

strophion

The elaborate girdling effects used in establishing the drape of the chiton were obtained by winding long lengths of ribbon around the figure. The earliest figure-controlling girdle, or *strophion*, was made of three rather wide bands of cloth. These were wound snugly about the body, one just under the bust, one at the waist, and another around the hips.

COSTUME TRIMS
embroidery

Greek women attained great skill in the art of embroidery. Favorite motifs included stars, floral patterns, zig-zag, fret, key, spiral, guilloche, honeysuckle, palmette designs, and simple parallel bands. Often stars or floral forms were scattered all over the chiton fabric. The more rigid designs were used as hem borders. Though it is not known for certain, it is believed that the overall patterns were printed rather than embroidered.

HAIR STYLES
Men and Women
kepos
Hectorean
Theseid
monk

Men and women took care in grooming their hair. Men's styles divided into four categories: *kepos*, curls tumbling over the forehead; *Hectorean*, combed back from the face curling in back; *Theseid*, short bangs over the forehead with long locks in back; and the monk cut, cut round of ear length with no part. Trinkets and ribbons or metal bands decorated the male coif. Ribbon hair trims were worn low over the forehead. These were usually

Archaic chiton (540-530 B.C.)

tied at the back. Very early styles included braided plaits of hair bound around the head, holding a crown of curls on top. Carefully arranged bangs covered the forehead in this style.

women
Women regarded their hair as a crowning glory. General early styling included wearing the hair in a knot on the top of the head with ringlet curls masking the brow. Later hair fashion dictated a large bun worn projecting outward from the back of the head. This bun was bound by the snood or sphendon scarf and wound with ribbons. The chignon was a vast bun of hair worn at the nape of the neck or projecting to some distance from the back of the head. The scarf or snood also secured the knot of hair featured in this coif. Cascading locks of hair hung from the end of the bun of hair, distinguishing it from the snood-covered style. The simplest style left the hair falling free with a flattened pompadour pushed well over the forehead. Athenian women generally wore their hair in a knot at the nape of the neck, while Spartan women pulled the hair to the crown of the head, tying it in place with ribbons. Brides of the Doric period shaved their heads as a sign of submisssion. Husbands often shaved the heads of unfaithful wives as punishment. Wigs and false hair pieces, gold, silver, or bronze bands were also used in caring for hair. A bleach of potash, a rinse of yellow flowers crushed in water, perfumes and pomades were other hair grooming aids. Washing procedures are not known, but oils were used to add luster to the hair.

Additional pictorial resources

1. painted ceramic—Cup of Pistoxenoa—(chlamys) 500 B.C., Louvre, Paris

2. sculpture—Delphi Charioteer—(male chiton) 475 B.C., Delphi Museum, Delphi

3. bas-relief—fragment of Parthenon frieze—(tunic), 445 B.C., British Museum, London

4. sculpture—Dancing girl—(peplos), undated, Museo Nazionale, Naples

5. bas-relief—Ariston funeral steli—(armor and tunic), c. 500 B.C., National Museum, Athens

6. sculpture—Tanagra figurine—(tholia), Hellenistic period, Louvre, Paris

7. sculpture—Tanagra figurine—(deplos), Hellenistic period, Louvre, Paris

8. sculpture—Demosthenes by Polyeuktos—(himation), undated, Ny Carlsberg Glepothek, Copenhagen

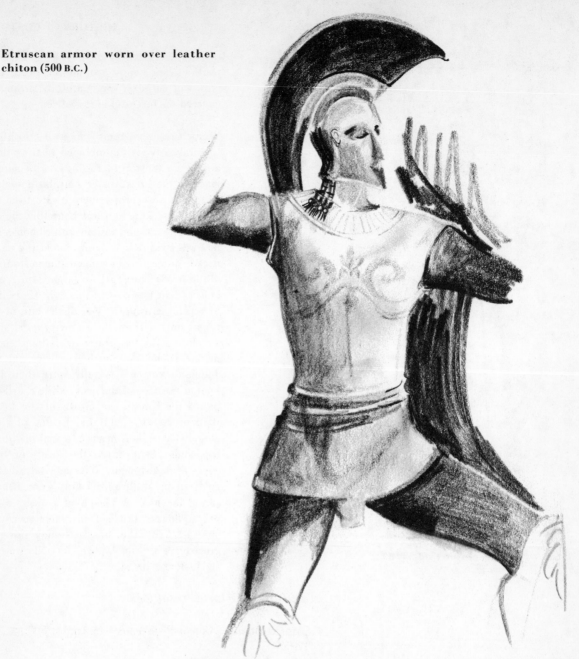

Etruscan armor worn over leather chiton (500 B.C.)

Chapter 4

ETRUSCAN STYLES

*T*HE *Etruscans were unique among the tribes who populated the Italian peninsula. Their civilization developed prior to the unification of the inhabitants of this land by the Romans. Their exact origin is controversial. Similarities between their language and the languages of other tribes of the Mediterranean area indicate that they may have been a consolidation of groups which had immigrated to the central region of Italy and which may in turn have intermixed with the Indo-Europeans who settled in the area after the Bronze Age. Archeological excavations point to the influence of many ancient cultures. Contributions to the Etruscan civilization were made by Greek, Phoenician, Cypriot, and Mycenean peoples. The time lapse associated with this* *central Italian group is set between the thirteenth and seventh centuries B.C.*

These pre-Roman peoples occupied an area northwest of Latium. By warring and pirating they expanded their territorial holding, penetrating as far south as the Caelian, the third Roman hill. The political foundation of Etruria was based on a form of feudalism with a king at the head. The fleets of these warriors, pirates, and seafarers sailed the Mediterranean harassing Phoenician and Greek merchant vessels. They also voyaged northward as far as Marseilles. Sea trade and agriculture supplied their economic prosperity.

The Etruscans were expert builders, constructing strong city fortifications, temples and tombs. They developed a sophisticated system of highways which were remarkably engineered. They built an excellent sewer system, the Closca Maxima. They were adept at metal-working, pottery-making, cobblering, and goldsmithing. Their architectural decoration evidenced a gay virtuosity, using colorful wall paintings in interiors and terra-cotta tiles on exteriors. Their sculptural forms, however, indicated a strong Grecian influence. The twelve cities forming the Etruscan League imported a number of luxury items from Greece, including jewelry, costume forms, and utilitarian objects. They themselves were skilled in using bronze and made a variety of housewares from this metal.

In general the Etruscan character was moody and cruel, hidden by a false gaiety. Many of the men and women were licentious. They were also vain and concerned with physical appearance. This was a society which preferred to go about nude in public. There are records indicating that their behavior was at times shameless and obscene. Overindulgence was the rule, particularly among intellectuals, artists, and musicians. Some men were exceedingly effeminate, while women were dynamic with masculine characteristics. Livy, shocked by Etruscan women, remarked that they went abroad "unblushingly" attending banquets, reclining on couches, relishing the repast with their male companions. Unlike their female Greek contemporaries, they attended concerts, boxing matches, races, and other sporting events. These women were given many masculine privileges.

The religion of the Etruscans was based on beliefs contrasting with their outward behavior. It was sombre and superstition-ridden. It involved such extremes as revelation through mystical signs and belief in eternal life. Worshipers bound by the religion of Etruria had faith that, through observation of matches between fighting birds and examination of animal entrails, the will of their gods would be revealed. The Etruscan religion also involved a firm conviction that there was a life after death. This belief pattern closely resembled the Egyptian religious dogma. Great tombs and sepulchers were, therefore, built for the dead. These were designed in the same style as the dwellings of the living. As their territorial boundaries were extended, the Etruscans chose a supreme location as the residence for their favored dieties, namely the fourth hill of Rome, the Capitoline. It is curious that peoples so bawdy and ribald should be believers in a faith that espoused a life after death based on the actions of the secular world.

During the sixth century B.C., despite their religious faith and worldly behavior, the power of the Etruscans waned. By the fourth century this vital people had succumbed to the power of Rome. Their society was completely obliterated as it was absorbed into the Roman cultural pattern. The lasting contributions made by the Etruscans were few. Those utilized by the succeeding Roman civilization included the curule chair, the costume form that was to become the toga, and the engineering fundamentals of their temples. Some authorities credit them with leaving a rudimentary alphabet. The Etruscans, for all their gay and abandoned behavior patterns, their attention to physical beauty, refined techniques in metal work, and aggressive territorial expansion, are not remembered for their efforts which encompassed some five centuries.

BASIC GARMENTS OF THE ETRUSCANS (1300 B.C. — 700 B.C.)

TUNIC
(1300-700 B.C.)
Men and Women

The tunic, the simple, short-sleeved garment common to all early peoples, was also worn by both sexes of Etruscans. Because of their concern with revealing the human form, this basic costume of Etruria was narrow, close-fitting and short. Bas-reliefs and wall paintings indicate that the snug male tunic barely covered the posterior.

PERIZOMA
(1300-700 B.C.)
Men

The *perizoma*, or tight-fitting trunk, was worn with a waist-length tunic. Made as any simple pants form, this brief costume covered the figure from waist to buttocks, outlining the latter because of its extremely close fit. The short legs of this clothing item had small inverted V-shaped side vents. Occasionally these vents were curved and quite large, the opening extending almost to the waist. Bands of contrasting color trimmed this style, bordering the leg opening and the curved vent.

LOINCLOTH
(1300-700 B.C.)
Men and Women

These people wore the scant loincloth so common to the costume forms of all ancients. It was made from a long, thin length of cloth and worn between the legs, secured about the waist by twisting the ends together.

TEBENNA or TRABEA
(c. 1200-700 B.C.)
Men and Women

Said to be the forerunner of the Roman toga, the semicircular *tebenna* or *trabea* was an Etruscan garment innovation. The knee-length tebenna was wrapped around the figure in the same manner as the Greek male himation. The oval or circular form was folded in half. It was placed under the left arm with this fold at the top, and wound about the body in a spiral fashion, with the curved edges creating interesting draped effects. It was made of woolen cloth which was usually white and had gay

Patterned chlamydon, male

decorative borders of red or blue. A black bordered tebenna was worn exclusively during a period of mourning.

CHLAMYDON
Men

The *chlamydon* was a simple, wound garment of lightweight patterned fabric. While rather formless itself, it was pulled taut about the body, revealing the natural curves and forms of the figure. This was a garment worn primarily by young men, perhaps for festivals only. It had decorative borders as well as the overall, random patterns embroidered or painted on the cloth from which it was cut.

SKIRT
(c. 1100 B.C.)
Women

Women wore a decorative, full, bell-shaped skirt. The fabric of this garment was covered with an ordered pattern of crosses or dots. Skirts made of striped material arranged to create horizontal bands about the figure were also worn. Bands of contrasting color decorated the hem. This garment was ankle length and similar in many ways to the bell skirt worn by Cretan women, though much fuller.

BLOUSE
Women

An elaborately styled blouse, with a yoke, was worn with the full gathered skirt. It was made of

Blouse and gathered skirt

Tunic, long peplos, and scarf (female, second century B.C.)

intricately cut pieces, particularly the sleeves. These were designed with curved cuffs and bands of contrasting colors encircling the arm, as well as long floating ribbons attached at the cuffs. Sleeves were elbow length and often bell-shaped.

CHITON
(c. 1100 B.C.)
Men and Women

This extensively worn garment was the Etruscan adaptation of the Greek chiton. Women's styles were made of very thin, transparent fabrics of extremely dark hues. These fabrics were covered with random or ordered patterns which were either geometric or floral designs. The female chiton was further decorated with bands or geometric borders around the hem.

Men also wore the chiton, but the male style fitted the figure closely. Leather chitons of scant length, patterned after the Greek male Archaic style, were worn by warriors under their armor.

OVERDRESS
Women

The overdress, which was seldom if ever belted and covered the figure from the shoulder to mid-calf or the ankles, was made in much the same way as a tunic but with inset sleeves which had a somewhat flared cuff (possibly formed by rolling full-length sleeves to the elbows) and a broad but shallow neckline.

This garment was sometimes worn over the blouse and skirt costume for added warmth, with the high standing blouse collar projecting over its broad low neckline. The longer versions had a band trim, sometimes extended down the center front, around the neck. Pleated insets on the side seams often added fullness to the skirt of the overdress at the hem.

SCARF
(1300-1100 B.C.)
Men and Women

The Etruscan scarf was made from a long rectangular length of cloth and was an adaptation of the Greek himation. This wrap was brightly colored, often red, yellow-orange or royal blue. A sawtoothed border design of yellow or brown was the distinctive decorative element of this wrap. The wearing pattern for each sex corresponded to the manner established by its counterpart in Greece.

LACERNA
Men and Women

The *lacerna* was a short, circular cape worn by the lower classes. It was made of rough, heavy woolen cloth and had a center front opening extending from the simple round neck to the thigh-length hem. This too was a borrowed garment form based on the Greek tribon.

Short overgown and floor-length chiton, female

ACCESSORIES
(1300-700 B.C.)
Men and Women headwear tutulus

Few people wore hats; however, the conical *tutulus* was used by some women. This oddly designed hat form had a tall cone-shaped crown with a small turned-down knob at the top. The small brim was worn upward, framing the face. The back of the head and hair was covered with a long, sacklike sheath or a gold net. This hat was perhaps a poor copy of the phrygian cap. It was worn well back on the head and was doubtless made of rather firm material such as felt or leather, for it held its shape even though projecting precariously outward from the back of the head.

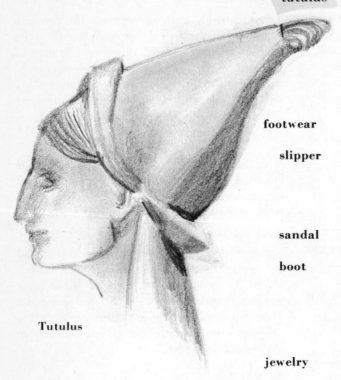

Tutulus

footwear

slipper

sandal

boot

Etruscans were accomplished shoemakers. Three basic forms of footwear predominated; the slipper, the sandal, and the boot. The slipper was made of one piece of felt or cloth in a simple shell form that covered both the sole and the top of the foot. The fabric colors used included red, green, and brown. A variation of this slipper had instep laces and was open at the toe and heel. Etruscan sandals were rather delicate footwear with thin straps and binding laces, attached to a leather sole. Boots were sturdy and made with leather soles and tops. The body of the boot covered the foot and the lower leg. The section that covered the foot and the back of the leg was laced together with thongs.

jewelry

Much of the Etruscan jewelry was imported, though they too created handsome body ornaments. They are credited with the lost art of soldering powdered gold to jewels. In an affluent society, the female Etruscan aristocracy possessed great casks filled with gold rings, brooches, fibulae, bracelets, clasps, and earrings. Earrings were an important accessory and dominated the costume by their enormous size and length. There were three-inch long pendants with snakes or human heads as the design theme. Gold and precious stones etched with engravings of the images of small birds or animals, arabesques, and floral volutes were used extensively in this craft.

HAIRSTYLES
Men and Women

The earliest female hairstyle was simple with the hair falling about the head and body to the waist. Later the hair was trained into corkscrew curls about the face and arranged into small pencil braids in back. Hair was also formally waved over the brow and drawn back, plaited into a floor-length braid that was then encased in a long cloth sheath. The hair in back was also enclosed in a gold net that was secured just behind the ears. In this coif a jumble of curls, originating from waves drawn smoothly over the forehead, fell in front of the ears. Coronets and wreaths of golden leaves were the primary head decorations. Blonde hair was much admired and Etruscan women used bleaches to attain it.

Men wore their hair rather short, with curls over the entire head and sizable sideburns. They also pulled the hair back from a center part and formed two club pugs behind the ears. This was a very early style. Some men wore a chin fringe beard or a sparse jawline beard ending in a stiletto point at the chin.

Additional pictorial resources

1. sculpture—head of a woman—(tutulus), c. 500 B.C., Ny Carlsberg Glyptotek, Copenhagen

2. sculpture—figure of a woman—(tebenna), undated, Museo Etrusco, Gregoriano, Vatican

3. wall painting—dancing figures—(blouse and gathered bell skirt), 600 B.C., Tomb of Triclinium, Caera

4. statuette—female figure—(tunic and lacerna), 800 B.C., Civic Museum, Chiusi

5. bronze statuette—female figure—(chiton), 700 B.C., Metropolitan Museum of Art, New York

6. wall painting—male figures—(trabea and scarf wrap), undated, Tomba Archeological Museum, Florence

7. statuette—male figure—(tebenna), 600 B.C., British Museum, London

8. bronze statuette—male warrior—(perizoma and helmet), 800 B.C., Archeological Museum, Florence

9. wall painting—female figures—(chiton skirt section and tebenna), c. 600 B.C., House of Vetti, Pompeii

10. wall painting—male figures—(tunic), 500 B.C., Archeological Museum, Florence

Palla used as a head covering (19 B.C.)

Chapter 5

HOW THE ROMANS LOOKED

*T*HE centuries of Roman influence extended from hundreds of years
before the birth of Christ until well into the early Christian era.
Roman civilization can be divided into three major periods: the
Kingdom (750-509 B.C.); the Republic (509-30 B.C.); and the Empire
(30 B.C.-A.D. 476). The Kingdom takes us from the legendary founding
of Rome by Romulus to the expulsion of the last Etruscan king of Rome
and the establishment of the Republic, a patrician-dominated state
governed by two Consuls. During the period of the Republic, Rome gained
supremacy over the neighboring Italian city-states and by the third century B.C., after the Punic Wars, it controlled most of the Mediterranean,
with outposts as far north as the British Isles.

48

The Roman Empire came into being after the assassination of Julius Caesar under his nephew, Octavius, who ascended to the throne as Augustus. The ensuing two hundred years of the Pax Romana was the golden age of Roman culture. The arts flourished during this time, especially under Augustus and Nero, with the greatest achievements in the areas of architecture and sculpture. The grandiose, ornate, yet disciplined structures of Roman architecture lend insight into Roman character and culture. These vast structures—the Baths of Diocletian, the Basilica of Maxentius, the buildings of the Forum, the House of the Faun in Pompeii, and the many arches, such as the Arch of Titus—are also evidence of the Romans' skill and mastery as designers and builders. Though an engineering feat, the great arch-supported aquaduct system of Rome is, in addition, an architectural achievement and one of such durability that it is still being used today.

The sculpture of Rome was dominated by portraiture, which attained a remarkable degree of realism. Although the Romans greatly revered Greek sculpture and some Roman sculpture was simply an imitation of Greek works, there are marked differences between Greek and Roman sculpture taken as a whole. While the Greeks were concerned with capturing the harmony of the whole physical being in union with the soul, the Romans were more intent on portraying the detailed features and outward appearance as an expression of human character.

Besides being a time of cultural advancement, the period of the Roman Empire was also one in which the Romans further expanded their domain to include lands from England to the Orient, forming the largest unified state the Western world has ever known. However, a slow decline began at the end of the second century A.D., culminating in the sacking of Rome by the Ostrogoths, a barbarian tribe from the north, and in the transfer of the capital to Constantinople.

Roman culture reached a high level of sophistication before its decline, however. The Romans established a highly organized system of law. Their military ability was unchallenged. Highly skilled in sports, they devoted much time to physical conditioning. Both men and women were fastidious and used the public baths to insure good health, for pleasure, and for conducting business. Women came to the baths in the morning accompanied by slaves carrying oils and unguents in glass balls hung from cords. The ritual of the bath was begun with exercise, followed by a rest period in the sudatorium, then the hotter calidarium, a cooling-off period in the tepidarium, and finally an icy cold bath in the frigidarium. During all these elaborate procedures, slaves massaged their mistresses with instruments of ivory, copper, iron, or silver. Men, following a similar ritual, went to the baths in the afternoon for conversation and business negotiations.

The Romans enjoyed pomp and splendor. They were preoccupied with amassing vast fortunes. These dominant interests were interwoven in their festivals and ceremonies as well as their daily activities and they dictated their social order. Attention to luxurious dress played an important role in the lives of women of wealth and social status. Their interest in elaborate costumes influenced men, who became equally concerned with wearing apparel of elegance and with their general personal appearance.

Roman armor

Traveling was a lavishly attended matter and luggage included every-thing which they thought was required for their comfort, from gold and silverwear to furniture.

During the formative stages of this society, men ruled the home. How-ever, by the period of the Empire, women were educated and were able to read both Latin and Greek; they also became well versed in philosophy and literature, avidly reading the novels of the day. In addition, they were aware of the arts of Rome—of the dance, of singing, and visual forms. In time, women controlled the home activities of spinning, storing and taking inventory of provisions, and the early care of children. "Domina" of her house and "regina" to her husband's clients, the Roman matron was not part of public life nor of his business dealings.

Christianity had its beginning during the reign of the Emperor Nero and as time passed, the number of Roman Christians increased. Before the Christian influence, Roman religion was pagan, based on a belief that the forces of nature were spirits. Formal worship ceremonies were brief, yet their religion played an integral and practical part in everyday life. The Romans believed that if they paid regular patronage to the spirits, they would be protected and blessed by them. The Romans worshipped such deities as Saturnus, god of planting, Fides, god of faithfulness, and Terminus, the god of territorial limits. In time, Greek gods were adopted and renamed. A female underworld goddess, Matura, represented with a child in her lap, was to become the Madonna of Christians. Of great importance was the god of the home. The sacred fires of this god were attended by six vestal virgins. These fires were kindled anew each year in the Forum, and home fires were relighted by flames brought from them.

BASIC GARMENTS OF ANCIENT ROME
(500 B.C.— A.D. 400)

TOGA
(500 B.C.-A.D. 200)
Men and Women

The most commonly worn garment during the Roman era was the *toga*. It was worn by men and women, boys, and girls and was a derivative cos-tume copied from the Etruscan tebenna or trabea. The toga was designed in three basic forms; the simple rectangle of woolen cloth, the semicircle of linen or woolen fabric, and the folded oval with a woven band of contrasting color through the center. The toga was draped and wound around the body in much the same manner as the Greek himation. In the Roman style more of the chest was exposed by starting the draped winding at a point just above the waist on the left side. A spiral effect was created by wrapping each layer higher on the body, with each successive wrap drawn less taut. A pouch or pocket was formed in the folds that developed about the waist. At times this excess of material was twisted inward, secur-

Boy's toga praetexata

ing the toga more firmly about the figure. The right arm was always exposed, while the left was usually covered. The final section of the toga was drawn up over the left shoulder, wrapped about the left forearm, thrown casually over the shoulder, and hung loosely down the side or over the left arm. The wearing style and manipulation of the free end indicated the sophistication of the wearer. Because the draping of the toga was according to personal preference, the spiral was often created by arranging the winding layers in the reverse order. This was particularly true when the band-trimmed toga was worn. This cumbersome garment was so difficult to arrange that a slave assisted. The toga was worn over either the tunic, the nude body, or the figure clad in a subligaculum. Men frequenting the Forum often protected their heads with the left arm bound in the end of the toga, for heated arguments often turned into brawls in this gathering-place.

toga praetexata

toga picta
toga virilis

toga candida

toga sordida

Many toga forms evolved which connoted rank and social position. These were: *toga praetexata*, white with a purple border, worn by emperors, priests, magistrates, censors, and boys and girls below the age of fourteen; *toga picta*, purple with embroidered gold stars, worn by generals; *toga virilis*, natural wool color, worn by freemen; *toga candida*, wool color made whiter by chalk powder, worn by candidates, who also chalked the exposed portions of the body to symbolize purity of character; and the *toga sordida*, brown, worn by plebeians.

TUNICA
(500 B.C.-A.D. 400)
Men and Women

The simple T-shaped *tunica* was the same design as the tunics worn by contemporaries in neighboring lands. Made of linen or wool of natural color, the tunica was worn belted and slightly bloused over the girdle. The male tunica was thigh length while the female style touched the floor. The long style worn by women was basically an undergarment made of yellow or natural colored linen, though in later periods green, sea green, flesh pink, and azure blue were used.

tunica lati clavi

tunica palmata

The tunica also became an indicator of status. The *tunica lati clavi* worn by consuls, senators and priests had two vertical bands embroidered or appliqued on the front. The width of these bands, placed on either side of the neck, also designated the importance of the wearer. The *tunica palmata* was worn by generals for celebrations honoring victories. This purple garment was decorated with gold palm leaf designs and a gold border at the

Toga virilis, male; stola and palla, female (50-40 B.C.)

Tunica, toga praetexata (Roman senator, 100 B.C.)

Stola and palla (Ostia, Museo Ostiense)

tunica tularis

hem. The *tunica tularis* was also a festival garment trimmed with a Greek fret border at the hem and random patterning of animal images in gold embroidery.

STOLA
(c. 130 B.C.-A.D. 400)
Women

The basic garment of Roman women was the *stola*. It too, was a borrowed style of wearing apparel whose origin was the Greek chiton, perhaps of the Ionic period. The basic difference between these two gown forms was the sleeve. The Roman stola may well have had the sleeves sewn into the main body of the garment. The draping of the sleeve was formed by gathering the fabric along the seam which was placed on the top of the arm. The stola was double and triple girdled in the same manner as the female Greek chiton. Evolving into a true dress form, this costume was not pinned on the shoulders, but had shoulder seams made in the conventional manner of present times. The blouse section was full, draped in many intricate arrangements, and flounced over the girdling. The girdle

succincta cingulum

at the hips was called the *succincta* and the one under the bust the *cingulum*. This graceful garment was always floor length.

TALARIS
(510 B.C.-A.D. 400)
Women
inseta

The *talaris* was a floor-length gown made very much like the tunica of the empire. It was modified in design by the addition of a gusset, or *inseta*, in the skirt. This created a short pleated train. The decorative tunica, with deep fringe around the hem, was worn during the last period of this society. It was made from many different types of cloth, including fine wool, linen, cotton and silk, in a wide range of colors.

SYNTHESIS
(c. 200 B.C.)
Men

Romans enjoyed elaborate feasts, lounging on couches, savoring every morsel. The most sophisticated diners donned a garment called the *synthesis* when attending these lavish eating orgies. The exact construction of this dining costume is vague but it seems to have been a combination of a tunic top and a skirt draped like a toga.

DALMATICA
Men

The *dalmatica*, or dalmatica tunica, was a late arrival on the Roman costume scene. It was a floor-length overgarment, with full-length sleeves open wide at the wrists. While it was primarily a male garment, older women also used this item of apparel for warmth.

CASULA
Men

The outer wrap called the *casula* was a poncho or simple cape. It was made from a square or rectangle of woolen material with a slit in the center for the neck and was worn loose with no sleeve arrangements devised.

Talaris with inseta, over tunic and pulla

SAGUM
Men

Roman soldiers used a blanketlike form called the *sagum* which they placed about the body in much the same way Greeks wore the chlamys. They also used the sagum as a knapsack or as a tent, depending on the circumstances.

PALUDA-MENTUM
Men

Plebeians or commoners and men when traveling wore the *paludamentum*. This was a rough, rugged wrap, similar in form to the chlamys.

LAENA
Men

Among the many outer garments worn for warmth by Roman men was the *laena*. This garment was a large circular cape. It was made of heavy woolen cloth, lined with a gaily colored fabric and may have been a duplicate of the Grecian lacerna.

PALLA
Women
PALLIUM
Men

A rectangular length of woolen fabric worn wrapped around the figure and arranged in the same wearing style as the Greek himation was known as the *palla* when worn by women and the *pallium* when worn by all classes. The female version of this outer wrap was gaily colored and patterned. The fabric was often covered with random designs of intertwining floral motifs. Fringe was used as a border trim. Men wore the pallium about the figure in the same manner as the masculine version of the Greek himation.

CARACALLA
Men and
Women

The ankle-length outer tunic, open from neck to hem, usually designed with an attached hood, was called the *caracalla*. This garment was worn only if the weather was cold.

PULLA
Women
supparium
clicula

The adult female toga was called the *pulla*. Other simple wraps used by women included a shawl or *supparium* and the *clicula*. The latter was an elbow-length cape.

CAPES
Men and
Women
bardocu-cullus
lacerna

cucullus

birrhus
paenula

The large travel capes, the *bardocucullus* and *lacerna*, were used for travel and during cold weather. The hooded bardocucullus, a peasant's garment, was made of coarse wool material in dark somber colors. This cape had modified sleeves. The lacerna, also hooded, was short and sleeveless. Side slits acted as armholes. The hood section was called the *cucullus*. This short wrap was fastened at the throat with cord ties. Colors of the fabrics used in making the lacerna were usually black and brown. When red cloth was used, this same style was referred to as a *birrhus*. The *paenula* was made from a full circle of woolen cloth with a hole in the center for the neck. This huge travel cape also had a hood attached and was often designed with a slit extending some distance down the front from the neck opening.

Cucullus, caracalla, crepida, and feminalia

Bardocullus

FEMINALIA
(40 B.C.-A.D. 300)
Men

The *feminalia* were the Roman adaptation of the crudely shaped breeches worn by Gaulish men. This pants form was tight-fitting, thigh length and worn beneath the tunica. The feminalia were originally worn by foot soldiers as protection against cold during the campaigns in Gaul, but were not accepted as a suitable male garment until the Empire period, at which time they were used more for horseback riding than as everyday apparel. Portrait sculptures of the later Roman periods indicate that these pants were a primitive form of knee breeches, secured about the legs at the knees with tapes or thongs. The exact cut of the main body of these garments is not known, for none have survived from the time of antiquity.

UNDERWEAR
(c. 200 B.C.-A.D. 300)
**Men and
Women
subligaculum
subucula
licinium**

The *subligaculum* (a form of loincloth) was worn beneath the male tunica or toga. If weather demanded, the *subucula* (a close-fitting, short tunic) was used. The loincloth of linen worn by men was known as the *licinium*. Like the subligaculum, it was worn between the legs and held in place by knotting the ends together. The licinium was the official garment of the Roman athlete, who wore

**loincloth
mamillare
strophium
pagne**

no other costume, weather permitting. Underwear for women consisted of a loincloth and the *mamillare*. The latter was a tight band bound about the breast. The *strophium* and *pagne* were garments worn beneath the stola at the public bath, while participating in the exercises which were part of the bathing ritual or in gymnastic events. These garments combined made a very early version of the bikini bathing suit. The strophium was a simple band brassiere, the pagne brief trunks.

**ACCESSORIES
Men and
Women
  headwear
  galarus
  causia
  pileus
  petasus
  flammeum**

Roman hats and headcoverings developed many forms. These included: the *galerus*, a close-fitting cap; the *causia*, a hat with a low crown, ear flaps and broad brim; the *pileus*, a cone-shaped cap worn by plebeians and slaves; the *petasus*, a straw sun hat worn by women and senators to the Roman Circus and outdoor sports events; and the ceremonial wedding veil, the *flammeum*, worn by the bride "atop six pads of hair and covering the brow," encircled with a wreath of marjoram, verbena, myrtle, or orange blossoms.

footwear

Tunica and thong sandal (A.D. 350, Rome, Museo Nazionale della Terme)

Footwear of this period was designed to suit the demands of the occasion, ranging in style from high boots to silken slippers. Roman shoe forms for the most part covered the foot. The earliest of these was the simple soft leather *cabatina* made from a sole cut two inches larger than the foot size and drawn up over the foot by a thong which was laced over the instep. The street shoe or *cacei* also covered the foot, had a separate sole and top, instep lacing, and was tied about the ankle with the knot in the back. Patricians wore these shoes made of elegant leather and gold or silver ornaments. The spiked soled soldier's boot was called the *caligae*. Another rugged boot, the *pero*, had many variations, one of which identified senators. The senatorial style was made of black leather decorated with a silver "C" (for *Consul*) placed behind the ankle on the heel. Women wore a white boot laced with colored silk straps. This female boot was called the *phaecassium*. Women wore the simple slipper or *solea* about the house as well as sandals with four straps, one of which was worn between the first and second toes. About the house men wore a shell-shaped slipper called the *campagus*. Among the many boot forms developed in the latter years of the Roman civilization were: the *caceus*, a high boot laced on the inside of the lower leg and fitted with a tongue; the *muleus*, similar to the caceus, but laced with red colored thongs and worn only by emperors; the *gallicae*, a knee-high closed boot; the *espadrilles*, a boot

cabatina

cacei

**caligae
pero**

**phaecas-
sium
solea
sandal
campagus**

**caceus
muleus**

**gallicae
espadrilles**

crepida
soccus

with the straps laced through eyelets, or a sophisticated version of the Greek *crepida*. The *soccus* was an elegant and decorative slipper that appeared during the last years of this civilization when trade with the Orient had introduced fabric made of silk fiber. This colorful shoe in reds, greens, yellows, or white was a delicate shell shape.

jewelry

fibulae
stiletto
pins

brooches
buttons

In a society that was so fond of rich and sumptuous personal adornment, jewelry items were numerous. Pins in the form of fibulae or stiletto pins were richly decorative. The former had three dominant shapes; the "T," the harp, and the arrow. The Romans were perhaps the first to create the brooch pin form and to use jewel encrusted buttons as costume decorations.

necklaces

bracelets

Much of the heavy massive Roman jewelry was imported from the Near East and was less graceful than that worn by the Greeks. Necklaces were designed with diamond, sapphire, garnet, and opal settings. They were also fashioned from cylindrical beads of amethyst and chrysoprase. Ropes of pearls, heavy gold plates encrusted with pearls, inlaid with colored paste or enamel, and highly polished stonewear set in a tracery of gold filigree were other neckwear forms. Roman bracelets were equally massive and made of the same materials as the necklaces. The serpent wound about the arm was one of the more simple forms. Nero awarded bracelets to heroes of the state, much as chest medals are given today for meritorious acts. Pompey has been credited with initiating the popularity of these arm decorations, which ranged from the single circle of metal to the huge, jewel-set, hinged and clasped forms of later periods.

rings

The ring was one of the most unique jewelry items of this era. The iron ring was perhaps the original Roman accessory. Later rings were made of gold. At one period, after a defeat, the wearing of rings was banned. When the ban was lifted, iron rings were again worn as a sign of mourning. Seal rings, key rings, thumb rings, summer and winter rings, poison rings—some functional, some decorative, some lethal—were used. Summer rings were small but winter rings were massive, worn on the thumb, and many were three inches long, very wide and very heavy. Key rings were generally used by women, to lock or gain access to the household stores in their charge. The segment that fitted the lock was hinged to the shank and was folded back over the outside of the thumb when not being used. Poison rings were made with a minute vial and a decorative hinged lid. The lid could be lifted surreptitiously and the lethal contents poured into the victim's goblet. This was a handy way to dispose of an enemy or to have the means of suicide available when needed.

hand held accessories umbrellas fans mirrors gloves watches

Umbrellas, fans, mirrors, watches, and gloves were all used by Romans. Gloves were worn during a meal or large feast when all in attendance dipped their hands into the same bowls of food. Wearing gloves was thought to offer some sanitary protection. Watches (really miniature sundials) were carried or worn on the person suspended from small chains. All other hand-manipulated accessories were designed after similar objects used by the Romans' contemporaries living about the Mediterranean.

HAIR STYLES Men and Women

During the early periods, Roman men wore their hair long and also wore beards. Later hair styles were short and carefully curled. During these later periods beards were also short and carefully waved. The hair was usually clipped to lie in flat curls or waves, and golden wreaths of laurel were used as head decorations.

cauls nets

Styles of female coif developed from the simple free falling waved or plaited fashions to rather high pompadours made of corkscrew curls. The hair in back was caught up in nets or cauls of gold, or wound with ribbons which bound it in place. During the period of the Empire, hair was parted in the center, waved and puffed out, circling the head. Wigs were formed in the same style. At one time late in the third century B.C. the hair was arranged into shallow waves from a center part, drawn to the nape of the neck and plaited into three flat braids. These were then brought up over the back to the front, covering the part. Another style of the same era had two small buns on the neck. This style was held in place by a large oval clip. Braids wound coronet fashion atop a mass of closely waved hair brought well over the forehead were fashionable during the second century. Cauls, diadems studded with diamonds and emeralds, and jewel-encrusted *stephone* added elegance to a wide variety of female hair fashions.

stephone diadems

Additional pictorial resources

1. sculpture—figure of woman, seated—(stola and pulla). Empire, Museo del Campedoglio, Rome
2. mosiac—female figures—(strophium and pagne), 400 B.C., Piazza Armerina, Sicily

3. wall painting—bride—(flammeum), undated, Villa of Mysteries, Pompeii

4. fresco—slaves and young women—(tunica, pulla, palla and sandals), undated, Museo Nazionale, Naples

5. bas-relief—warriors and slaves—(toga and tunica), undated, Villa Alvani, Rome

6. actual articles—sandals, c. A.D. 100, London Museum, London

7. sculpture—Emperor Trajan—(armor), undated, Louvre, Paris

8. sculpture—Aedila—(long tunica and pulla), A.D. 300, Museo del Conservatori, Rome

9. sculpture—Augustus—(toga and tunica), undated, Louvre, Paris

10. sculpture—Tiberius—(toga and chiton-like tunica), undated, Louvre, Paris

11. wall painting—actors—(caracalla), undated, Museo Nazionale, Naples

12. wall fresco—female figures—(pulla, tunica and palla), undated, Museo Nazionale, Naples

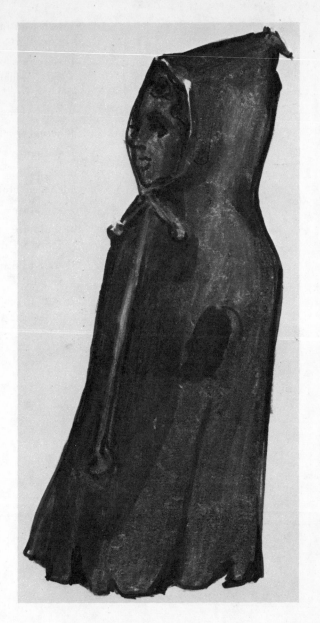

Chapter 6
COSTUMES OF NORTHERN TRIBES

*W*ILD, *fierce men with intrepid spirits braved the last remnants of the retreating Ice Age. Neither written records nor archeological findings are available to explain how men came to be living in the vast inclement regions of northern Europe. The southward migrations of the Celts, Goths, Franks, and other tribes culminated in the invasion and sack of Rome.*

The invasions and migrations of all these tribes, with their variety of origins, formulated the future of Europe. No one will ever know just how far the influence of these restless tribes reached or what modifications resulted from their movements while searching for better living conditions. Modes of living changed through the interaction of vastly different

60

primitive cultures, and from these changes emerged a totally new and vital social order.

Records of trade intercourse indicate that some of the more subtle influences and those with less world-changing impact were reflected in forms of dress. For example, men of southern Europe adopted a garment similar to the breeches or braccae worn by the men of northern Europe. Until the time of these contacts, men of the southern region did not wear any form of leg-covering trouser. The two-legged garment, which had originated in Persia, was introduced into the clothing culture of northern Europe in the course of invasions via the Central Steppes, through Teutonic lands, and into Gaul. Body coverings made of skins in their raw state were discarded for more convenient and more protective forms. Knowledge of weaving techniques radically altered the costumes worn by the northern tribes. They in turn contributed novel dress ideas to those with more sophisticated habits. Among these were the braccae, which became the feminalia (femoralia), and the use of furs as cloak linings. One common garment, the tunic (colobium), was represented in every culture, refined or primitive. From the Neolithic period, one of rudimentary body coverings, to the early Bronze Age, when wearing forms that could be called clothes were invented, man was concerned with covering his person with costumes both decorative and functional. All garments of the northern tribes satisfied these qualifications.

Rhino and loincloth (300-100 B.C.)

Vest colobium, singlet (or belted tunic) with saw-toothed edged hem and braccae

BASIC GARMENTS OF NORTHERN TRIBES (1200 B.C. — A.D. 400)

LOINCLOTH
(1200-200 B.C.)
Men

During the Bronze Age, men wore the simple loincloth made from an unshaped piece of doeskin. The skin was worn between the legs and looped over a leather waistband, with the ends hanging down loose front and back. Later the belt was made of lengths of braided cloth. By the thirteenth century B.C. the shape of the loincloth was rectangular and the free hanging front panel was knee length. Still later versions were made from a folded square of fabric, worn much like an infant's diaper. The two side ends were tied together over the one pulled between the legs. This rude style was an undergarment worn by both men and women.

BRACCAE
(1200-30 B.C.)
Men

paison

The *braccae* evolved from the loincloth when leg windings held up by bands bound around the leg were added. The braccae (or braies) were made from leather or crudely woven cloth, in an inverted U-form, gathered at the waist and belted with a thong or braided cord. In cold weather they were tied at the ankle or cross bound up the legs to the knees. *Paison* were made in the same way,

Vest type colobium worn over tunic with gathered neckline (100 B.C.-A.D. 300)

but were much fuller and cross bound up the legs as far as the thigh. At first the Romans thought these garments ridiculous and referred to them as *gallia narbonenis* or *gallia braccata*.

TUNIC
(1200-300 B.C.)
Men and Women

Both men and women wore the tunic, which was slim, had either long or short sleeves and was usually floor length. Men also wore a thigh-length style tucked into the braccae or paison or worn on the outside girdled at the waist. Women seldom belted this basic garment. The hem was often trimmed with fringe or a "toothed" edging. The former was the result of raveling out the lower edge of the material and the latter was made by cutting a series of V-shaped cuts around the bottom of the tunic. If the tunic was made for winter use it was lined with fur, which was allowed to show at neck and hem. Many layers of tunic were worn at one time as protection against the cold. Later versions were amply cut, pleated about the figure and belted about the waist. A double girdle was also created by winding the braided cord once about the waist, once about the hips, and tying it low in the front. The singlet, or short belted tunic, and the sleeveless *colobium* were male style variations of this simple costume. The colobium was often slit from neck to hem, making a long vest, sometimes lined with goatskin and worn with goatskin braccae.

singlet colobium

SKIRT
(1200-200 B.C.)
Women

The skirts worn by females of these northern tribes were made as they were donned. A rather long piece of coarse woolen fabric was placed around the body, covering the rib cage. It was then gathered or pleated, with a belt holding the pleats in place and at the same time securing the skirt around the figure. The belt was often double-girdled.

BLOUSE
Women

A simple blouse with elbow-length sleeves was worn with the gathered skirt. It covered the upper body from the shoulders to just below the bust. The band-trimmed neckline was round with a center slit extending a few inches down the front. This blouse, which was worn outside the skirt, had a fringed hem.

CAPE
Women

From the time of the Bronze Age and for several centuries, women wore a semicircular cape of coarsely woven wool. The straight side was worn around the neck with the edge rolled or folded back, forming a crude collar.

Paesula and foot cov-
ering

Skirt and blouse with knit hair covering (women of northern tribes)

Cape over tunic of
reindeer hides (100
B.C.-A.D. 300)

Camisia, rhino, gallia braccata, and pileus (300-100 B.C.)

Sagum (or sale), gartered paison, bracelets, and brooch (100 B.C.-A.D. 300)

SAGUM
Men
  lacerna
  paesula

  bardocu-
  cullus

The *sagum* was a male wrap of woolen cloth worn about the shoulders and fastened at the throat with a fibula. Other simple wraps were the lacerna and the paesula, which were long shawls draped around the figure in the same manner as the Greek himation. The hooded cape of this time was called the bardocucullus. The animal skin wrap, the earliest of all cape forms, was called the *rhino*. During warm weather the skin side was worn inside, while during winter months it was reversed.

UNDERWEAR
Men and
Women

In time women discarded the loincloth and wore a waist-length shirt, or *camisia*. Men wore this same garment for added warmth, with or without the loincloth.

ACCESSORIES
Men and
Women
  headwear
    pileus
    cap
    tiered cap

Many Gallo-Roman people wore the round pileus. Celts and Teutonic tribesmen wore round caps made by an early form of crochet. Seafaring males adopted two-tiered caps, similar to those worn by men in present-day navies. Women used the larger, more protective, broad-brimmed hat styled much like the petasus.

  footwear

    slippers

    gallicae

The earliest foot coverings were made by binding animal skins to the feet with strips of leather. Later styles were made in the same way as the soft leather Roman slipper. The sole, cut larger than the foot, was drawn up over the toes by a thong which was laced through a series of slits, laced over the instep, and caught through the leather that covered the heel. *Gallicae* were simple boots made of two pieces of leather shaped like the profile of the foot, large enough to allow for its width. These basic soft leather boots were usually ankle high and sometimes had small rolled cuffs. They were worn with crude gaiters, primitively knitted woolen socks, and paison.

  jewelry
    rings
    bracelets
    amulets
    fibulae

    coronets

Rings, bracelets, and lucky amulets were made of bronze and decorated with an enameled surface or set with bits of stone. Rings were worn on the fingers between the first and second joint. Fibulae were usually disc-shaped with an openwork or pierced design on top attached to the simple pin on back. Metal headbands or coronets set with large stones were also worn by tribal chiefs, members of their families, and by warriors of undoubted loyalty.

HAIR STYLES
Men and
Women

Hair styles were originally created to make the wearer have a ferocious appearance. Such awesome male styles were made by shaving the head

Female tunic and typical early hair
style for women (100 B.C.-A.D. 300)

smooth except for a top knot bound by thongs at
the crown or long trailing locks streaming out
behind. Long corkscrew sideburns and thin
mustaches added more fierceness. Full uncombed
heads of hair with full beards, long hair brushed
back from the brows and long locks falling from
rough center parts were other ways these early
men of the north wore their hair.

Women wore their hair long, often reaching the
ground, in long plaited braids starting from center
parts and brought forward to be braided with strips
of colored fabric or caught up in net snoods. The
snood was placed beneath the hair in back, tied
over the crown with thin cords, and then the hair
was gathered in the net section. The net was held
in place by another pair of cords tied low over
the forehead. Women also wore their shoulder-
length hair hanging free. The more carefully
arranged coifs were held in place by simple coronets, or bronze bands, set with bits of stone or
semiprecious gems.

Additional pictorial resources

1. actual garments (blouse, skirt, basic tunic), c. 200 B.C. Ny Carlsberg Glyptotek, Copenhagen
2. statuette—young boy—(bardocucullus), undated, Louvre, Paris

Very little remains of this culture, exact dating is rare. The Ny
Carlsberg has the largest collection relating to this time period.

Saccosz

Chapter 7

DRESS OF THE DARK AGES

*B*ARBARIAN *invasions played a significant role in the transforma-
tion of Europe after the fall of Imperial Rome. For several
centuries Europe suffered the onslaught of marauding Slavic,
Teutonic, and Hunnish bands while other tribes still in a crude stage of
cultural development moved across the continent. The inherent characteristics of the Vandals, Alemanni, Lombards, Franks, and Saxons, particularly their love of freedom and ideals of personal loyalty, were
directly reflected in the social and political order between the fourth and
ninth centuries. As these restless nomadic tribes finally acquired terri-
tories on which they could establish a more stable society, small numbers
of families banded together in village communities around which they*

cultivated the land. The village, or pagus, was the cultural center. Here the laws under which the people lived were formulated and, for a time, the old pagan religion, a polytheistic form of worship honoring Wodin, Thor, and Freya, was practiced. These communities established by the various tribes developed into separate kingdoms, which were eventually united under Charlemagne. Formalized classes of nobles, commoners, and serfs evolved.

Meanwhile, Constantine I moved the capital of the Roman Empire to Constantinople (Byzantium), which was to be the fashion and cultural center of Europe until the time of the Crusades. Constantine tolerated Christianity, and, after a brief setback under his successor, Julian the Apostate, it was accepted as the state religion during the reign of Jovian.

The influence of the Church spread in line with the organization of the Empire. The Bishop of Rome ruled in the West and the Metropolitan in the East. Learning was confined to the monasteries. The population was burdened with heavy taxes and was powerless under the paternalistic rule of the Roman Empire. The agricultural class (small landowners and free laborers) was degraded. Though serfs were able to attain freedom from slavery somewhat more easily than before, once it had been gained they were forced to eke out a miserable existence on a small plot of land. The serf or poor freeman, descendant of the proud invaders of the north, lived a burdensome servile life.

Costume styles during this period were influenced by the mixture of many cultures. Roman costume—the sleeved stola and the open-toed crepida—was adopted in Byzantium. The rich fabrics of the East were made into sumptuous court costumes in the West. Complex oriental design motifs were seen on the fabrics used at the Byzantine court. Traders from the Adriatic, the North Sea, and the Rhine traded with the merchants of Byzantium. In time the silken cloth of the Near East was to change the costume habits of the whole of Europe.

BASIC GARMENTS OF THE DARK AGES (400—800)

Cloak with tablion, paragaudion, breeches, and boots (500)

PARAGAUDION
(400-600)
Men

The *paragaudion*, or short tunic, was worn by men, whether members of the ruling class or commoners, during the Dark Ages. It was worn outside the paison and belted at the waist. The sleeves were long, with cuffs which were either embroidered or made of bands of contrasting color. Royal males wore a purple paragaudion heavily embroidered with thread of gold. The belts, both functional and decorative, were leather.

TUNIC
(400-600)
Women

The female tunic of this period was long and flowing. In northern European areas it was made with rather extended sleeves which were worn

Tunic (600: Trinity College, Dublin)

Lorum, supertunic, and stola (400-600)

folded into deep cuffs or falling over the hands for warmth. The tunics worn in Byzantium were made with less fullness and had narrow sleeves fitting tightly about the wrists. They were made of rich multicolored silk fabrics. These fabrics were originally woven in the Far East, carefully unraveled and rewoven into lighter weight materials more suitable to the warmer climate of Constantinople. Eventually the manufacturing of silks was local and under the jurisdiction of the area's rulers.

tunica

The *tunica*, like the tunic, was an outer garment, used by both sexes. It was varied in style but was basically a knee-length slender garment with short sleeves that covered half of the upper arm or reached to the elbows. The tunica skirt had two deep side slits starting at a point just below the hip and extending to the hem. The simple round neckline, sleeve cuffs, slits and hem were trimmed with embroidery or bands of color. Kings of Byzantium wore a floor-length version of this garment, made of decorative heavy silk cloth, called the *saccoz*. The tunica was made of either plain colored wool or elegant material, depending on the rank of the wearer. The *talaris tunic*, of similar design, was exclusively a priestly garment embroidered with traditional Coptic motifs.

saccoz

talaris tunic

STOLA
(400)
Women

The stola was the primary garment included in the female wardrobe during the early period of the Dark Ages. This full, girdled gown was designed with long, full sleeves, either wrist length or extending below the hand. It was girdled about the waist and often worn beneath the tunica. The fabrics used in making the stola were rich silks, wool, or coarse linen depending on weather conditions and the affluence of the wearer.

GOWN
Women

The gown was a slim, long dress with elbow-length sleeves and a throat-hugging neckline. Made of white material or of natural colored linen, it was often worn as an undergarment beneath the stola.

SUPERTUNIC
Women

The Dark Ages were devoid of many creature comforts, not the least of which was a heating system. In northern Europe people adopted the practice of wearing many garments at one time as a means of keeping warm. The supertunic, designed in many different styles and lengths, was one such item of apparel. Basically it was a tunic with small cap sleeves, loose fitting, gathered in at the waist with a girdle, and with a drawstring at the neckline holding it snugly about the throat. The lengths varied; to the hip, to the thigh, to mid-calf.

Mantle (seventh century: Trinity College, Dublin)

Chlamys, tablion, and maniakis (500)

WRAPS
Men and
Women
mantle

cloak
chlamys

clavus
tablion

paluda-
mentum

palla

pallium

SCARF
Men and
Women
loros
thorakios

lorum

trabea

BREECHES
(400-600)
Men

All wraps of this period were forms of capes. The Byzantine mantle was semicircular, open from the tight round neck to the hem, and clasped with a brooch at the throat or clavicle. String ties with tassels of gold sometimes replaced the huge pin fastening. The more important the wearer, the more sumptuous this garment became, with Byzantine nobility wearing jewel-encrusted silk mantles, while those living farther north and of lesser status wore mantles made from rough woolen fabric. The cloak was made from a rectangle of material and, like the chlamys first worn by the ancient Greeks, was fastened on the right shoulder. Both of these wraps were worn by men during this period. The cloak, however, had two distinctive decorative devices: the *clavus* (two vertical bands) and the *tablion* (a rectangular inset of contrasting color positioned on the diagonal). The tablion was a frontal decoration placed about waist-high near the edge. It was appliqued silk, usually embroidered with a single spreadwing bird. The *paludamentum* was a Byzantine version of the Roman toga. It too was decorated with a tablion. When worn by royalty, it was purple with a gold silk tablion covered with designs made with pearls. Both men and women wore this wrap. A slender shawl, the *palla*, made of brilliant green, red, orange or gold colored silks, was worn crossed over the chest, often with a large round collar over it. The male version of this same slight wrap was called the *pallium*.

Many decorative scarfs originated in the center of Orthodoxy and were used by royalty throughout Europe during the Dark Ages. Some of the many forms include: the *loros*, worn wrapped around the body and tucked into a broad belt; the *thorakios*, also wrapped about the body and decorated with a shield made of precious stones and pearls; the *lorum*, narrow panels front and back originating from a shoulder-wide circular collar; and the *trabea*, a long thin length of fabric worn across the shoulders and crossed over the chest.

While still a major part of male attire, breeches remained a very crudely constructed garment for much of this period. They were functional, covering the lower section of the torso and the legs, but were not decorative, nor did they greatly alter the silhouette, for generally the long male outer garments concealed them completely. Toward the latter part

paison

of the sixth century they lost some of their baggy shape and were cut to hug the leg somewhat. Peasants, serfs, and commoners continued to wear paison, bound at the ankle or stuffed into the tops of boots.

UNDER-GARMENTS
Men and Women
shift

nightgown

undertunic

The shift or undertunic, worn next to the body as an undergarment was a long, straight, shapeless tunic without sleeves, generally made of unbleached linen. This simple costume was floor-length when worn by women, but only covered the body to mid-thigh when used by males. It was also used as a nightgown. Both sexes removed their outer garments, but left on their shifts while sleeping. The male undertunic, also hip or thigh-length, had long sleeves gathered into a small cuff. There is no data giving credence to the use of the loincloth at this period, however, a simple cloth duplicate of the outer breeches was worn by men.

ACCESSORIES
(400-700)
Men and Women
footwear
slippers
boots

hose

leg windings

crepida
calceus

Shoes were made of soft leather, had pointed toes and were made from a foot profile pattern. Eastern European footwear was made of colored leather or silk. Royalty wore slippers of purple silk trimmed with pearls or embroidery, often both. These slippers showed eastern influence in their turned-up pointed toes. High, soft leather boots were made in many styles. The ankle-high boot was worn with the top folded over to form a snug cuff. Both men and women wore this style, while the higher boots were worn exclusively by men. Hose were important costume accessories for all people, regardless of sex, wore brightly colored stockings. Men also used leg windings bound around the leg in a spiral or wound up the leg in an overlapping criss-cross fashion. This basic form of leg covering was made from a long slender strip of woolen cloth, put about the leg to the knee with the end or ends tucked into the winding to keep them up. The open-toed *crepida* and the laced *calceus* were worn by workers.

headwear
turbans
stemma

cap

Headwear worn by women in eastern Europe included large decorative turbans, hung with ropes of pearls, or the cloth *stemma* constructed over a wire frame. The stemma was worn low on the forehead, standing erect with a slight flare at the top, tied with cords at the back of the head and decorated with jewels and pearls. This head covering was worn by men and women. The hat forms of the northern European areas continued to be designed in simple cap or skull cap shapes.

jewelry
rings

Rings of the nobility and the episcopate were massive, with engraved inscriptions, the sign of the

Lorum worn over granatza (400-600)

cross, and the owner's initials or coat of arms. Ecclesiastical rings were symbols of authority and the mystical union of the priesthood and the church. A ring engraved with the image of St. Peter in a boat holding a net was the traditional ring design for the Bishop of Rome. It included the pope's initials as an integral part of the design, for his ring was used as his seal and signature on all official documents. Upon his death, his ring was smashed so that no forgeries of papal bulls could be made. Each newly elected pope was given a ring, thus insuring the authenticity of each episcopal communiqué.

necklaces Beautifully made necklaces, a synthesis of Greek and Roman styles, were worn by the rich. These were made of gold with enamel or paste set in lively colors, or of pearls, gold beads, and deeply chased golden beads set with precious jewels.

bracelets Bracelets were made of wide hinged bands set with cameos or enameled designs. While belts worn by the folk of northern Europe were simple leather or cord ties, royalty and their peers in the east used jewel-covered metal girdles. These were made of small square or round segments, pierced and set with large semiprecious stones, and hinged cleverly to fit easily around the waist.

hand held accessories Only in the southeastern sections of the civilized world were fans or hand held shading devices used. Gloves were worn as badges of distinction by kings and bishops in the northern areas. Royal and episcopal gloves were made with large flared cuffs and covered with gold embroidery and pearls. Priests and bishops wore white linen or silk gloves during the reading of the mass as a sign of the purity of the wearer.

HAIR STYLES
(400-800)
Men and Women Women wore their hair hanging free or braided, concealed by the turban or hidden under a heavy veil or headcloth. Men's styles were worn short, covering the ears, falling from the crown naturally rather than being parted. Small chin beards and mustaches were also worn though some men were clean shaven.

Additional pictorial resources

1. actual article—(comb and jewelled coronet), c. 700. Museum of the Basilica of San Giovanni, Monza

2. manuscript illumination—procession of female figures—(stola and palla), c. 600, Marciana Library, Venice

3. mosiac—Emperor Justinian with Bishop Maximianus—(mantle with tablion, clerical tunic with clavi), Sixth Century, San Vitale, Ravenna

4. canon page—Gospel of Rabula—(loros, paragaudion and chlamys), late Sixth Century, Laurentian Library, Florence

5. Joshua Roll—Joshua Meeting the Angel before Jericho—(tunic, paragaudion and chlamys—male; coif and stola—female), Seventh to Eighth Century. Vatican Library, Vatican

6. actual articles—(hose and sandals)—Seventh Century, Musée Jurassien, Delmont

Mantle and dalmatic tunic

Chapter 8
MORE MEDIEVAL MODES

*T*HE *chaotic period which followed the death of Charlemagne in 814 also saw the birth of many new trends. The feudal system spread from France throughout most of Europe and was established in England by the Norman Conquest. The castle dominated the country landscape as the church did the city. In return for the protection afforded by the castle, vassals were required to serve their lord as mounted soldiers in time of conflict, while serfs and peasants were obliged to serve as foot militia. Around the base of the castle walls, peasants and serfs built groups of crude windowless huts, which eventually grew into village settlements. Life was hard and social patterns primitive. A king or nobleman might live in one room with wife and horse, while the peasant's* *hovel housed family and livestock. Men of the upper classes jousted or hunted for relaxation. As living conditions improved, the ladies of the castles and their maids embroidered and wove tapestries or watched tournaments in which their lords and knights exhibited their war skills.*

Christianity was now the established religion, although this period also saw the rise and spread of Islam. The church was at first ruled by bishops and archbishops selected from the nobility, while peasant priests conducted the village churches, married, and worked the fields with their neighbors. During the eleventh century priests were forbidden to marry. After this ban they moved into monasteries to ponder theological dogma and concentrate on other types of learning. The church played an important part in preparing youths for knighthood. Schooling in chivalry was divided into three phases: the aspirant to knighthood served as a page, then as a squire, and finally, after fasting, a night of vigil and prayer, and confession, was knighted by his lord in an imposing ceremony. He took an oath to defend the church, his lady and his lord, and promised to succor the poor and the meek. Chivalry represented the church's attempt to fuse the Teutonic ideals of manhood with those of Christianity.

The Byzantine influence which at first dominated art was superseded by the Romanesque, which blended Eastern aesthetic concepts with the vigor of Celtic and Lombard elements. Art forms involving human figures were frontal, stylized, and rigid in posture. They combined pagan mythology with Christian imagery. Byzantine architecture was richly ornamented with decorative mosaics depicting somber saints. Romanesque churches, characterized by their round arches, featured dramatic scenes from the scriptures on their portals and elaborate silverwork and tapestries within. Manuscript illumination as practiced by monks in the newly founded monasteries reached a high refinement. These art forms too were treated in a flat style, devoid of perspective or chiaroscuro. The style so typical of this era flourished between 500 and 1200, continuing through the transitional phases to the Gothic period.

Costumes worn in northern Europe during this period were designed for warmth but also served as status symbols. The Byzantine influence was seen in richly ornamented garments. Basic garb showed little change, but the nobility was elegantly clad.

Gonelle, cloak, and chlamys (permission, Trustees of the British Museum, London)

BASIC GARMENTS OF THE MEDIEVAL PERIOD (700 – 900)

DALMATIC TUNIC Men
The dalmatic tunic was a long garment with long sleeves, round neck slit in front, and embroidery encircling the neckline, the cuffs and the hem. Characteristically slender, it had slashes at the sides of the skirt and very deep armholes. Young men wore a thigh-high version of the dalmatic tunic with elaborate embroidery on the upper sleeve and blouse section. It was girdled with a

wide belt worn low on the hips. Peasants wore a variation of this tunic made of coarse cloth, with short sleeves and a large oval neckline. The side slits in the skirt extended from the hips to the hem, allowing the laborer to draw it up and tuck it into his belt while at work.

Peasant smock and femoralia (400-600)

GONELLE
Men

smock

braies

tibialia
femoralia

The *gonelle* was also a type of tunic with the waist bloused over the belting, a full thigh-length skirt, and snug sleeves trimmed with braid at the cuffs, hem, and neck. Later the sleeve form changed into a funnel shape with the large opening at the wrist. The smock, a loose-fitting garment gathered to a shallow yoke, was worn unbelted. Both of these male outer garments were mid-thigh to knee length and worn over *braies* or *femoralia*. Braies were short, snug fitting breeches, hidden by the gonelle, and worn with *tibialia* or winding bands covering the lower legs. Femoralia were long, baggy pants often cross-bound up the leg, tied about the ankle or knee or allowed to flap about the legs. Peasants customarily wore these shapeless breeches with the smock tucked into them and firmly belted around the waist.

STOLA
Women

Just as the smock worn by males was a remnant garment from the previous centuries, the stola was held over into the eighth and ninth centuries as a female main apparel item costume. This sleeveless dress, patterned after the male Archaic chiton, was pinned on the shoulder with fibulae. Late in the period it acquired a longer fuller skirt and a hook and pin device arranged on the center braid trim of the skirt to keep it up out of the woman's way as she worked. A strange law of the time decreed that if a man touched a woman's arm (other than his wife's) he would be brought to trial and fined. The amount of the fine was determined by the point on the woman's arm that was touched. The higher up the arm the male's touch had trespassed, the higher the fine levied.

Peasant with gonelle and cross-laced braies

GUNNA
Women

kirtle

The *gunna* or gown was a floor-length female garment. It was a slender, smooth-fitting dress with a low square neck and deep slits or slashes in the skirt. The sleeves, at first full with wide wrist openings, later became more slender and longer. They were worn crushed up about the forearm. The gunna was girdled by a decorative belt with tassel tips, wound once about the waist, then about the hips, and secured with a fibula or brooch. Under the gunna women wore the *kirtle* or an undertunic of ample cut and high round neckline. The kirtle was visible above the low square neck opening of

Kirtle and gunna with tippets on sleeves (800)

Male gonelle, hood, and hose; female gunna

Gonelle, hose, and crackows

overgown

the gunna and through the gunna skirt slits. Over the linen-lined gown and kirtle ladies donned the overgown, knee length and with elbow-length sleeves. Gown and overgown were usually made of handsome fabrics, woolen and heavy silks for winter wear, ribbed satin or linen for summer. Peasant women wore the same types of garments made of rough homespun materials.

WRAPS
Men and
Women
   capes
   mantles
   palla
   chlamys
   sale

Cloaks, mantles, and rectangular capes continued to be the same styles as they had been for some centuries. Women wore the ancient palla and men the chlamys. The *sale* or shoulder cloak, later fitted with a hood, was elbow length and more decorative than functional. It often had "toothed" or serial V-cuts about the cape hem and hood face opening.

ACCESSORIES
Men and
Women
   footwear
   shoes
   brodequins
   heuze
   slippers

Shoe and boot makers had become highly skilled and a wide variety of new forms and perfected older styles were used. *Brodequins*, or high shoes with laces, made of leather, were heavy footwear worn by the lower classes, while the upper class wore the *heuze*, a boot made of soft leather, laced and fitted with a tongue beneath the center opening. The nobility wore soft silk slippers indoors, and women wore soft leather slippers tied or buckled at the ankle both in and out of doors.

hose

Between the fourth and the tenth centuries, hose were made of knitted material in a tube shape. Tapes sewn to the tops served as simple garter supports, possibly tied to a cloth belt worn around the waist under the gonelle or kirtle. Men wore their hose either under their breeches or pulled up over them. In warm weather the working classes wore their stockings crushed down over their boot tops.

Female bliaud and wimple

headwear
veil

chinstrap
headrail

guimp

This period saw the beginning of unique hair-concealing headwear for women. Veils were used extensively in many shapes and sizes: long rectangles draped over the head and wound around the neck; small shoulder-length veils made from a square of cloth held in place with a coronet or larger styles draped loosely over the head, covering head and shoulders reaching to the waist. In time the chinstrap and headrail were added. The former was a folded piece of cloth, usually linen, long enough to bind the head from under the chin to the top of the head, where it was securely pinned. The latter was a similar piece that was bound around the forehead and fastened in back. Over all of these face-framing bindings was worn a silken veil or *guimp*.

Hood with attached shoulder cape

Armor with dish helmet (800)

hoods

Head coverings for men remained constant and were cap forms with variously shaped crowns, round or pointed but generally brimless. Hoods attached to short capes also acted as protective headwear. They could be worn pulled well down over the face or pushed back or worn crushed about the neck and shoulders. The first hoods were made by forming a cone shape out of woolen fabric, sewing it and cutting a round hole in it some distance from the hem. It was slipped over the head and the face poked through the hole. Another early hood was made from a rectangle of cloth by taking the two top corners and folding them to the center of the lower edge. By making a seam where they met, a crude hood was fashioned.

jewelry
rings
bracelets
stiletto pins
buckles
fibulae

The most distinctive jewelry characteristic of this period in northern Europe was created in England. Rings, bracelets, and pins were fashioned by twisting golden wires together to the desired width and thickness. Stiletto pins, with large decorated heads, buckles with punctured or cutout geometric designs, and fibulae of similar design were also jewelry accessories that continued in use throughout this period.

HAIR STYLES
Men and
Women

Hair fashions changed little until the end of this period, when women bound their hair close to the head in braids or twisted ropes which were then wound into small pugs at the nape of the neck and covered with guimps.

Additional pictorial resources

1. bas-relief—Altar of Rotchis—(gonelle and braies), Eighth Century, Church of St. Martin, Cividal

2. bronze bas-relief—warriors—(gonelle and helmet), 600, National Museum of Antiquities, Stockholm

3. book illustration—Book of Job—(gonelle, boots—male; stola—female), Bibleothèque Nationale, Paris

4. bronze statue—Charlemagne—(dalmatic tunic, cloak and circlet), 800, Louvre, Paris

5. actual garments—(hose, shoes), 600, Musée Jurassien, Delmont

6. mosiac—Salome—(gunna and kirtle), c. 900, St. Mark's, Venice

7. manuscript illustrations—figures of five women—(stola and palla), undated, Marciona Library, Venice

8. detailing of painted sarcophagus—men and women in procession—(gonelle, mantle—male; gunna, mantle—female), undated, Bairgos Museum of Catalan Art, Barcelona

Cotehardie (1100–1200)

Chapter 9

COSTUMES OF THE GOTHIC PERIOD AND THE CRUSADES

*F*ROM 1095, when Pope Urban II promised those taking part in the First Crusade that their journey would count as full penance, till 1272, when the Ninth Crusade ended in failure, the European scene was dominated by the Crusades. Although the original aim of "elimination of heathens, infidels and all that were not believers" had not been achieved, participants who were fortunate enough to return home had broadened their horizons. New standards developed as intellectual endeavours, religious concepts, and personal standards of heroism and honor changed. New trade routes had been established. With trade on the increase, a system of money replaced barter. A new economy was born.

79

Gonelle, mantle, and tibialia (1100: Courtesy Victoria and Albert Museum, London)

Supercotehardie, hose, and bonnette

Many of the kings, barons, and knights who had participated in the Crusades had squandered their wealth to mount and finance these expeditions. The power which had rested with the nobility, both temporal and ecclesiastical, disappeared together with their wealth. By the end of the thirteenth century commoners—townspeople and serfs—were clamoring for peace and order. Rulers who needed money and wealthy tradesmen formed an alliance which put an end to feudalism, and placed the power in the hands of the monarchies while giving freedom to the cities. Although they were still to some extent dependent on the kings for protection, cities were released from their direct obligations to assist in providing that protection.

The power of the papacy, very high at the beginning of this period, was contested by the rulers of France and England as well as the Holy Roman Emperor. These struggles delayed the unification of Italy but fostered the rise to power of the city states of Venice and Florence.

Meanwhile in the lower echelons of the Church, groups of friars and monks were forming orders with specific aims. Thus, the Franciscans went about in pairs as humble missionaries, while the Dominicans preached, and both as mendicant friars or "begging brothers" collected alms. All combated heresy and sought to spread the teachings of the church.

Romanesque art forms in varying degrees of evolutionary development continued through the earlier period of the Crusades. The most notable characteristics of the Romanesque style, which appeared about the year 1000 and continued for two hundred years, were cut block construction, round arches, and vast vaulting systems that related vault, support, and abutment. Aesthetic concepts overlap chronologically. Thus the Gothic (emerging c. 1150) and Romanesque art forms appeared concurrently for a time. Gothic influences were dominant between the twelfth and fourteenth centuries. The towering, sky-piercing cathedrals built at this time were embellished with lacelike stonework, gargoyles, and elongated figures of saints ingeniously integrated into the pillar supports. These multispired cathedrals were the work of vigorous, civic-minded people, a material expression of their intense religious faith as well as of their intellectual capacity. Design and engineering innovations resulted in intricate vaulting, thinner supporting walls, flying buttresses, and jewel-like stained glass windows in the clerestories. Notre Dame, Chartres, Canterbury, and the Duomo in Milan illustrate the nationalistic styling trends which were developed.

Between the eleventh and fourteenth centuries costume was greatly influenced by the crusading expeditions to Asia Minor. Rich fabric made into long garments and particolored clothes were the most characteristic of these design trends. The practice of using the family colors in clothing, originated by the servants of noble houses, was eventually adopted by the nobility themselves. Upper class garments were heavily embroidered. This art of stitchery and its extensive use were the result of the long days, months, and years which women whiled away in this activity while their lords were away on the Crusades. The association with eastern pomp and splendour increased Europeans' taste for opulent and sumptuous personal adornment. During the final phases of this period this taste was to be developed to excess.

BASIC GARMENTS OF THE CRUSADES AND GOTHIC PERIODS (1000—1300)

Female laced bliaud with head covering composed of chinstrap and headrail

Surcoat over armor (800-900)

BLIAUD
(1000)
Men and Women

chainse
cainsie

braies

The *bliaud*, or *blialt*, replaced the gonelle as the basic outer garment for men and women. The male style was made like a tunic with long wide sleeves. It was tightly belted. In earlier wearing styles the top portion of the garment was pulled up and bloused over the belt, hiding it. At first the female bliaud was made and worn in this same manner except that it was floor length. Later, the bodice section was designed with side lacings extending from the underarms to the hips. When these lacings were drawn tight, the bosom, waist, and torso were emphasized. The sleeves, originally designed with modest proportions, became excessively large. This fullness and length were at one time so exaggerated that huge knots were tied in the sleeves to keep them from dragging on the ground. Beneath this outer costume was worn a *chainse* or *cainsie*. This basic linen undergarment was also a tunic design. It was ankle length when worn by women and shorter for men. Because clothing was worn for warmth as well as for personal decoration both men and women wore floor-length bliauds during the colder months. Men wore braies and tube hose with either the long or short styles of these garments.

COTEHARDIE
(1100)
Men and Women

super-
cotehardie

A significant clothing innovation was developed during the twelfth century. This was a *cotehardie*, the first true coat to be designed. It was knee length, tightly fitted, with inset sleeves and closely set buttons on the center-front closing. The hip-length version was called the *supercotehardie*. As in the evolution of any garment styling, changes occurred and pockets became an integral part of this costume. These were long vertical slashes, bound with braid or embroidery, placed thigh-high on the center of each of the front panels. The ladies' cotehardie had a fitted bodice and a long, many-gored skirt. This sumptuous garment with its excessive skirt length and width was held up in front, giving the wearer a pregnant profile and a swayback contour. Some of these gowns had two vertical slits placed low on the skirt fronts. These allowed the wearer to slip her arm through them, thus catching up the bulk of the skirt, lifting the front hemline. This made walking easier and eliminated holding great bulky quantities of fabric in the hand to create the desired silhouette. Sleeves in the females' cotehardies were snug and

Liripipe, hood with dragged edge cape,
cotehardie and crab-edged crackows
(Crusades)

**HOUPPE-
LANDE**
(1300)
**Men and
Women**

SURCOAT
(1050-1250)
**Men and
Women**

tabard

sewn more tightly about the wrists after the garments were put on. Women carried small scissors suspended from a cord attached to the girdle so that they might snip these wrist stitchings if need arose. When out walking or playing in the woods, they frequently cut the threads at the wrist and "went about with unsewn sleeves," to quote one chronicler. It was also the custom to snip out the entire sleeve and award it to a favored knight as a good luck charm during jousting tournaments. He wore it attached to his shield or helmet.

The *houppelande*, worn by both sexes, was a voluminous outer garment with enormous conical sleeves. The neckline fitted snugly about the throat. The skirt, sometimes calf length for men, always floor length for women, was slit front and back. The distinctive design feature of this bulky costume was the deep rolled pleats that radiated from the tightly belted waist upward to the shoulders and downward to the hem. The blouse was extremely full in some versions and only slightly bloused in others. The long, funnel sleeves were trimmed with fur or the "dragged" design, a series of deep scallops or deep V-shapes, a modification of the "toothed" edge of earlier times. A belted or unbelted short houppelande was worn by younger men. The sleeves of this garment were often short in front and long in back. Made of elegant fabrics, often particolored, but on rare occasions with heraldic designs, these long or short costumes were worn primarily by the upper classes. Simpler versions in rough wool were later adopted by the middle and lower classes.

The *surcoat* was first introduced as a cloth poncho form and was worn over armor to protect against the glare of the Arabian sun. It was a long rectangle of fabric folded in half, with a hole cut in the middle for the neck. It had no sleeves or side seams and was simply tossed over the head and girdled with the buckler. The red cross emblem of the Crusades was a later decorative addition, placed on the front and back panels of this ankle or knee-length overcostume. Later, when warriors of the cross returned, it was introduced into the civilian wardrobe. Many elaborate and decorative additions were made. The side seams were closed for a few inches above the hem; the neck, deep armholes, and hem were fur-trimmed and the garment itself became rather full and gathered at the shoulder seams. It was made of heavy velvets and silks. A short cap sleeve variation, the *tabard*, was particolored, emblazoned with the family coat of arms,

Cyclas worn over sorquenie; hair dressed in the reticulated style

and served primarily as a ceremonial costume. This shorter form was also worn by young pages. The female garment of the same design origin was called the *cyclas*. This was an overgown made with a wide, full, four-gored skirt, a thin center panel in the front, and a larger panel in back. The neckline was wide and oval-shaped, trimmed with fur, as were the front panel, the inside of the back, and the edges of the deep armholes. Nonfunctional buttons were additional trims included on the front panel, or *plastron*. The *sorquenie*, worn with the cyclas, was a close fitting bodice with tight sleeves that extended over the back of the hand. This garment covered the figure to well below the hips but had no skirt attached. Cyclas and sorquenie carried out the particolor theme, with the former divided down the center skirt front, one half carrying the colors of the male side, the other those of the female side of the family. Beneath both of these garments ladies wore sleeveless tunics with high little necks and side lacings to insure that they fitted smoothly and snugly under the bodice. The bodice was also laced, back or sides, to reveal the curved contours of the female figure. The full skirts of the tunic extended well below the hip-length sorquenie.

cyclas

plastron
sorquenie

tunic

GARDE-CORPS
(1200)
Men and Women

The *garde-corps*, while in general design and construction the same as the male and female cotehardie, had one distinctive detail—a long band of fabric attached at the elbow of the tight-fitting sleeve. This sleeve streamer of gaily colored silk (occasionally fur) developed out of the custom of wearing a veil or cotehardie sleeve, given as a charm, tied to helmet or shield or tucked into the articulating plates of the armor at the elbow. This streamer was called a *tippet*. In turn, the narrow tippet became a wide, long panel, two or three feet in length. Another name change occurring because of sleeve detailing was the *corset*. Made after the houppelande pattern, the corset sleeves were either flaring wing sleeves or large, full sleeves gathered to cuffs but left open at the seams under the arms.

tippet

corset

Particolored cyclas; chainse and circlet; sleeves of sorquenie

DOUBLET
Men and
Women

pelican

gipon
jupe

justaucorps

A number of undergarments which had originally been worn for the extra warmth they provided, eventually became visible male costumes. The *doublet* used by both sexes was such an article of clothing, given this name because it was made of duplicate layers of material. It was sometimes quilted or tufted to keep the two linen layers in place. The doublet neckline was high and round, the body of the garment fitted smoothly, and the full-length sleeves were tight. The *pelican* was made to a similar design with animal fur sewn between the fabric layers. The *gipon* or *jupe* was always quilted and made with tight, long sleeves, while the pelican was cut more like a waist-length vest. The *justaucorps* was originally worn under armor, but was later adopted by civilians. It too was made of linen, and had long slim sleeves and a tight body with a high round neckline. The justaucorps was made in several lengths, but the slim sleeves were all that were ever visible, showing beneath the short tunic sleeves. By the end of the thirteenth century these garments became the upper body covering for males and were made of a variety of fine fabrics.

Garde-corps with tippet sleeve; hood (crushed about shoulders) of dragged edge liripipe

Court costume forms (English: fourteenth century, permission The Metropolitan Museum of Art. Fletcher Fund, 1927)

Peasant cotteron, apron, with head-rail and chinstrap covering the head (1200)

Corset (sleeves), chemise, and turban (1400)

COTTERON
(1200-1400)
Men and Women

The *cotteron* was a simple smock worn by peasants of both sexes for some centuries. Short, belted cotterons were worn by men, while women wore longer ones reaching the ground. These were belted by a rectangle of cloth that acted as a girdle and as an apron. For additional warmth, peasant women wore several cotterons, one on top of the other, often each one of a different color and length. If the longest was worn on top, the woman might draw it up at the sides, tucking it into the apron girdling, thus keeping it out of the way while she worked.

DALMATIC TUNIC
(1100-1400)
Men

The dalmatic tunic, floor length, and fur trimmed, continued to be worn throughout the centuries by older men. It was varied by sleeve design, either full at the wrist and snug at the armhole or the reverse, and by girdling. If belted, it had a wide decorative belt, but many wore it hanging loose, tied only at the throat by tassel-trimmed cords. Short tunics with long or elbow-length sleeves were worn by the poorer classes.

MANTLE
(1000-1100)
Men and Women
  chape
  chasuable
  balandran

  à parer

  housse
  hérigaute
  garnache
  cape
  jackets
    cotte
    gamboisée
    gambeson
    hoqueton

Cape or mantle wraps continued to be used as garments for warmth and protection against the weather. The *chape* or *chasuable*, circular or rectangular cloaks, with no collar, tie or brooch fastenings at the throat and lined with fur, were the most common. The *balandran* was a full circle mantle used as rainwear. It was often fitted with a shoulder cape and deep face-hiding hood. The shoulder cape was edged about the hem with the "dragged" design. The *à parer* was also a circular cape that tied at the neck and had slits on the sides for armholes. Other lighter weight wraps included: the *housse* and *hérigaute*, both variations of the surcoat; the *garnache*, with a full back panel and two long tabs in front crossed over the chest; and a small, hip-length, circular cape. Jackets such as the *cotte gamboisée*, *gambeson*, and *hoqueton* were usually padded garments with high necklines, tight sleeves, and closed down the front by closely spaced fastenings. These latter styles came into use late in the thirteenth century and continued in style well into the fourteenth.

ACCESSORIES
(1000-1300)
Men and Women
  headwear
  cole
  calotte
  barrette

Headwear for men during these centuries developed from simple protective forms such as the hood into elaborate decorative forms of which the *chaperon* is but one. The simple cap shapes included: the *cole*, fur-lined with ear-covering tabs but no chinstrap; the *calotte*, a skullcap made of four or six pie-shaped pieces; the *barrette*, a wool cap made of four rigid segments worn by clerics

Garnache with chausses and crackows. Other poncholike garments were the housse and the hérigaute (ninth to thirteenth centuries)

Hérigaute, female cotehardie with gorgette at throat, and sun bonnet (fourteenth century)

Tabard, hose, boots, and barrette (1200)

Gown, mantle, and wimple headdress (German: c. 1300, permission The Metropolitan Museum of Art, Gift of J. Pierpont Morgan. 1917)

bonnette

and professors; and the *bonnette* of the late four-teenth century. The bonnette had a jaunty air about it and was designed with a tall conical crown that came down well over the head. This crown was turned up in back and shaped into a pointed bill brim in front. Feathers and embroidered headbands were used as trimming. Young men carried these bonnettes on their walking sticks. To show off their stylish graces they would, with a flick of the sticks, deftly don these dapper hats.

aumusse liripipe

The *aumusse* and *liripipe* were styles that evolved from the conical hood with the face hole. The liripipe had a shoulder cape, and its attenuated hood peak, often ten or twelve feet long, could be wrapped about the neck like a scarf. This hood was made from two profile sections sewn together along the top, the full length of the liripipe (as the long point was called) and down the center back of the shoulder cape. The front was left open so that it could be pinned snugly under the chin as protection against the winter's cold. Later versions were made with a profile pattern hood and an attached cape that was closed in front. It was from this style that the chaperon developed. This was a type of turban made by drawing the cape section up to the head, carefully pleating it, and then winding the long point around and around. It was firmly secured by pulling the end of the liripipe through the binding layers. The scalloped edges of the cape made a cockscomb effect if carefully arranged. Both men and women wore this type of headcovering, often topping off the liripipe-formed chaperon with a stiff decorative doughnut-shaped hat called a *roundlet*. It was also worn over a simple skullcap.

chaperon

roundlet

Female chaperon and roundlet

veil chinstrap headrail wimple gorget

The veil and circlet, the chinstrap, headrail, and wimple or guimp; and the *wimple*, headrail, chinstrap, and *gorget (gorgerette)* were female head coverings used over a long period. The gorget, the last bit of veil draping to be added to ladies' headwear, was attached to the chinstrap below each ear. This veiling covered the neck, falling free or tucked into the neckline of the gown.

reticulated headdress cauls

By the fourteenth century, head coverings and hair styles were closely related. The reticulated headdress consisted of a pair of braided coils of hair over each ear covered with cauls. *Cauls* were nets made of fine gold wire strung with pearls or set with precious jewels. A wimple was worn over the head and a gorget attached to the cauls

crispine

Reticulated headdress (French: late fourteenth century, permission The Metropolitan Museum of Art, gift of George Blumenthal, 1941)

hennin

frontal

horned hennin escoffion

was draped about the neck. Later a *crispine*, or *crispinette*, was added. This was a tight golden headband worn well down on the forehead, with cauls attached on either side. A gold wire net was also used to hold the hair at the back of the head. The reticulated headdress took many forms, all of them based on the positioning of the buns of hair on either side of the head. Sometimes these buns were shaped like horns and positioned over the temples; at other times they were round, flat coils, and sometimes they were even shaped like half-globes. In time the buns reached excessive proportions, projecting far out from the sides of the head or towering into peaks well above it. Veils of fine white or colored linen were usually draped over all of these many variations. Eventually heart or butterfly-shaped golden frames, draped with diaphanous veils and trimmed with ribbon streamers, replaced the cauls covering the buns of hair.

The tall conical *hennin* was introduced late in the fourteenth century. This strange headgear, shaped like an enormous dunce cap, was often more than ten feet long. The hennin was made from a stiff cone, pointed or truncated, and at first modestly proportioned. It was covered with black velvet or colored silk and was worn over a tight-fitting cap of linen that partially covered the cheeks. This little cap may have been tied under the chin and the hennin anchored to it with stiletto pins at the crown. As the hennin became more elaborate, long floating veils and ribbons were attached at the peaked end. The small caps also became larger, with the face-framing brims greatly enlarged and formed into a number of arched or pointed shapes extending well beyond the sides of the face. When the visible cap was discarded, the hair on the forehead was plucked to well back on the top of the head. A velvet-covered wire, possibly as a means of holding this ungainly headgear in place, was attached to the front edge of the hennin and curved over the forehead. The sides of the face at this time were framed by the *frontal*, a rigid wire netting covered with either velvet, gold, or stiff sheer linen. The horned hennin, or *escoffion*, was made of two curved cones extending as much as three feet beyond the head at the temples. These cones were made of heavily starched voile stretched over a frame or of a gold webbing. Large delicately colored lightweight veils were spread over this, and bows and streamers of ribbons attached to the points of each horn. Little flags or small veils were also used as horn tip decorations. The term "hennin" applied to all of these huge and rather ridiculous head coverings was in fact not the name originally given, but one used derisively.

Crackows

Patten

footwear

crackow

pattens

poulaine

hose

The pointed-toed shoes of this period had, by the late thirteenth century, been extended so far beyond the toes that they had to be stuffed with straw. The style had been first introduced in Cracow, Poland, and became known as *crackows*. This shoe was a simple slipper form held on by an ankle strap. Others were half-boots or ankle-boots with snipped or "crab" designs around the cuffs, worn folded down or straight, covering the leg to the calf. *Pattens* were at first oval pieces of wood with a toestrap, used to protect the soft leather crackows from the mud and muck of the streets. Later they were lengthened into pointed scooped shapes, much the same as the shoe sole shapes. Two small blocks of wood were fastened on the underside of each *poulaine*, as this type of shoe protection was called, and an instep strap held them on.

"pair of legs"

closed hose

full bottom hose
codpiece

chausse

As the male outer garments became shorter, legs and leg coverings became more important to the whole costume. The tube hose were replaced by linen hose made from two leg profile pieces, sewn together. These were held up by tapes tied to a waistband. Under the hose was worn a shapeless pair of linen "legs" which were stitched through the crotch, hemmed at the top and gathered by a drawstring around the waist. In time, the outer hose were joined and called "closed hose" or a "pair of legs." This was an uncomfortable and impractical arrangement, for no extra material had been added. Young men, the first to adopt the hip-length cotehardie, who wore closed hose were rather restricted in their movements. Both secular and religious leaders demanded that, for the sake of male modesty, closed hose must be worn with the shorter upper garments. In time, better knitting techniques were developed as well as the introduction of the full bottom hose and *codpiece*. The leg sections of these limb coverings were made to fit more smoothly by means of a series of small darts, hidden by embroidery, around the ankles of the hose. As the doublets and supercotehardies came into general use, the hose or chausses were first worn over the breeches, but eventually these became only brief trunks and were then discarded in favor of the full bottom hose. Both these styles of leg coverings were attached to the doublets or jupes by cord laces with metal tab tips.

Cotte gamboisée, "pair of legs" or full bottom hose, and codpiece

jewelry
necklaces

belts
bracelets

pins

Necklaces made of gold chains replaced bead neckwear. Double rows of jeweled plaques alternating with double links of gold made massive decorations for both men and women. Belts and bracelets were ornately engraved with filigree, set with stones or enameled designs, all characteristic of these forms of jewelry accessories. *Agrafa, fernails* (brooches), stiletto and *tasseau* pins in many designs were used as mantle fastenings or as costume decorations.

HAIR STYLES
(1000-1300)
Men and
Women

For the most part men wore short, bobbed hair, shaved well up on the neck to a point just below the curve of the skull. During these centuries, women's hair was concealed under wimples or elaborate hennins, but after the totally hair-concealing headwear fashions were finally discarded a style similar to the classical Greek coif, with the hair pulled back tightly and bound with plain or flower-bedecked ribbons, was adopted. These styles of the late fourteenth and early fifteenth centuries were very smooth in appearance. The hair was drawn back from a plucked forehead, with no curls. Often it was built into structures which towered above the head or which were shaped much like half a loaf of French bread projecting from the back of the head. During this period women's hair styles could take many forms to suit the fancies of individual women.

Additional pictorial references

1. miniature—profile of man—(leripipe and houppelande), c. 1000, Tacuinum Sanitatis

2. painting (anon.)—three women—(cotehardie and kirtle), undated, Corret Museum, Venice

3. miniature—cobbler's shop—(bliaud, chausses, calotte and barrettes), undated, Metropolitan Museum of Art, New York City

4. painting (anon.)—Allegory—(gown or female cotehardie and roundlet), c. 1200, Hall of the Palazzo Comuale, Padua

5. wall painting (anon.)—procession—(chaperon, bonnette and general costume styling), undated, Trevulzio Collection, Milan

6. fresco (anon.)—women of court—(reticulated headdresses, houppelande with dragged sleeves, cyclas and mantle), c. 1330, Castle of Manta, Saluzze

Huque, fur-trimmed (ermine), worn over chain mail—note dragged edge

Chapter 10

RICH DRESS OF THE RENAISSANCE

*T*HE *Crusades, followed by the Hundred Years War, had served to set the stage for the period known as the Renaissance. The new spirit of this age is epitomized by a pledge given by lords of petty states to their elected kings: "We, who are each of us as good as thou, and who together are far more powerful than thou, swear to obey thee if thou dost obey our laws, and if not, not." This oath seems to express a new attitude, one involving a humanistic philosophy and stressing the importance of the individual.*

The Renaissance period was marked by an economic revival, expansion of learning, and sea-going exploration, all of which spurred intellectual

91

development. Dante, Petrarch, Savonarola, Luther, and Machiavelli are a few of the notable individuals who played important roles during this intellectually explosive and humanistic period. Although theological dogma had controlled learning for centuries, "an era of truth" developed as thousands attended the newly established universities.

By the end of the fifteenth century the military might of the Tartars and Turks and the growing influence of Islam under the Ottoman Empire had changed the social organization of eastern Europe and Asia Minor. As wealthy merchants and bankers acquired more power the role of the nobility diminished. Important commercial families like the Este, Scaliger, Visconti, and Medici formed a new tyrannical aristocracy, controlling much of Europe. The trading centers of Venice, Genoa, Marseilles, Bruges, and Antwerp established a new powerful capitalism. Gold currency was reintroduced, with resultant economic stability.

Subtle changes appeared in art and scholarship, leaning toward more secular subjects. People took pleasure in life and in the pursuit of learning. Pictorial manifestations of these attitudes can be seen in the works of Jan van Eyck, Rogier van der Weyden, Veneziano, Bosch, Giovanni Bellini, Sandro Botticelli, Donatello, Michelangelo, da Vinci, Raphael, and many other contemporary masters of visual imagery. A rebirth of interest in Greek classicism had begun in the Republic of Florence. Its force was felt throughout Europe. Ideals of beauty were in flux and standards set earlier by the poet Dante and the painter Giotto were accepted, modified, and reshaped into a Renaissance style. Artists of the importance of Pesellino, Pollaiuolo, and Jacopo Bellini turned to designing costumes and textile patterns. These Italians may have been among the first fashion designers.

Sleeve detail, modified manches pertuisse sleeve

As the Renaissance began to flower, women's gowns were in general long, flowing, and intricate, characterized by national and individual styling details. Men's fashions were equally diverse in styling as design preferences were expressed within each country. Some of the particularly nationalistic trends were matters of detailing, but in each country, principality or dukedom clothing was, for the most part, elaborate and sumptuous. The Renaissance period dates roughly between 1300 and 1600, but the cultural impact and influences stimulated by intellectual curiousity began to attain momentum during the fifteenth century. Concepts emphasizing individualism and individuality spread from Italy to France, Spain, Germany, the Flemish and Dutch areas, and finally to England. These influences affected commerce, concepts, and clothing as the spirit of the age and the ideal of virtu spread across the continent. Intellectual giants of art, philosophy, and literature and explorers of courage and daring paraded through the Renaissance. The many changes these men initiated remodeled their world.

Lady's robe with bandier and heart-shaped hennin; male haincelin, chausses, and chaperon with roundlet (Franco-Flemish: fifteenth century, permission The Metropolitan Museum of Art, Rogers Fund, 1909)

Gown with bandier, chemise sleeves, and reticulated (horned) hair style with veil (1435)

Robe with skirt caught up on trousspir; starched butterfly hennin (fifteenth century)

BASIC GARMENTS OF THE RENAISSANCE (1400—1500)

ROBE
(1400-1500)
Women

gorgias

bandier

parament
troussoir

à la francoise
mancheron
bassard

points

demiceint

chemise

corset
blanchet

The many visible layers of outer garments that had been worn by women for several centuries were, by the fifteenth century, replaced by the robe, or gown. Designs for these voluminous, graceful gowns varied from country to country. General traits included a short-waisted bodice that flattened the bust, deep square neckline, fanciful elaborate sleeves, and long, many-gored skirt with a train. The protruding stomach silhouette continued in fashion and was achieved by sewing small bags full of horsehair, or other padding, in front just below the high waistline. The deep, square neckline was modified by a filmy gauze insertion called the *gorgias (gorgette or touret de col)*, or by a lattice of thin velvet ribbons trimmed with pearls at the intersections. A *bandier* or wide belt was worn around the figure under the bust. Embroidery was used extensively, particularly around the neck. This colorful and artfully stitched decoration was called *parament*. To add to the forward curve of the figure, the skirt was often caught up and pinned with a *troussoir* or simply gathered up by the hand. The intricate sleeve designs were given names to designate their styling, such as: *à la francoise*, full, straight, with deep cuffs or revers; *mancheron*, tight elbow-length sleeve, and *bassard*, a half-sleeve extending from the wrist to the elbow. Flared funnel sleeves, à la francoise, and mancheron were all tied to the bodice at the armhole and were interchangeable. When both mancheron and bassard were worn, the full sleeve of the softer linen chemise was carefully puffed out between them where they were tied at the elbow. Ties of sturdy silk ribbon with metal tips, called *points*, were laced through eyelets at the edges of the parts of many garments as a means of keeping them together. Points were both decorative and functional, and were used on garments worn by both sexes. In addition to the cloth bandier, a second belt or *demiceint*, made of hinged metal plaques, was worn low on the hips. From the long end that extended almost to the toes dangled keys, scissors, a mirror, or other accessories necessary in a lady's life. While the gown or robe became the dominant visible garment, women continued to wear many clothing items underneath. The *chemise*, a full tunic with high neck and long sleeves gathered into small band cuffs, was generally worn next to the body. On top of this was worn the corset, which had a low neckline, short sleeves and a rather full skirt. The long *blanchet*, or indoor coat, fur-lined and with full funnel sleeves, was worn for warmth, as was the cyclas, or female surcoat, patterned after those worn during the previous period. Both of the overgarments were designed with long full skirts and trains. The blanchet was a dual purpose costume, serving as a dressing gown as well as a house coat. The houppelande continued in use as an elegant, high-necked garment for either indoor or outdoor wear. The rolled pleats so characteristic of this garment were now stitched in place, accenting the high waistline and broader shoulder line of this period.

cyclas

houppelande

Bag-sleeved houppelande (1405)

Italian unbelted long houppelande (fourteenth century)

Pourpoint with à grandes assiettes and full bottom hose, male; robe with mancheron, female (c. 1515, permission The Metropolitan Museum of Art)

POURPOINT
(1400-1500)
Men

caraille
à grandes
assiettes

manches
pertuisse
shirt

cotte
gambeson
jaque
doublet

The *pourpoint*, developing from the doublet in the fifteenth century, became the major male garment. It was made from carefully cut pieces and, for the first time, armhole and sleeve matched accurately. During the first years of its use, the pourpoint accented the natural contour of the figure. It was designed with a high standing collar called the *caraille*, center front closing, and a short or waist-to-hip circular peplum called *à grandes assiettes*, made from four semicircular panels. The doublet sleeve was also important in male costuming. These sleeves were varied and intricate, and during the early phase of the pourpoint were tight, wrist length, and slightly padded for warmth as was the rest of the garment. As styles changed, and the pourpoint became very short, the sleeves were enlarged with padding, raising and broadening the shoulder line. This added to the silhouette illusion of long slender legs and a masculine broad-shouldered torso. Sleeves ranged in design from balloon shapes to inverted padded cones puffed at the shoulder to the *manches pertuisse*, gathered at both wrist and shoulder with the underarm seam left open. Under the pourpoint, men wore a linen shirt. It was a full blouse gathered to a round neck and tied with cords at the throat. The shirt sleeve was full, gathered to a narrow cuff. The cotte and gambeson were tuniclike undershirts, worn with pourpoint or *jaque (jack)*. The latter was a heavily padded doublet which was often made with thirty inner layers of lining. The jaque was rather loosely fitted and had very simple sleeves.

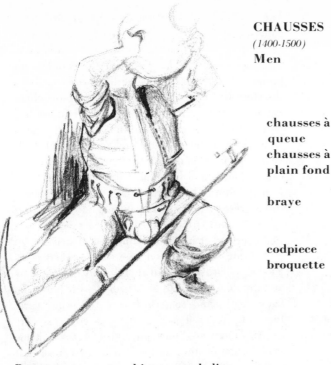

Peasant garments: shirt, vest, lodier with codpiece

CHAUSSES
(1400-1500)
Men

chausses à
queue
chausses à
plain fond

braye

codpiece
broquette

Hérigaute variation, pourpoint with manches pertuisse sleeves, chausses à queue, and "devil's finger" shoes (poulaines)

In time the pourpoint and jaque became so short that the à grande assiettes extended only a little distance below the waist. The long hose, worn for some time tied by tapes to the waistband over the braies, satisfied neither the church's demands for modesty nor the male's demands for a neat, smooth, long-legged silhouette. The older *chausses à queue* were discarded and replaced by *chausses à plain fond*, or full bottom hose. These were made by sewing a triangular piece of fabric between the legs of the chausses in back and adding a small inverted triangle, called the *braye*, in front. The braye was tied on either side by points. Later it was greatly enlarged by padding and called a codpiece or *broquette*. This style of chausses à plain fond closing was used for many years in a number of different variations. The leg coverings (chausses) of this period were an adaptation of the hose of previous years, made with the portion covering the outer leg several inches longer (reaching almost to the waist) while the inner portion extended from toe to crutch. A two-part panel, or waistband, was attached (often by ties) to the longer outer chausses section. This was brought over the stomach and laced together. The codpiece was fastened to this band and to the hose at the crotch. At first introduction it was a basic triangular or truncated triangular piece of fabric similar to that used for the hose section. Later, this chausses à plain fond closing (or hose-joining device) became very decorative and exaggerated. At the height of its elaboration it was slashed and padded, a large crescent or bun shape suggestive, in some instances, of the male sex organ which it covered. This larger, more prominent style, often used as a purse to carry small coins, was attached to the chausses at the crotch and at the waistband by metal-tipped cords or ribbons. The codpiece joined the two chausses or stockinglike leg coverings in front, and the back was covered with two larger triangles of material. These triangles, sewn or tied to the longer side of the hose, were inset with the points downward and the bases at the waist. They were seamed together in the center back, forming a complete covering for the posterior. As hose knitting techniques were perfected, it was no longer necessary to have a small series of darts around the ankles, and there was no longer any need for the decorative embroidery used to hide them. This embroidery, known as "clocks" (fanciful patterns extending from the anklebone well up the calf of the leg) was used as a hose decoration a long time afterwards, but its function of camouflaging tucks or darts had disappeared.

The combination of the hose, triangular inset back panels, and the codpiece created a trouser form resembling present-day tights or the leotards worn by ballet dancers. The design of the codpiece or broquette was never affected by criticism from the church—only the evolution of fashion eliminated it as a prominent decorative and functional part of male attire. It continued to be used as a front closing device until the breeches of later years (such as Venetians and Spanish slops) became so large and full that it was no longer functional. Before the introduction of these larger, fuller breeches, men wore pants or a brief trouser-type garment. Often a small padded crescent was tied over the chausses à plain fond at a point on either side where the codpiece was fastened. This padded roll rose upward in front to the hipbone and then descended to be attached with points in back. *Lodier* and *boulevard* were the other early types of "upper stock," as the crescent pads were called. They were short unpadded breeches made in the same manner as the full bottom hose, but with legs that just covered the upper thigh. Made of heavy silk, or leather if worn by peasants, lodier were worn over the chausses à plain fond. Under these were worn shapeless linen braies.

lodier boulevard upper stock

Jerkin with slashed sleeves, stock, upper stock, codpiece, and slippers

Robe longue and paletat with fur revers, square-necked doublet, turban, and beaver hat, also duck-billed slippers (fifteenth century)

HOUPPE-LANDE
(1400-1500)
Men

CABON
(late 1300-1400)
Men

The male houppelande included a tall standing collar, bag sleeves that were full and gathered at the shoulder and wrist, deep radiating pipe pleats, and a tight belt. This garment was buttoned from the tight neckline to the waist, with the belt worn quite low about the figure. The full floor-length style was generally worn by older men who also used *robe longue*, the knee-length cote-hardies or houppelandes rather than the hip or waist-length pourpoints.

Late in the fourteenth century the *cabon* was introduced, prompted by a design called the *cafton* brought from the Far East. It was an outer garment with "crossed fronts" (double-breasted). This long jacket coat had a fitted waist and gathered skirt. The sleeves were long and tight. A belt was sometimes worn with the cabon, but this accessory was not essential in creating the tight-waisted silhouette. In some versions it was made with an attached hood.

Houppelande with dragged design sleeve; roundlet head covering (fifteenth century)

Robe longue and liripipe (French, Burgundian: fifteenth century, permission The Metropolitan Museum of Art, gift of J. Pierpont Morgan)

ORNAMENTAL WRAPS
Men and
Women
   tabard
   huque
   paletat
   jounade
   giornea
   montiline

The people of the Renaissance devised a number of ornamental wraps for their elaborate ceremonial festivities. These wraps included: the *tabard*, particolored and embroidered with heraldic emblems; the *huque*, made of two fur-lined decorative panels; the *paletat*, a jacket with *manches pertuisées* (slit sleeves); the *jounade*, made with two floor- or ankle-length panels; and the *giornea* or *montiline*, a two-panel floor-length ceremonial costume with a deep V-neckline.

ACCESSORIES
(1400-1500)
Men and
Women
  headwear

Hats and headcoverings remained similar in style to those of the late Gothic period. The chaperon, sugarloaf cap, hennin, and reticulated headdresses continued in vogue.

  footwear
    crackow

The pointed crackows, discarded for a brief time, reappeared with even longer pointed toes. They became so lengthy that walking was impaired, and

Male houppelande, boy's doublet (Italian: fifteenth century, permission The Metropolitan Museum of Art, The Jules S. Bache Collection, 1949)

Chaperon, pourpoint with heavily padded sleeves, and chausses à plain fond

Blanchet, horned (escoffion) hennin (fifteenth century)

**poulaine
heuze**

**botte
patten**

**jewelry
neckwear**

belts

rings

**hand held
accessories
gloves**

the tips were held up by a thin chain extending from the toe to the calf of the leg. These pointed shoes were referred to as either crackows or *poulaines*. High boots, *heuze*, with instep laces, buttoned or buckled at the ankle, were made of soft leather in a variety of styles. Women wore soft leather fur-lined boots indoors during the winter months. The *botte* or *bottes à relever* were simple bedroom slippers. Pattens, the simple wooden oval shoe protection, and *chopines*, the tall platform shoe protection with wide toe strap, were used out of doors.

Neckwear became massive and two or three great chain, plaque, and pendant ornaments were worn about the neck at one time. Late in the fifteenth century jeweled collars that covered the shoulders were worn by men. Families of great wealth employed artists with prodigious talents to do nothing else but create these elegant baubles. Belts were equally important to the look of the total costume during the Renaissance and were designed in a similar way. There were also wide leather belts fastened with large jewel-encrusted buckles from which dangled fan, key, mirror, scent box and seal, attached by a golden chain.

Rings, popular to the point of excess, were worn in multiplicity. Every finger was adorned with at least one gold ring. Diamonds, sapphires, and rubies were used as settings. The Grecian charm ring was revived and believed to have "magical powers." These charm rings were made with mystical words or symbols engraved on them or set with animal teeth and worn on the thumb. Signet rings, rings of twisted gold and those with stylized floral patterns were but few of the many ring designs used.

Gloves of the fifteenth century were made of doeskin, sheepskin, or hareskin. Because of the demand for gloves, entire villages in France built their economies upon the manufacture of these accessories. Glovemaking achieved a high degree of sophistication and gloves were made with separate fingers, thumbs, and with wide embroidered cuffs from leather tanned in such a way that the scents added to the finished gloves were retained. Perfumers were in abundant supply and their products were used liberally. To quote one chronicler of the time, "Hair, shoes, fans, and gloves gave out sweet odors . . ." for it was believed that ". . . strong odors refreshed the brain."

walking sticks

Walking sticks, made of rare woods with carved heads, were a short-lived fad in the middle years of the fifteenth century. They were carried by women and were ornamental rather than functional.

escarcelle

Escarcelles or purses were carried or worn suspended from belts, by both men and women. Two forms predominated; a canvas bag made from a rectangular piece of fabric with tassels hung at the corners and richly embroidered with animal designs or scenes of romantic tales; or a draw-string pouch, also heavily embroidered. These purses were first used to hold missals.

fans

Fans were not an important accessory during the Renaissance and were either "a round form which folds" or shirred. They were often carried by a servant who whisked annoying insects away from his master. The servant carried the fan suspended by a chain or cord attached to his belt.

HAIR STYLES
(1400-1500)
Men and Women

Hair and headcovering fashions changed very slowly for both men and women during this period. By the end of the fifteenth century men wore their hair in shoulder-length bobs, discarding the round cap and shaved neck style that had persisted for some years. Long bangs covered the forehead at this time and the hair was worn straight or gently waved, curving inward at the ends.

Gown with bag-supported skirt front, showing bandier, and hennin with trailing veil

BODY SUPPORT
(1400-1500)
Women
busc

The *busc* (busk or *busque*) was the first in a series of garments that were designed to control the female figure. It was introduced first in Italy late in the fifteenth century and was made by sewing several layers of fabric together. These were then stitched or quilted to give stiffness to the simple body-encircling band. It was laced snugly in back and assisted in creating the flat-chested appearance typical of the female silhouette of the period. This corset was made of rich, heavy silk, replacing the woolen material used in making the cotte, an earlier figure-forming garment. A still later refinement was the addition of whalebones sewn between the layers of the busc, which were stitched or quilted in the required positions. The busc, thus boned, had more rigidity and gave even more figure control, particularly in the area of the bust. The tight lacings pulled the body in at the rib cage, decreasing the girth of the figure in that area. Usually simple ribbon ties were used as shoulder straps. These were attached to the top hem of the busc, a pair in front and a pair in back, knotted in a bow on each shoulder.

Additional pictorial resources

1. bas-relief—Figure on Florentine—(houppelande and chausses), c. 1400, Victoria and Albert Museum, London

2. painting—"The Birth of the Virgin," Fra Carnevale—(gown, gown with mancheron bassard, surcoat, wimple, turban and cyclas), c. 1400, Metropolitan Museum of Art, New York City

3. illumination—"Jewish Wedding," Jacob ben Essen Manuscript—(houppelande, particolored chausses à plain fond, fur-lined houpplande with manches pertuisées and gown), fifteenth century, Vatican Library, Rome

4. painting—"Legend of Ursula," Carpaccio—(points, pourpoint, with puffs and slashes), 1495, Metropolitan Museum of Art, New York City

5. painting—"Miracle of St. Giles" (anon)—(square-necked pourpoint, cotte or gambeson, lodier, heuze and broquette), 1495, Metropolitan Museum of Art, New York City

6. painting—"Marriage of Boccaccio Adimari and Lisa Ricasoli," Cassone Adimari—(chaperon, roundlet, chausses and huque), fifteenth century, Academia, Florence

7. painting—"Portrait of a Lady," van der Weyden—(butterfly hennin with wire frame), 1450, National Gallery, Washington, D.C.

8. painting—"Virgin and Child with Donors," Memling—(hennin, velvet falls, bandier, busk-flattened bust), 1470, National Gallery, London

9. painting—"Portrait of a Lady," Pisanello—(turban, female houppelande with tall collar), 1424, National Gallery, Washington, D.C.

10. painting—"Predella on his Presentation in the Temple," Fabrino—(turban, dragged sleeved houppelande—male; bag-sleeved houppelande, wimple—female), 1423, Louvre, Paris

There is a vast pictorial resource in the major collections in this and other countries; this list presents only those with the most typical costumes.

Chapter 11

FLAMBOYANT FASHIONS OF
THE HIGH RENAISSANCE

*T*HE *sixteenth century was a century of discovery, of church
reform, of high artistic and literary achievement, and of
political upheaval. It also witnessed the birth of capitalism as
as we know it today.*

*Encouraged by ambitious rulers, not always their own sovereigns, sea-
faring men from all of Europe ventured over uncharted routes to new
lands, which they claimed in the names of the monarchs they represented.
The struggle for control of the oceans was the natural consequence of
navigational exploration. It had begun with the first tentative expedi-*

Spanish gown with pendent or double funnel sleeve (1525)

tions sponsored by Prince Henry the Navigator of Portugal along the western coast of Africa in 1470. Christopher Columbus's voyages to America, Amerigo Vespucci's exploration of the eastern coast of South America, and Vasco da Gama's epic voyage along the east coast of Africa all took place at the end of the fifteenth and the beginning of the sixteenth centuries. By 1522 Balboa had discovered the Pacific, Ponce de Leon had landed in Florida, Magellan had circumnavigated the globe. In the early part of the century Spain ruled the oceans, but by 1588 the exploits of Sir Francis Drake and the defeat of the Spanish Armada had established England as the "ruler of the waves," a title she was to retain until well into the twentieth century.

This was also the century of the Reformation and the Counter-Reformation, of the separation of the Church of England from Rome and the family feud between the Catholic House of Guise and the Protestant House of Bourbon in France. Erasmus in Holland, Luther in Germany, Colet in England, Zwingli and Calvin in Switzerland, established their various forms of Protestantism, laying the groundwork for a new social order. In Spain there was a revival of the Inquisition, now used to search out and prosecute Protestants and other heretics rather than Jews and Moors. The eventual effect was an intellectual and economic blight which led to the decline of Spanish influence and power through the ensuing centuries. The Council of Trent and the Counter-Reformation halted secessions from the Catholic church and a new religious "balance of power" was established. In 1534 St. Ignatius Loyola founded the Jesuit order. The movements of Huguenot refugees from France and Catholic refugees from England led to the beginning of the colonization of North America.

The restoration of Rome, ravaged by invasions, political turmoil, and plague, was undertaken under the auspices of Popes Julius II and Clement III. At the beginning of the century Michelangelo was working on the ceiling of the Sistine Chapel and Raphael was painting the Sistine Madonna. In 1546 Michelangelo was appointed chief architect to complete Bramante's plans for St. Peter's church. The central dome was completed from his drawings by 1590.

The French invasion of Italy under Charles VIII had introduced the French to the aesthetic wonders of Italy. Francis I brought Leonardo da Vinci, Cellini, Raphael and others back to France, where they exerted an important influence on French art.

By the end of the sixteenth century all Europe had felt the impact of the philosophical concepts of the High Renaissance. Malory, Marlowe, Bacon, Spenser, and Shakespeare in England, Rabelais in France, Machiavelli in Italy, even the morality plays of the period, expressed the belief that man lived after his own pleasure, delighting in having his body "gay and fresh." Every aspect of life reflected these concepts. It was the demand for silks, cottons, and spices from the Orient which inspired the Spanish and Portuguese explorers' search for a new passage to the Orient. Meanwhile Italy was the principal supplier of these luxuries. As trade expanded between nations and continents, once again fusing cultures and affecting clothing styles, the rich fabric which Marco Polo and his successors brought back from China, the gold and jewels seized by the conquistadores, were added to the splendor of the already opulent Renaissance costumes. Moreover, elegant clothing was no longer restricted to the nobility, and the wealthy commercial families also flaunted the latest fashions.

During the last decade of the sixteenth century, Titian's grandson, Cesare Vecellio, produced innumerable fashion plates so that all who were interested and financially able might be dressed in the latest fashion. These styles from Venice appeared in DEGLI HABITI ANTICHI E MODERNI and established many style trends. In DIVERSARIUM NATIONUM HABILIA Pietro Bartelli presented fashions to the people of England, Germany, Spain, and Hungary in the form of illustrations. They showed garments similar to those of previous centuries, styles that were international, details that were nationalistic, but all were elegant. The new silhouette, carried

Fifteenth century armor

out in rich fabrics, was seen in all its bejeweled, slashed, padded and corseted splendour at the "Field of the Cloth of Gold" when Henry VIII of England and Francis I of France met near Calais in 1520. The raiment seen at the courts of Elizabeth I, Philip II of Spain, and the other European rulers at the end of the century was no less elaborate. For the wealthy, at least, the High Renaissance was a flamboyant fashion period with the dominance of the individual evident in every garment and in the many variations of design and detail.

BASIC GARMENTS OF THE HIGH RENAISSANCE (1500–1600)

DOUBLET

(1500)

Men

   jerkin

   vest

    "stuffs"

    puffs and slashes

During the High Renaissance men wore four types of short jackets; the doublet, the jerkin, the vest, and the peascod jacket. The doublet, vest and peascod jacket were made with two layers of fabric and interlining of padding or "stuffs." The outside was made of heavy silk, while the lining was linen. The padding was usually horsehair though sometimes it was straw. The thickness and position of these "stuffs" changed as the male silhouette was modified. At first during this period, the upper part of the figure was made to appear square, bulky, and broad-shouldered by heavily padding the sleeves. Puffing and slashes in them increased the illusion of a strong, masculine figure. This decorative trim, puffs, and slashes had been introduced, if the legend is to be believed, as a means of honoring the soldiers who defeated Charles the Bold. These returning warriors, tattered and ill clad, had stuffed silks and tapestry bits into the slits in their clothes, or donned the garments of the defeated dead. Many of these pieces of apparel were too small for their new owners and split along the seams. As a result, the soldiers' garments beneath puffed out between the slits. The people of Germany, seeing the soldiers in their haphazardly mended and borrowed clothes, in admiring imitation slashed their own sleeves and puffed out their amply cut linen shirts and chemises through the slits. It readily became a vogue, and slashes were made in the sleeves of outer garments with small hot irons, the linen shirt sleeve fabrics were then meticulously pulled through. In time, the whole garment was covered with puffs and slashes, permanently created by rich fabrics. The linen shirt, however, continued to be arranged between the bodice of any outer garment (male or female) and the tied-on sleeves.

Paned Spanish slops, doublet with slashed sleeves

Peascod doublet with neck ruff, pumpkin breeches, codpiece, futera, plumed bonnet

vest

The vest was a lightly padded doublet, with or without sleeves. It may have been merely vest fronts held together by a narrow band across the back of the neck and buttoned down the front.

peascod jacket

The peascod jacket was a long-waisted padded pourpoint or doublet worn during the last half of the sixteenth century. The upper body section fitted the back and sides closely, while the front was heavily padded into a convex curve. In profile, the silhouette of the torso bowed into a low curve. This jacket had a high standing collar while the earlier doublet and vest necklines were either square or oval revealing the shirt worn underneath. The frontal view of this costume tapered from broad shoulders to a low, narrow, pointed waist. The fronts sloped to the fitted side seams. (Armor of this period had the same configuration, suggesting that the shape was developed as a defense against the thrust of a sword.) The peascod jacket had a small stiff peplum extending three or four inches below the waist. Sleeves for most garments were tied on with points, which for a time acted as decoration as well as a means of holding sleeves to the main body of the garment. As this fashion detail faded, padded crescents, or *ropillas*, were tied over the lacings that held on the sleeves. Sleeve styles varied from the larger puffed or balloon sleeves of the bulky silhouette period: to padded inverted cone-shaped sleeves gathered and puffed at the shoulder; to the padded ball forms covering the upper arms worn over slightly padded full-length sleeves; to slightly padded full-length sleeves typical of the peascod jackets. Hanging sleeves, long, wide and fur-trimmed, were also worn laced on with the doublet sleeves. These were called *cuerpo boxo*.

ropillas

cuerpo boxo

jerkin
haincelin

bag sleeve
manches
pertuisse
tube sleeve

The jerkin was an intermediate evolutionary style of *haincelin*, or short houppelande. The haincelin, an outer wrap worn by young Renaissance dandies, had been designed with a variety of sleeves; the bag sleeve, the manches pertuisse, and the wide tube sleeve. The thigh-length outer wrap of the sixteenth century was made by gathering the main body of the garment to a deep yoke. Generally worn loose with the fronts folded back into deep lapels, the jerkin assisted in creating the square silhouette characteristic of the early sixteenth century. Sleeve styles were the same as those of the doublets, and there were also sleeves that had cross slits at the elbows or a long vertical slit on the outside. Arms could be withdrawn from the long cumbersome sleeves through these slits, allowing more freedom of movement. Fur collars, cuffs and linings were an important part of these large coats.

shirt

Often all three of these garments were worn at one time. A linen shirt with bishop sleeves, high round gathered neckline, or square, embroidery-edged neckline was worn next to the body. The round gathered neck eventually evolved into a small ruffled collar, which in turn became the **ruff** Spanish ruff.

BREECHES
Men
    upper stock
    pumpkin
    breeches
      lower stock
    hose

The chausses continued in style until the middle of the sixteenth century. A small padded roll, the upper stock was gradually enlarged to cover the buttock and became known as pumpkin breeches. Below these brief padded, slashed, and puffed breeches were worn the lower stock, thigh-length tubes, with hose covering the rest of the legs and feet.

Spanish cape, ruff, chausses en bourse (1660)

Doublet, upper stock, and chausses, ferreruolo, and beret (Italian, Venetian: sixteenth century, permission The Metropolitan Museum of Art, gift of Lionel F. Straus, Jr., in memory of his parents, Mr. and Mrs. Lionel F. Straus)

**Jerkin, vest, venitians, and canons
(sixteenth century)**

**Vest, leather lodier, of Flemish peasants
(1520)**

codpiece

The codpiece became an elaborate functional pro-
tuberance, joining the two halves of the upper
stock above the crotch. Throughout much of this
period this device seems to have been symbolic of
some of the excesses and "gratifications of human
desires" (as an affronted cleric declared) in which
men indulged. This puffed, slashed, padded, grotesque breeches closing continued in style despite
censoring and banning by the church, until
breeches became so huge with padding that the
codpiece was lost from sight and discarded. Horsehair or bombast were also used as breeches padding
and in shaping pumpkin breeches (globe-shaped) or
venetians (pear-shaped) or trunk hose (balloon or
oval-shaped). Trunk hose were varied in styling by
the addition of long strips of fabric attached at the
waistband and at the breeches cuff. These were
called "paned" trunk hose. *Canons (canions)* or
half-hose were also worn with the trunk hose.
Late in the period, the padding and bombast were
removed from the breeches. This style became
known as Spanish slops and was calf-length, often
made more elegant when paned with a contrasting
color.

**bombast
venetians
trunk hose**

**paned
canons**

Spanish slops

**GOWN
Women**

Gown styling during the sixteenth century changed
radically from the high-waisted styles of the previous period. In general they were made of several parts which, when combined formed a
complete gown. The *saya* was one three-piece costume made up of a *vaquero* (bodice), bell skirt
(worn over a farthingale), and cuerpo boxo (separate sleeves or hanging sleeves). The bodice was
a female version of the doublet or pourpoint with
tight-fitting sleeves. The waist was long, tapering
to a point below the normal waistline. An under-
bodice, called the *jubon*, was tight and worn beneath the vaquero. The latter, in time, was laced
in front, the lacing hidden under a *stomacher*, a
decorative and functional device that was tied over
the lacings and held the busc (busk). During this
period the busc was a V-shaped piece of whalebone
or wood used to flatten the bust and hold the figure erect. It was inserted between the two layers
of fabric that formed the stomacher. The *ropa*,
semarra (Italy), *marlotte* (France), and *vlieger*
(Holland) were other names given to ladies' gowns.
They all combined the three primary costume
parts to form the gown, using the Dutch waist
which made the bodice appear square and short-
waisted.

**saya
vaquero
bell skirt
cuerpo boxo**

jubon

stomacher

busc (busk)

**ropa
semarra
marlotte
vlieger
Dutch waist**

As feminine styles of the High Renaissance
changed, the outer skirt was slit in the center

kirtle
farthingale

ruff

under-proper

Venetian gown (sixteenth century)

front to reveal the kirtle skirt beneath. Farthingales which added girth about the hips were at first bombasted or deeply pleated cartwheels tied about the waist. Their shapes were a matter of nationalistic design preferences and became elaborately constructed skirt supports made of tapes and whalebone or tapes and reed bands or bombasted doughnut-shaped hip cushions. Necklines were truncated V-shapes in England, high throat-encircling collars topped by a little ruff in Spain, and in France inverted V-shapes with a tall Medici collar framing the head. Each country developed this detail to suit its taste. Starched pleated ruffs, which developed from the drawstring gathered neckline of the male shirt, became the dominant detail of both men and women's costumes. At first only small lace ruffles encircling the throat, they eventually grew into huge pleated wheels of lace. These were so large that a wire frame, or under-proper, was needed to support them. These huge collars caused considerable problems when eating and spoon handles were lengthened to facilitate getting the food over them, from plate to mouth. Huge lace collars, standing high in back and attached to the corners of square necklines, were also supported by delicate wire frames. These collars were either fan, heart, or wing shapes and often studded with seed pearls and shot through with golden threads.

Gown with stomacher, farthingale, and standing collar, supported by under-proper (British: sixteenth century, permission The Metropolitan Museum of Art, gift of J. Pierpont Morgan, 1911)

Saya with cuerpo boxo and partlet—note lacing (Italian: c. 1506, permission The Metropolitan Museum of Art, gift of Henry C. Marquand, 1890)

Gown with partlet and chemise (1550-1560)

**kirtle
petticoat**

partlet

**chemise
shift
under-
knickers**

Beneath the three-piece gowns women wore kirtles, petticoats or skirts, made of handsome fabric. They were visible through the inverted V-opening of the outer skirt. Additional female underwear included; the *partlet*, a fine linen or silk underwaist with full, soft, gathered sleeves trimmed with lace cuffs; the chemise, a long linen one-piece tunic with tight sleeves; the shift, a long silk tunic; and underknickers. The latter were full baggy pants, and at first they were considered indecent because courtesans had originally used them made from gold or silver fabrics. These Renaissance ladies of easy virtue wore them beneath the split gown skirt without wearing underskirts or kirtles. It was Catherine de Medici who made underknickers popular and proper. Although the shift was sometimes used as a nightgown, the wearing of clothing at night was also not considered respectable until Margaret of Navarre began to wear black silk shifts when she retired to accentuate her extremely fair skin.

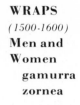

WRAPS

(1500-1600)

**Men and
Women**
  gamurra
  zornea

  chamarre

  casaque

The *gamurra* was a woman's wrap made by combining the surcoat and houppelande. It was sleeveless, with full floor-length skirts made of silken fabrics and lined with fur or contrasting colored silks. The *zornea* was a male outer garment, fur-trimmed and made of elegant material. It was much like a large cape, but was worn tightly belted at the waist and had wide, full sleeves. The *chamarre* was another masculine wrap made of silk and fur lined. The sleeves of this short full coat were made with large puffed wings attached at the shoulders, encircling the upper arm. The *casaque* was a thigh-length overcoat tied in the front with bows and with deep side vents or slits.

Gown and balzo (rebalzo) head covering, female; haincelin, male (sixteenth century)

Chamarra, casaque, trunk hose, jerkin, plumed beret, and slippers (1548)

Gamurra

Balandran (sixteenth to seventeenth century)

cape

ferreruolo
boemio
balandran
futera
capa
Spanish
cape

ACCESSORIES
(1500-1600)
Men and
Women
  headwear
  balzo
  (rebalzo)
  hood

The casaque sleeves were either closed and full-length or were designed with long slits that exposed the forearms, revealing the rich fabric of doublet sleeves beneath. Capes were the major decorative wrap used during the last half of the sixteenth century. They were either long or hip length and were known by several names; *ferreruolo, boemio, balandran, futera, capa* and Spanish cape. The Spanish cape was hip length and of circular cut. Worn as an accessory, it was made of heavy velvet lined with a contrasting color of silk. The surface decorations included gold lace and complicated braids. It was worn, as were most of these capes, slung over one shoulder and tied with silken cords under the other arm, giving a dramatic dashing accent to the total male costume, though ladies also selected this wrap form.

During this century head coverings changed radically. The huge hennin totally disappeared. It was replaced briefly by the *balzo (rebalzo),* a large dome-shaped toque. This hat completely covered the hair and accented and slenderized the neck. Forms of hair-concealing hoods were introduced at the beginning of the sixteenth century. These were designed with many variations, all nationalistic in origin. Basically they consisted of a veil,

Balzo

Gabled headdress

touret

lappet

gabled headdress

French hood

Stuart cap

bonnets

or *touret*, of black velvet lined with contrasting silk, generally white or red. In the next form change the veil was cut on the sides in front of the ears, forming lappets which fell over the shoulders in front, with the back of the head covered by the remainder of this heavy veiling. Later, these side pieces were folded up and pinned onto the top of the head. In the French variation of this hood, the veil was made of stiffly starched linen and arranged into large imposing wings. The English, during the time of Mary Tudor, modified the hood into the gabled headdress. This style consisted of the veil and a pointed or gabled shape framing the face and covering the cheeks. A white or gold coif, frilled and stiff, hugging the face and hair, was worn under this type of hood. The French hood was worn well back on the head revealing the hair in front, the back hair was caught up in the back in a caul or black velvet bag. The cap section of this hood was made with a small curved or heart-shaped brim. The small white cap with heart-shaped brim, the Mary Stuart cap, was the final hair-concealing hat form of this period. Elizabeth I popularized the wearing of tall crowned bonnets with small brims decorated with plumes and ribbon headbands. Large jeweled brooches held the feathers to the crown, standing erect or trailing off the brim at the back.

Male costume of the sixteenth century; outer garment, probably the cabon (Italian, Brescian: 1525-1578, permission The Metropolitan Museum of Art, Purchase, 1913, Joseph Pulitzer Bequest)

Men wore conical bonnets with puffed crowns and feather trims, flat small-brimmed pancake berets and, late in the High Renaissance, tall-crowned beaver hats with small snap brims.

footwear

duck's bill

Late in the fifteenth century, the point-toed poulaine was discarded and replaced by the broad-toed slipper known as the *duck's bill.* Just as crackows had once grown to ridiculous lengths, so the duck's bill became excessively wide. At one time these ankle strap slippers measured twelve inches across the toes. They were worn by men and were made of silks, brocades, and velvets, heavily embroidered, padded, slashed, and puffed. To keep from walking on their own toes, men were forced into a duck's waddling gait. Women's shoes were soft ankle strap slippers with puffed and slashed round toes. Because women's footwear was neither visible nor important to the total silhouette, as was men's, it never reached outlandish proportions. A shoe style with a raised heel attached was introduced late in the sixteenth century. The heel was placed well toward the arch and was spool-shaped. The toes of this style, while square at the tip, were rather narrow. A T-strap held the shoes which were sometimes decorated with large ribbon rosettes to the feet. These shoes were a natural outgrowth of the tall single pedestal *chopins* worn particularly in Italy. These elevated-toe slippers were raised to extreme heights; often the platform was twelve inches high. They were worn indoors, and ladies using this decorative but awkward footwear had to have assistance when walking. Another late sixteenth century shoe style was a T-strap, round-toed sandal raised by two heels, one under the ball of the foot, the other under the heel. During the reign of Elizabeth I, a platform sole (about one inch thick) became popular.

Chopin

chopins

hose

The invention of a knitting machine by William Lee revolutionized hosiery making. Hose were less costly and better fitting. They were an essential item in the male wardrobe and, though hidden by the saya skirt, were an integral part of the female costume. The colorful leg coverings came in bright blues, reds, yellows, and greens, often embroidered with gold thread on the instep and up the shin.

jewelry

watches

Neurenberg

egg

Watchmaking attained perfection during this century in England and on the continent. The *Neurenberg egg,* a fat oval timepiece; finger watches; earring watches, made with gold, crystal, or enameled cases; and many which were fitted with tiny chimes that "chimed sweet tunes" on the hour, were some of the types of watches worn. These costly accessories were always worn where they might be seen and admired. Ropes of pearls, gold chains with a series of large precious stones and large rings, worn on the index finger, were typical neck and finger jewelry of the late sixteenth century.

neckwear

rings

hand held accessories fans flag fan

disc fan screen fan

Fans changed radically during the sixteenth century, particularly towards the end. They were made in the shape of flags or weathercocks rather than the customary semicircular forms or pleated circles of the past. The small rectangular blades of these fans were made of plaited straw, painted linen, parchment, vellum, or silk. Disc or screen fans became popular about 1550, and the folding fan, made of leather with deep permanent pleats, was also used. The handles of all of these fans were made of gold and beautifully chased or set with precious stones. The circular pleated fan, when folded, concealed the pleated section in the silver, gold, or ivory handle. Fans were used so extensively that master gilders were kept constantly busy decorating them.

**MASKS
(1550-1603)
Women**

**loup
loo**

**oval mask
full face
mask**

Prior to the late sixteenth century masks were a prop used exclusively by theatrical performers. The masks made for cosmetic purposes in mid-century were small and colorless. They were first worn as eye shades while riding horseback. In France they were called *loup*, in England they were referred to as *loo*. However, it took little time for the charm and mystery associated with the mask to take this fashion accessory out of its totally utilitarian role. By 1558, and continuing to the end of the reign of Elizabeth I, the fashion mask was worn by all elegant women when they went "abroad" (out of doors). The short, eye-covering mask gave way to larger oval masks made of velvet. Finally, a full, face-concealing mask of "fine white cloth" was introduced and was generally accepted. Many devices were developed for keeping the mask in place after the original, hand-held smaller versions went out of style. String ties, velvet ties, wire bands (much like early spectacles bows) were used. One of the strangest devices was the stave and button arrangement attached to the inside of the full face mask. The button was held firmly between the teeth, keeping the mask in its face-hiding position. Women wore masks to prevent the detection of their identity when attending the bawdy and prohibited theatrical productions which were popular during the period or on other occasions, such as an engagement with a secret

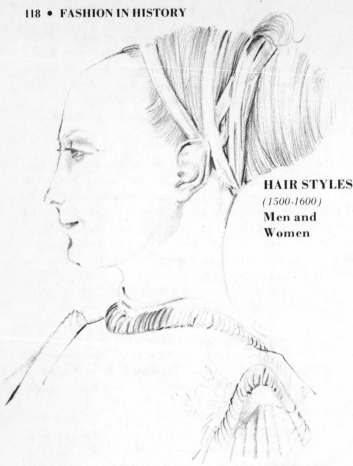

Renaissance hair style, copy of classic Greek coif

lover when mystery was paramount. There were also many who wore masks to protect their heavily rouged and powdered faces. Glass was sometimes fitted into the eye openings to keep out the dust and grime while "riding to hounds." The mask continued in vogue during these centuries of intrigue, serving both as a utilitarian and camouflage accessory.

HAIR STYLES
(1500-1600)
Men and Women

During most of the sixteenth century men's hair was styled in a close, head-shaped bob. Some men wore their hair in an ear-length bob, flared slightly behind the ears, with rather long sideburns. Thin mustaches and stiletto beards covered the face but most men were clean-shaven, and a lad's first shave was a matter of ceremonial festivity.

During the Elizabethan period, tight, crimped curls, shaped into a head-encircling bubble, were in vogue. Wigs made in the same coif style were also used, imitating the "Faerie Queene," who was forced to use wigs because she had lost her own hair due to illness and high fever. Earlier in the High Renaissance, females wore their hair parted in the center, pulled back, and covered with some variation of the hood.

BODY AND SKIRT SUPPORTS
Women
corset
cotte

The busk (busc or busque) was the V-shaped piece of whalebone or wood used in the stomacher. The "pair of bodies" also acted as an additional body support to mold the figure into the narrow elongated torso considered the height of feminine pulchritude in the late sixteenth century. The *cotte*, an earlier figure-controlling garment, was made of quilted layers of silk or linen with whalebone sewn between these layers to ensure that the proper female form was achieved. Later a metal cotte or gambeson, lined with quilted silk or linen padding, was introduced. This diabolical figure-forming garment was hinged on one side and laced with ribbons tied in bows on the other. Ribbon shoulder straps were used to further ensure the proper positioning of this armorlike underwear. It was no wonder that women, confined by such figure-controlling gadgets, soon became known as the weaker sex.

farthingale
bourrelet
verdingales
tray
farthingale

The gown skirt was supported by: a *bourrelet*, a roll of felt tied around the waist, and *verdingales*, a hip level hoop; or a *farthingale*, a tape and wire hoop, larger in the back than on the sides in the final stages; or a tray farthingale, a wire skirt support that held the gown out perpendicular to the waist, dropping the skirt in a straight rather than

a belled line to the floor. These were both transitional and contemporary farthingale forms. National preference dictated the shape while acceptance of various styles generally depended on the speed of fashion communication between national zones. Earlier farthingale styles had included a pleated and padded peplum form secured at the waist over the gown skirt. In later styles these skirt supports were composed of hoops that were flat in front, semifull in back, extending well out beyond the hips at the sides.

Saya with bolstered farthingale (vaquero) and cuerpo boxo (1581)

Additional pictorial resources

1. painting—"Portrait of Bartolomeo Panceatichi," Panttormo—(doublet with puffs and slashes, and bonnet), sixteenth century, Palazzo Vecchio, Florence

2. painting—"Ball at the Court of Henry III of France," (anon.)—(slashed upper stock, peascod jacket—male; gowns with leg-of-mutton sleeves, stomacher, farthingale, ruff, and pendant sleeves—female), sixteenth century, Louvre, Paris

3. painting—"Philip II," Titian—(duck's bill slippers, codpiece, pumpkin breeches, peascod jacket, and cuerpo boxo), sixteenth century, National Museum, Naples

4. painting—"Henry VIII," School of Holbein—(doublet, duck's bill slippers, Venetian breeches, lower stock, chamarra and ostrich feather-trimmed bonnet), 1537, Collection of the Duke of Devonshire

5. drawing—"English Lady with Rosary," Holbein—(gown with bell sleeves, partlet, and gabled headdress), 1527-1536, British Museum, London

6. painting—"A Horsleydown Wedding," Hoefnagel—(gown, kirtle, Stuart cap, and general costumes of the period of many classes of people), 1569, Hatfield House, Salisbury

7. actual garment—(bonnet, white leather hat trimmed with passementerie) late sixteenth century, Deutsches Leder Museum, Offenbach

8. actual garments—(slashed and puffed doublet, Spanish slops with canons and hose) c. 1600, Victoria and Albert Museum, London

9. actual garment—(chopins, Venetian style), sixteenth century, Musée Bally, Schoenenwerd

Bodice fastening

Chapter 12
THE OPULENT FADS OF THE BAROQUE

*T*HE *death of Elizabeth I and the accession of James VI of Scotland as James I of England ushered in the Classic era, which would in turn lead to the era of the Enlightenment. James's insistence on "the divine right of kings" encountered opposition from the Parliament. Under his successor, Charles I, opposition developed into revolt and civil war, ending with the execution of the king and the ten years of the Commonwealth. After this period of Puritan rule the pendulum swung back again and repression gave way to licence. The end of the century saw a renewal of civil war in England, ending with the accession of William and Mary and the passing of the Bill of Rights, which finally limited royal power and created the constitutional monarchy which survives in England today.*

In 1581 the Dutch, under William the Silent, had finally gained independence from Spain. Spanish power in Europe finally came to an end with the Peace of the Pyrenees in 1659. The rule of the "Sun King" in France began in 1643, and by 1652 the struggle between the English, French, and Dutch for supremacy at sea had started. The end of the century saw Peter the Great attempting to westernize Russia and the yielding up of much of her European territory by Turkey.

The amazingly versatile Leonardo da Vinci might be said to have laid the foundations of modern technology. Newton published his theories of motion and gravitation in 1684 and around the same time Christian Huygens introduced the use of pendulums in clocks. William Harvey discovered the principle of blood circulation in 1628 and in 1632 Galileo confirmed the Copernician theory of astronomy.

Cervantes, Milton, Molière, and Racine were among the forerunners in an age of great literary production. In architecture, the fire which destroyed most of London after the Great Plague gave Sir Christopher Wren his opportunity to erect many of his exquisite buildings although his plans for the reconstruction of London were not carried out.

The melding of the aesthetic ideals of the Renaissance with classical concepts of beauty established a new compositional order in art. The church, always influential in prescribing the form and subject of religious art, had continued to be a controlling factor throughout the Counter-Reformation. Artists seemed content to unite Renaissance forms and classical art by copying the spatial organization they found in the masterworks of these previous periods. Many were apparently satisfied to redo, in their own painting style or technique, whole compositions created in the past. The Madonna theme so dominant in the previous period was replaced by the crucifixion. Roman and Greek sculpture provided the compositional arrangement of many of these paintings. The Baroque art form introduced a sumptuous and sensuous combination of shapes, lines, and colors that created extravagant architectural embellishments, paintings, and sculptures. The work of Rubens is typical of the richly curvilinear Baroque style. The realism of the Flemish School was brought to the height of refinement by Hals, Rembrandt, Vermeer, and Van Dyck. Poussin, painting classically ordered allegories, and Velàszquez, recording the Spanish court scene and national victories, are also representative of the artistic achievements of the seventeenth century.

French male costume, justaucorps and plunderhose with bavaroise

The social and aesthetic concepts of the age were reflected in costume. Soft gowns, with floppy lace collars, lace sleeve cuffs, bodices and sleeves adorned with "points and bunches" (tab-end ribbons and ribbon rosettes) were characteristic of women's clothing. Cavaliers and gentleman fops dressed in loose-fitting garments decorated with many ornaments. Silks, brocades, and softly tinted broadcloths were used as fabrics for justeaucorps. High flop-topped boots, hose with lace cuffs, and plumed hats with tall crowns and large swooping brims were typical of men's clothes during the Baroque period. Such excesses of dress reflected their wearers' gay existence. From time to time sumptuary laws, some of which even went so far as to attempt to regulate the number and dress of lackeys, were passed. Costume trends had in the past filtered down from the nobility to the commoners, but during the seventeenth century the newly affluent *merchant and banking classes, as well as the landed gentry, markedly influenced costume choice and style. For a comparatively short period Puritan standards also dictated costume forms, particularly in England and other predominantly protestant areas.*

BASIC GARMENTS OF THE BAROQUE (1600 — 1700)

DOUBLET
(1600 -c.1620)
Men

The loosely fitting doublet of the early seventeenth century was unpadded. It was designed with wrist-length sleeves slightly puffed and slashed, it had a rather tall-standing tight collar, and was fastened in the front with closely spaced round buttons. When this garment was designed with a normal waistline, it often had a snug band

Slash-sleeved doublet, falling lace collar, breeches with braid trim; rosette-trimmed heeled shoes (Flemish: seventeenth century, permission The Metropolitan Museum of Art, The Jules S. Bache Collection, 1949)

long
doublet

justaucorps

veste

rochet

Pantaloons, justaucorps (1639)

section around the rib cage and a tab peplum. Later it was styled with a very short, square waist and a peplum that was shallow at the hips, extending into a deep V in the center front. The high collar was eliminated and the peplum lengthened, made of trapezoidal sections arranged to overlap one another. The sleeves of the later variations of the doublet were large bishop sleeves, gathered full sleeves with a deep tight cuff, or paned, gathered sleeves. Many times, arm-length slashes bordered with braid revealed the full bishop sleeves of the linen shirt beneath. In the evolution of the doublet it became a hip-length coat, with the silhouette of a truncated triangle. The long doublet was worn fastened at the neck with the fronts falling open in an inverted V. The sleeves were amply cut with slashes, points and bunches, or paned trims. More often, however, it was a serviceable rather than decorative coat. The *justaucorps* was a decorative outer garment much like the long doublet. It was first designed with elbow-length sleeves slashed from the shoulder to the hem. They were elaborately trimmed with ribbon fringe, points and bunches (the typical decoration of the period composed of ribbon streamers with metal tips and ribbon rosettes), and lace or braid. The justaucorps gradually lengthened to the calf and was worn over the full linen or lawn shirt, veste and huge flared breeches. There were slits or vents in the side seams, allowing this shapeless coat to cover the petticoat breeches. The *veste* replaced the doublet late in the century. Worn as an accessory, it was often made of silk brocade or other rich fabrics that matched the justaucorps. At first it had narrow sleeves matching the fronts, though the back was made of linen. In time, the sleeves were omitted. The *rochet* was a very short bolero jacket with elbow-length sleeves similar to those of the justaucorps. It was square in silhouette, with a round collarless neck buttoned or tied at the throat beneath the large falling lace collar characteristic of the period. This decorative abbreviated jacket was trimmed with looped ribbon fringe or points and bunches around the hem, at the shoulders and on the sleeves. The rochet was worn either in the normal fashion or tossed casually over one shoulder.

BREECHES
(1600-1700)
Men
gregesque

Male breeches developed into many ridiculous and strange forms during this century. The puffed venetians of the sixteenth century continued or returned to vogue and were called *gregesque*. These were pants forms made of two pear shapes covering the body from the waist to the lower

Saya, female; petticoat breeches, plumed hat, male (French: 1684-1721, permission The Metropolitan Museum of Art, The Jules S. Bache Collection, 1949)

Venetians en bourse with la braye, cassock, and lace neckcloth (1663)

pantaloons
venetians
en bourse

petticoat
breeches
rhinegraves

la braye

knee
breeches

bavaroise

thigh. Pantaloon breeches or *venetians en bourse* (without padding) were also popular early in this century. These were full and baggy, calf-length or ankle-length. They were worn with the legs hanging loose or stuffed into boot tops. Petticoat breeches or *rhinegraves* were one of the excessive styles of male attire during the seventeenth century. The legs were made with deep pleats or by gathering long lengths of fabric to form two shapeless tubes. At one time they appeared to be a skirt worn over puffed, padded, lace-trimmed upper hose, with the lace showing below the rhinegraves. The petticoat breeches were fully lined and were decorated with points and bunches or looped ribbon fringe around the waist, down the sides and the leg hems. Deep ruffles were also added at the waist and leg hems as an embellishment. The breeches closing, *la braye*, was created by arranging ribbon fringe to form an inverted triangle where the two legs met. Knee breeches, rather ill-fitting at first, were introduced after 1680. They were gathered to a waistband and held tightly around the knees with a buttoned or buckled band. The front closing of the knee breeches was fastened with large decorative buttons which were both elegant trimmings and functional closing devices. Later the *bavaroise* (la braye) was buttoned unobtrusively with a set of small buttons, three on each side of the flap type closing.

Brandenberg, long coat, periwig, and cocked hat

LONG COAT
(1680)
Men

waistcoat

The long coat which replaced the justaucorps when knee breeches were introduced was a slope-shouldered coat with knee-length or calf-length skirts. It was made with a cardigan neckline or high round neck and was fastened with buttons set closely together on the straight edges of the fronts. The sleeves of this coat were of modest size with wide deep cuffs elegantly trimmed with braid. The waistcoat of matching fabric, first with and later without sleeves, replaced the veste.

SHIRT
(1600-1700)
Men

The shirt was made with a full body section and long voluminous bishop sleeves. Sleeves and high round neck were trimmed with lace. The lace or lace-and-ruffle cuffs extended over the hand. The shirt collars ranged from the large cartwheel ruff, to the beautifully made shoulder-covering lace collar, to the square lawn collar that covered the chest in front and the shoulder blades in back. The shirt sleeves were often bound with ribbon and tied with points and bunches as additional decorations. This was a popular arrangement during the height of the rochet and rhinegraves fashion. Many of these superembellishments were discarded when the long coat was introduced along with the cravat neck trim, and wide waist-encircling sash with deep fringed ends.

Monteau and justaucorps; hurluberlu hair style (seventeenth century)

GOWNS
(1600-1700)
Women
  fiponne
  dishabillées
  negligée
  robe de
    chambre
  innocente
  battantes
  monteau

Women's gowns during the seventeenth century were known by a variety of descriptive names, including; *fiponne, dishabillées, negligée, innocente, battantes, robe de chambre,* and *monteau.* The last-named was a rich, elegant, two-part dress. Gowns had changed radically in style from those of the sixteenth century, and the monteau with its soft lines was typical. The farthingale had disappeared, as had some of the firm corseting. The stomacher became part of the bodice, but for a time remained stiff and pointed. The bodice was short-waisted and slightly fitted, with a tabbed or slashed peplum. Decorations included a soft fall ruff, the cartwheel ruff, and other collars similar to those worn by men. Deep, turned-back lace cuffs trimmed sleeves that were slashed and padded and puffed. The full, billowing monteau skirt was slit in front, revealing through the inverted V an underskirt of elegant silk. The gown was heavily decorated with points

Fiponne with flat collar (1628)

pretintaille

and bunches or *pretintailles* on the skirt, at the waist, and on the sleeves, which were bound with bunches and points at many places along the arms, creating double or multipuffed sleeves. The neckline, high and round in the first decades of the Baroque period, changed about midcentury to a rectangular shape. The gown of the 1680s later became more firmly corseted, and the farthingale skirt support of rather small proportions was reintroduced. The bodice waistline was lengthened, and was pointed both front and back. The extreme decolletage of the plunging neckline was often masked by a ruching of gauze or lace. The bodice, which was either pleated or gathered, appears to have remained separate from the full, bouffant skirt. In this period the skirt was drawn back from the center front opening, draped into large puffs, and held back with bunches of ribbon rosettes. The monteau gown characteristically had a long train throughout most of this period. Unlike the monteau, the dishabillées and robe de chambre, which were worn by elegant ladies in their homes, were designed with the skirt and bodice sewn together, or cut in one piece. They were loose-fitting, with floor-sweeping skirts. The robe de chambre was said to have been designed by Madam de Montespan to camouflage her pregnancy.

JUSTAUCORPS
Women

Women wore the justaucorps, or brief peplum jacket, with center front closing and slender sleeves for added warmth. The sleeves had a cuff, often of swansdown, one of the many types of decorative trims used during this period. A cloak or short cape with detachable hood called a *mantilla* was often worn in the garden at home as well as indoors. It was made in a variety of fabrics from four quarter segments of a circle. A drawstring cord at the neck was used to close it snugly around the throat.

mantilla

Gown with justaucorps

UNDER-
GARMENTS
(1600-1700)
Women
  jupe

The *jupe*, another name for underdress, was a handsome garment made of rich fabrics embroidered with silver and gold. The skirt of the jupe, visible through the V-opening of the gown skirt, became more important to the total gown design when the fashion of back-draping the overskirt came into vogue. The bodice, overgown skirt, and jupe should really be considered elements that constituted the entire formal costume for women. The jupe skirt was often trimmed to match the overgown decorations. During part of this century the farthingale was replaced by the wearing of several petticoats beneath the gown and jupe to

petticoat

fiponne

hold the skirt in the desired bouffant shape. As many as eight or ten underskirts were worn at a time. Though underwear, these huge gathered half-slips were decorated with ruffles and bows, all of which helped in adding to the girth of the overskirt. The fiponne, worn about the home with the justaucorps, was also used as an underdress. It had a full gathered skirt designed with a train and was worn as an underskirt in the last part of the century.

ACCESSORIES
(1600-1700)
**Men and
Women
headwear**

The high-crowned beaver hat was a luxurious male accessory of the seventeenth century. Though called "beaver," the hats were made of taffeta, velvet, and "hair of particular fine quality." It is believed they were first developed in Florence sometime during the previous century. These huge hats were costly, greatly admired, and an important part of the male wardrobes. They were considered so valuable that they were packed into specially designed boxes when not in use and willed to favored heirs on the death of their original owners. Pepys, the inveterate chronicler of the day, recorded that he received in such a way a hat which was valued at four pounds and five shillings, a huge sum at that time. Hats were worn indoors as well as out. They were decorated with great flowing plumes when worn by cavaliers or were extremely plain when worn by Puritans. These elegant and colorful broad-brimmed hats were an important part of a gentleman's posturing pattern. When "making a leg" (a deep solicitous bow) the hat was swept from the head in an eloquent, practiced gesture. Between 1625 and 1640, the brim was rolled up on the side or in the front and held in this jaunty position by a clasp. A great feather was stuck into the roll, its long fringed elegance cascading over the wearer's shoulder. It was an honor to be allowed to wear a hat in the presence of royalty, but few were accorded this privilege. Women wore hats of similar shapes and trims during the early 1600s. Later, to accommodate fuller and more fanciful coifs, women

**hood
shawl**

covered their heads with a simple hood or shawl with the ends tied loosely under their chins. One version of hood that appeared during the last third of the century combined a frilled cap and hood. The cap section was often made of gossamer fabric trimmed with lace, contrasting silk, or even fur.

**jewelry
earstring**

Earrings of pearls and gold plus the earstring, a silk thread with ribbon rosette, were worn by both men and women. The earstring was worn through

earrings

necklaces

rings

patches

one pierced ear only, dangling down at some length. Ear pendants were highly prized baubles of precious jewels and metals. Charles I, as he dressed for his execution, carefully selected the earrings he wore on his last day. Before he laid his head on the block, he removed each one with care and handed them to an attendant for safe keeping. Necklaces were extremely simple during this period of elaborate costumes and hairstyling. A single strand of pearls was preferred. Rings were also in little favor, though simple gold bands or gold rings with a single small stone were worn on the ring or index finger. Patches of taffeta cut in star, crescent, and circular shapes were coyly pasted on the cheeks of both men and women. These bits of black became the fashion late in the century and were to become a cosmetic necessity. At the height of their fashion patches were made into intricate forms—ships in full sail, animals, and other more eccentric shapes. Because a patch was apt to fall off during an evening of revelry in court, a small silver box full of replacements was carried. Patch boxes were fitted with tiny mirrors, a compartment for the extra patches, and a place for the adhesive needed to attach them to the face. The church, always with a wary eye on fashion excesses, failed once again to control costuming. The edict concerning patches did not eliminate the fad, and they continued in style for some decades instead of conventional jewelry.

hand held accessories feather fans pouch purses muffs

Small feather fans with repoussé handles of gold, silken pouch bags with silk cord drawstrings (used primarily for carrying missals to mass), and muffs were some of the hand-held accessories of this period. The muffs used by women were small at first, while those worn by men were huge fur pieces. They were attached to a large silk sash and hung down in front when not being used to warm the hands.

footwear

square-heeled shoes

Shoes for both men and women became important costume accessories, for during part of this century women's feet—for the first time—were somewhat exposed beneath the gown skirts. The raised heel continued in fashion and became eventually a large, rather clumsy shape placed well back under the foot. The top covered the entire foot, with a broad square tongue covering the instep and extending a little beyond the curve of the foot at the ankle. The shoe was latched or tied over the instep through straps formed by extensions of the heel-covering fabric. Brocades, embroidered velvets, and fine leathers were used in making the

Justaucorps, petticoat breeches;
bunches and fringe trim (1665)

shoe tops. Square toes, ribbon ties through A-shaped instep straps, wide shoe bows with lace ends, and "shoe roses," huge ribbon pompoms, and "rabbit-ear bows" (often twelve inches in breadth), were some of the styling characteristics of the shoes of this century.

mules Mules, high-heeled slippers with closed toe straps, fur-trimmed and made of brocades, were worn by ladies of the court. Heels and soles were often red.

pumps The pump was designed with an oversized tab that covered the instep and rose to ankle level. High boots with long, large leg-covering sections were worn with the pantaloons. The tops of these boots were worn crushed down, with the large floppy cuffs folded over them. Over the boot cuff was worn a large lace ruffle which was either the hose cuff or a separate item.

patten Pattens and pantofles (heeled scuffs) were used as
pantofle footwear and shoe protectors during inclement weather.

hose Hose were important to the male costume. They were made of linen with large lace cuffs or of silk fiber knitted into smooth-fitting leg coverings. The latter were often embroidered with "clocks," (decorative patterns extending from the ankles and up the calf).

neckwear

Neckwear was modified in line with the general costume styling changes. The cartwheel ruff and the large lace collar totally disappeared after the introduction of the long coat. The legend of the necktie's origin had its beginning in the seventeenth century. All members of a certain regiment, so the tale relates, from the lowest soldier to the highest ranking officer, wrapped a narrow scarf around the neck several times to fend off the slashing blows of the enemy's sword. These scarves were worn as amulets, supposedly charmed and capable of protecting their wearer. The regiment concerned, the Croats, when visiting Paris, enchanted the cosmopolitan French by the dashing appearance they presented with their "charm" neck wrap. The style was adopted as a novel neck accessory which the French dubbed "cravat" from the term *cravates* used to identify the regiment. Soon the fall collar with neck band and tabs gave way to this style innovation. In 1684, the cravat was again modified because of the wearing arrangements created by military personnel. The sudden and unexpected victory of the French at the Battle of Steinkirk caught the officers of the conquering regiment unaware. Unable to complete their elaborate toilettes, which included the meticulous wrapping of their cravats, they hastily put these around their necks, twisted the ends and tucked them through the buttonholes of their military jackets, securing the loose-hanging ends. This new wearing style was called the *steinkirk* and was quickly adopted even by some women.

cravat

steinkirk

HAIR STYLES
(1600-1700)
Men and Women

The coiffure styles of the ladies of the seventeenth century were many and varied. At the turn of the century, the hair was drawn back from the brow into a pug or bun made of a wound braid of hair. In 1625, the hair was arranged into a pyramidal shape by parting it in the center and puffing it out about the head. It was tightly waved or frizzed and stood out to the greatest distance from the head at ear level. After the puffed styles came a series of ringlet coifs called: the *hurluberlu,* or scatterbrain, a scatter of bunched curls from a center part; the *hurlupée,* a similar arrangement; *à la Fontanges,* or duchess, in which the hair was piled into two peaks from a center part and decorated with ribbons and a pleated hair accessory; and the *sultana,* a tall puff over the forehead draped with a scarf or ribbon bows. The fontanges was supposed to have been the coif style created when the wind played havoc with the coiffure of a lady of the French court. In haste she tried to remedy the damage by catching up her loose curls

hurluberlu

hurlupée
fontanges

sultana

with ribbons, to the immediate delight of the king. The fontanges style was in vogue from 1678 to 1701, despite criticism and later royal disfavor. Fontanges "caps" with a lace peak in front, and a small cap covering the back of the head in some versions were made in many ways and had many names such as; *effrontés*, revealing the ears; *guigne-galants*, worn with curls on the forehead; *guepes*, with precious stones in the hair; and *palissade*, a wide form, tilted forward.

fontanges
caps
effrontés
guigne-
    galants
guepes
palissade

For some time men wore their hair loose, long, and waved. This natural style may have been a reaction to more formal styles. During Louis XIII's reign, formally arranged coifs for men were again fashionable. Hair was combed from a center part and brushed into curls that fell over the shoulders. One lock was brushed forward and called the *moustache*, until the Duc de Luynes conceived the idea of tying it with a ribbon bow decorated with a precious gem. This added embellishment and the lock of hair was then called *cadenette*. Wigs became popular after Louis XIII lost his hair because of a severe illness. These "false heads," wigs, were full, long, flamboyant, and elaborate headpieces. The different styles included; the *peruke*, formal, elaborately curled wig; the *periwig*, less formal and somewhat less curly; and the campaign wig, twisted side pieces tied at the ends. Of the latter style Rondle Holmes wrote in *Academy of Armor*, "...this wig is knots and blobs, a dildo or cork-screw on each side with a curled forehead." Heated clay pipes were used to curl the hair. Elaborate and complex styles developed as wigs increased in popularity. One of these consisted of two tall curly peaks on either side of the center part, with two "full bottomed" side pieces and a back section that fell well below the shoulder blades. Powdering the wigs became the fashion about 1690. Keeping the wig properly styled was a time-consuming task that required special care. It was first brushed, then pomaded and finally powdered with white talc. Hair for wig making was in such demand that small street urchins were waylaid and "snatched bald." Horsehair was also used by perruquiers (wigmakers) to meet the demands for "false heads." The wig was worn over a shaved head for proper fit, but no attempt was made to conceal the fact that a person was wearing a wig. Combing and attending to the wig in public was an accepted practice, a proper activity according to the etiquette of the day. It was done with handsome combs and with great finesse.

moustache

cadenette

peruke
periwig
campaign
wig

perruquier

**BODY
SUPPORTS
Women
corps piqué
gourgandine**

Early in the seventeenth century, corseting was an integral part of the garment. The *corps piqué* was a firmly boned bodice, usually lined with heavy linen. The *gourgandine* was also an outer bodice stiffened with reed staves. For a brief time during the Baroque period little or no figure-controlling support was used. Toward the end of the century, however, when gowns were again designed with small, longer waistlines, the metal corset with inside padding, shoulder straps tied or buttoned to the front panel and hooked or laced in back, was again worn. These metal "prisons" flattened the bust and the stomach. Full breasts were not fashionable, and little girls were strapped into tight-fitting bands that held lead plates over their breasts to retard their development.

Additional pictorial resources

1. painting—"Marianna of Austria," Velázquez—(gown, jupe, and hurlupée coiffure), 1672, Prado, Madrid

2. painting—"Children of Charles I," Van Dyck—(children's styles, copies of adult fashions, funnel cuff, tab doublet and fall collar), seventeenth century, Sabauda Gallery, Turin

3. painting—"Portrait of Unknown Man," Terborch—(petticoat breeches, ruffle-cuffed hose, lace fall collar, long doublet), seventeenth century, National Gallery, London

4. painting—"Woman with Jug," Vermeer—(bodice or gourgandine, with tab peplum, slashed sleeves, fall collar and skirt held out by Catherine cartwheel), seventeenth century, Metropolitan Museum of Art, New York City

5. painting—"Portrait of the Artist and his Wife, Isabella," Rubens—(doublet, venetians en bourse, beaver hat, and hose—male; monteau with slashed sleeves, caul-covered coif, lawn cap and beaver hat—female), 1609, Bavarian State Collection, Munich

6. painting—"Philip IV," Velázquez—(long doublet, baldrick, padded venetians and rolled brim hat), 1644, Dulwich College Picture Gallery, Dulwich

7. painting—"James Stuart and his Sister," Largillière—(long coat, knee breeches and fall collar—male; monteau and fontange—female), 1695, National Portrait Gallery, London

Robe volante (eighteenth century)

Chapter 13
GOWNS OF A GRACEFUL AGE

*T*HE century which gave birth to the Age of Enlightenment, also
known as the Age of Reason, opened with the Great Northern War
between Russia, supported by Poland and Denmark, and Sweden,
and closed with the French Revolution. As the century ended, Napoleon
Bonaparte was establishing himself as First Consul of France. A series
of wars—the War of the Spanish Succession, the War of the Austrian
Succession, the Seven Years War, the Russo-Turkish War, punctuated
the progress of the century in Europe. On the American continent the
French and Indian wars were followed by the American Revolution. The
Declaration of Independence was signed in Philadelphia in 1776, in
1788 the Constitution was ratified, and in 1789 George Washington
became the first President of the United States of America.

The century of Frederick the Great of Prussia, Catherine the Great of Russia, Louis XV and Louis XVI of France, and the Hanoverian kings in England, also saw the passage of many dates which would be long remembered in the history of literature, philosophy, music, and art, to say nothing of science. Addison and Steele began publishing The Spectator in 1711. Diderot, Montesquieu, Voltaire, Rousseau, Adam Smith, Edward Gibbon, Edmund Burke, Thomas Paine, Alexander Pope, Goethe, Schiller, Gluck, Mozart, Haydn, and Beethoven—these are just a few of the names from this period which come to mind.

The intellectual ferment that had begun during the Renaissance continued through the eighteenth century. Man's geographical horizons had been expanded and now his intellectual horizons were also extended. The writings of Locke, Rousseau, and Voltaire exercised their influence on the political attitudes of the middle class, and the results were seen in the French and American revolutions.

At the beginning of the period France was the arbiter of European taste, subtly changing Baroque forms and refining them into the Rococo. Directions in art were controlled by princes, the wealthy bourgeoisie, and, to some extent, the Church of Rome. Rich merchants in Holland, England, Germany, and Flanders employed native artists, demanding a superrealism in their portraits, while painters patronized by the nobility developed a playful, flamboyant style involving sensuous curvilinear compositional patterns and romantic subject matter, which their patrons evidently preferred. The paintings of Watteau, Fragonard, and Boucher depicted people, cast in a rosy glow, participating in carefree activities in a misty, wooded environment. Watteau is credited with influencing costume designs, and a graceful gown with a full, gored panel back and full skirt was named after him. Colors in costumes and in paintings became rich, with near-musical overtones.

From 1750 till the middle of the nineteenth century the Neoclassical and Romantic styles developed almost side by side. A renewal of interest in classical cultures and in the medieval tales of the Holy Grail and King Arthur and his knights inspired changes in the forms of the visual arts. Rejection of established religion and the existing social order also had an indirect influence on visual imagery. The itinerant painters of America as well as the post-revolutionary architecture of this new country reflected the prevailing aesthetic concepts. Emotionalism, the expression of an experience, whether real or imaginary, motivated many creative individuals. West, Copley, Stubbs, Fuseli, and Blake created paintings typical of the close of this period, while in architecture Adam in England and Jefferson in America were typical of the return to classic simplicity after the complexities of the Baroque.

During the first three decades of the eighteenth century styles of dress were constantly changing, depending upon the whims of the French court. During the reign of Louis XV his mistresses, Mme de Pompadour and Mme Du Barry, directly influenced French dress and behavior. Other countries accepted the French fashion leadership and slavishly copied their modes. The demand for laces, elegant brocaded shoes, and rich silks for dresses and waistcoats established fashion as an important factor in the French economy. Both men and women were slaves to their rich,

Waistcoat, long coat, knee breeches, hose, heeled shoes, and periwig

cumbersome costumes, which literally dictated their movements. Court ladies were often forced to ride in their coaches or sedan chairs with their heads projecting awkwardly from the windows if the ceilings of the vehicles could not accommodate their towering coiffures. Men of fashion were also often subject to ridicule as they adapted their habits and activity patterns to the mode of the moment.

The fashion trends set by the French kings and queens and the kings' mistresses were epitomized in the practice of court ladies, wearing gowns designed like aprons, playing the role of milkmaid because Marie Antoinette had taken a fancy to this bucolic activity. These foolish occupations and the costume excesses which accompanied them were but a few of the contributing factors that led the citizens of France to revolt against the aristocracy. The self-centered concerns of the court had denied the rights of the common man. The overthrow of the nobility and all they stood for seemed a natural action.

The Industrial Revolution, which started in England around mid-century, brought about a radical change in the social order. The development of new machines for production and new methods of distribution of goods had an indirect influence on clothing. Fabrics were particularly sensitive to the changes introduced by the new inventions and trading systems. Cotton, previously an expensive luxury, was now imported from India, and later from the American colonies, and processed in the Manchester mills. Arkwright's cotton spinning loom (1769), the fly shuttle invented by John Kay, and the perfected weaving looms of Strutt (1785) contributed to the eventual industrialization of fabric making. The ready availability of silk from Coventry and wool from Norwich aided in creating a wide range of garments in a large variety of fabrics. Machine-produced cloth, the newly affluent merchant class mingling with the nobility, laborers and workers attempting to assert their rights—all these affected the social and political climate and also combined to create new forms of garments, new fashion trends. Under the lowering revolutionary clouds a free and romantic elegance reigned and, for a while, gay and frivolous moods prevailed in activity and apparel. But the desire for individual freedom was fermenting and was to be the most significant concept of the age.

BASIC GARMENTS OF A GRACEFUL AGE (1700—1795)

GOWN
(1700-1795)
Women

adrienne
sacque
robe de
chambre

The basic gown style of the late Baroque and Rococo periods, though given a variety of names, created a large, triangular silhouette, It is believed that an actress initiated the loose-fitting pyramidal form of this gown which she first wore while interpreting the role of Adriena. This gown was known as the *adrienne*, and like the *sacque*, *Watteau gown* and others, was designed with the bodice and skirt made together. The body of the garment, with its loose waist and full skirt, was

General costume styles of the eighteenth century (permission The Metropolitan Museum of Art, Harris Brisbane Dick Fund, 1932)

Sacque (1728)

Gown with Watteau back

Robe de Chambre and fontanges hair style (eighteenth century)

levantine
Watteau
gown

polonaise
sultane

robe volante

gathered to an oval neck. It was an evolutionary development of the *robe de chambre*. All of these gowns were created with wide skirts supported by a hoop underskirt. Some were open down the front from the neckline to the hem, as was the gown *à la levantine*, revealing the underdress worn beneath. The Watteau gown was made with a fitted front bodice and a panel created by deep box pleats in back. This panel was sewn to the side seams of the bodice which was laced in back beneath the panel. The *polonaise* and *sultane* were other names given these huge tentlike gowns that were fastened at the neckline and were left open to the hem to show the rich bodice or jacket of the underdress. These gowns usually had tight elbow-length sleeves. The underdress sleeves, with deep lace cuffs or horizontally pleated cuffs, were visible below them. Other sleeve styles included the flared or pagoda sleeves and sleeves with deep wide straight cuffs. Another more formal gown, the *robe volante*, had a boned, fitted bodice that dipped to a point below the waist. The points were sometimes found both front and back. The neckline shape varied from a wide square to a super ellipse, plunging low into an extreme decolettage.

Robe volante (British: 1727-1788, permission The Metropolitan Museum of Art, bequest of William K. Vanderbilt, 1920)

Mob cap, pierrot, tablier, and overdress with trompeuse about shoulders

**liar
caracasses
trompeuse
menteurs
lügner
fichu
mouchoir
tippet**

Filmy lawn or delicately woven cotton fabric concealed the low cut neck if the wearer was of advanced years or modest. This neck trim, which had a variety of names, increased in popularity and was worn loosely around the neck, brought down over the bust, crisscrossed and tied with silver cords or buttoned in back at the waist. To achieve the desired fullness over the bust, flattened by the boned bodice, a wire frame kerchief support was worn. The supported neckerchiefs were given rather sarcastic names such as: *liars, caracasses, trompeuse, menteur* or *lügner,* depending on the country. *Fichu* and *mouchoir* were the more formal terms used to indicate this bouffant type of neck trim. Tippets, worn generally in the same manner as the fichu, were the winter form of this accessory. They were usually tiny capes made of velvet or short black or white feathers. The skirt of the robe volante was full, supported by a hoop

La polonaise (1756)

Robe retousse dans les pouches with pagoda sleeves (French: c. 1728-1775, permission The Metropolitan Museum of Art, The Jules S. Bache Collection, 1949)

'A la Piemontaise

gown à la polonaise

robe retousse dans les pouches à la piemontaise

pettiskirt. This type of skirt support was constructed of thin circles of steel, graduating in size from smaller hoops at the hips to larger hoops at the hem. The steel bands were suspended from a waistband by tapes. These hoop frames were made in many forms, each with descriptive names. The elbow-length sleeves of the robe volante were snug and trimmed with a lace cuff that was shallow over the upper arm and dipping to a deep full cuff behind. By mid-century, the sack and its many variations gave way to the gown *à la francaise*. Before the introduction of this garment the polonaise had become a very formal gown. It was fastened high on the chest, had tight sleeves and a unique skirt. There were two polonaise skirt arrangements; one included tapes set on the inside that allowed the wearer to draw it up into puffs over the hips. The other style had slits on the skirt sides, and the front corners of the open skirt were tucked into them, also making a drape over the hips. These skirt arrangements were a prelude to the paniers of the gown à la francaise. The slit skirt style was called *robe retousse dans les pouches*, for pockets as well as slits were used to achieve the correct and fashionable hip puffs. Other late sack styles included the *à la piemontaise* with a free hanging panel attached at the back of the oval neckline. This pleated panel formed a floor-length

à l'anglaise

gown à la
francaise

la pièce
d'estomac

petticoat
falbala

robe ronde

fourreau

tablier

robe
redingote
gown en
chamise
à la criole

Pelisse

WRAPS
(1700-1795)

mantle or cape. As a characteristic posturing pattern, this pleated panel was held or carried at either side by the hands. The English version of this same style, but with a snug boned bodice, was called *à l'anglaise*. The bodice of this gown was intricately cut, made of many pieces that curved outward from a narrow waist to the armholes. It was laced in front to within a few inches of the low neckline. The gown à la francaise was the formal gown of the French court. It was designed with a tight fitting bodice laced in the front and the lacings hidden by *la pièce d'estomac*, or stomacher. This elegantly trimmed concealing device was V-shaped and embellished with bows and lace. The elbow-length sleeves had multiruffled cuffs. The skirt or overskirt encircled the figure to a point at the waist on the slightly elongated bodice covered by the stomacher. The smoothly fitting petticoat, with multiruffled skirt decorated with *falbala* and flounces, was seen between the edges of the fronts of the overgown. The neckline was either a deep U or a truncated triangle. A small ruffle or ruching was worn about the throat. Paniers swelled the skirts out beyond the figure at the hips. These paniers, or "hen baskets," as they were derisively called, reached exaggerated proportions. They extended often as much as six feet beyond the sides of the body. Just prior to the French Revolution a similar gown with a boned bodice was known as the *robe ronde*. The underdress worn beneath the sacque, robe de chambre, and similar overgowns, was styled in much the same way as these two gowns. All of them were elaborately trimmed with volants and falbala, bows and flounces.

Toward the end of the century each occasion had a special costume. Gowns became more slender and the fancy pinafore or *fourreau* was introduced. Some versions of this garment with "few or no bones in the bodice" had an apron skirt that was open in the back from the waist to the hem. They were worn over a sheath that had a very modestly gathered skirt. The overdress with the apron skirt, called the *tablier*, was usually white with a flounce around the hem. Other dress forms late in this period were: the *robe redingote*, a gown with a boned double-breasted bodice, gathered skirt, and long tight sleeves; *gown en chamise* or *à la criole*, a simple one-piece dress with slender sleeves and a generally thin silhouette.

A number of outer wraps, capes and jackets, were worn during the years of the eighteenth century.

**Justaucorps, knee breeches, ailes de
pigeon wig**

Women
casaquin
caraco
pierrot
polonaise
francaise
spencer
capes
pelisse
mantella

pélerine

The *casaquin*, a simple jacket, fitted in the front
and hanging loose in back; the *caraco*, a short
fitted jacket with tight sleeves and tails; the *pierrot*,
a short jacket with ruffled peplum in back; the
polonaise francaise, snug fitting waist-length jacket;
and the *spencer*, a version of a man's riding jacket
without tails. Capes were large and used for formal
occasions. The *pelisse* was a fur cape with half
sleeves. The *mantella* was a short velvet or taffeta
cloak with many frills of the same material and
small ruches used as decorative elements. Other
cape forms *(pélerine)*, made in a variety of silks,
patterned velvets, and furs, were large circular
forms tied at the throat with ribbons. The fabric
capes, with slits for armholes, were fur trimmed.

**JUSTAU-
CORPS**
(1700-1795)
Men

The long coat, or justaucorps, continued to become more popular as a part of the male "habit"
or suit. At first the justaucorps had been a calf-
length shapeless garment but soon detailing refinements were developed. At the turn of the century
the skirt of this coat had flat side pleats over the
hips. The front was straight with both of the open
edges trimmed with braid. Buttons and buttonholes were arranged close together from the collarless neck to the hem. Huge cuffs made from
the folded-back ample sleeves had a similar trim
of buttons and braid. The coat fitted the back and
the back skirt had a deep slit to make it more
comfortable when horseback riding. By 1730 the
pleats were enlarged and the total fullness of the
skirt was increased. The attempt at imitating the
hip fullness of women's gowns continued to influence the design of this male garment. Horsehair was used to extend the flare of the justaucorps
at the hips. Whalebone supports later replaced the
horsehair padding. The sleeves were rather full at
first, but became quite snug fitting as the hip
flare increased. Large decoratively embroidered
cuffs or facings and huge pocket flaps were characteristic of the coat for some time. There were
three basic cuff styles: broad and deep, open in
back; narrow, either open or closed front and
back; and broad with modest depth, closed in
back. The cuffs, frac, and justaucorps lining were
made of matching fabric. The name of this long

pourpoint

suit coat changed to *pourpoint* about the middle of
the century and slight modifications took place.
The skirt became slimmer and the fronts were
designed to create an inverted V opening. Braid,
embroidery and buttons, both functional and decorative, continued to be used as pourpoint trims.
Buttons, made of silk, horsehair or metal, were
used so profusely on male garments that they be-

Pourpoint with fronts and backs fastened at side seam; bag wig

came an important commercial commodity in England and France. For a time the bodice of the pourpoint was slightly boned and padded, but by 1750 this had disappeared and a more masculine silhouette developed. The "tail," or skirt, of the coat was folded front to side seam, back to side seam and clipped together, or the fronts were folded to the center back and buttoned together. This created a very large inverted V opening in the front. While this wearing style was used primarily for horseback riding, it was the typical style of military uniform coats. In 1760, the tails of the suitcoat were cut in a sweeping curve from the center front (at the chest) to the side seams. The collar, which was added when the name changed, continued to increase in size. Designed at first as a small straight band, it developed into a tall folded or doubled down collar. Collar, cuffs, and coat fronts were embroidered with gold thread. These rich, elegant garments made of velvets and brocades often had embroidered panels on either side of the front opening. This needlework would, at times, follow the same elaborate designs woven into the fabric, making them more pronounced.

FRAC
(1700-1795)
Men

le gilet
vest
veston

cordonnet

frac habillé

Essential to the overall appearance of the male habit, the *frac* (frock coat or waistcoat) was at first a duplicate of the justaucorps. The only essential differences were the proportions of the sleeves and skirts, which were more slender. In time the sleeves were omitted as well as the skirt in back. This new garment was known variously as *le gilet*, *vest*, or *veston*. At the introduction of the frac, it and the coat were the same length, reaching to the mid-calf. Eventually the le gilet was shortened, covering the figure first to the thighs, then to the hipbone, and finally to just below the waist. The line across the front was modified and the tabs extending below the waist were spread apart creating a small inverted V. The vest or waistcoat, at the end of the century, was decorated with *cordonnet* (triple thread embroidery) or printed braid. All coats and fracs had been buttoned (if buttoned at all, for they were not, as a rule, early in the century) high on the chest. By the time of the waistcoat they were buttoned at the waist only. Men of lesser social station wore broadcloth versions of these garments. The *frac habillé* and veston, while formal wear, were seldom decorated with embroidery, but were trimmed with large brass buttons and braid. The justaucorps and pourpoint were made in a wide range of delicate pastel colors while the frac habillé was made in more somber and darker tones.

Shirt and neckcloth; knee breeches with culottes à la bavaroise

Waistcoat with frac (1773)

BREECHES
(1700-1795)
Men

**culottes à
la bavaroise**

braces

les bretelles

Men's breeches were knee length. They were at first cut rather full in the seat, semifull in the leg and were rather ill fitting. These breeches were buckled or tied with ribbon at the knee. The center front button closing was discarded and replaced by a wide front panel, or *culottes à la bavaroise*. Patterns for knee breeches improved and they fit the figure smoothly. Tab and band replaced the tie fastening as a means of holding the breeches leg tightly over the hose. Buckles or a row of small buttons were used as fastenings. Breeches were made of elegant satin for the aristocracy and of sturdy broadcloth for commoners. Two ribbon braces (suspenders) were first used to hold up the breeches, later heavier fabric suspenders or *les bretelles* were worn. These were buttoned to the breeches on the inside of the waistband.

SHIRT
(1700-1795)
Men

Men's shirts continued to be made of fine linen with deep bishop sleeves, ruffled or deep lace cuffs, and a small standing collar or neckband. The body of the garment was gathered to a shoulder yoke. It was not open from the neck to shirttail, but only had a slit in the front from the neck to the chest. During the first decade of the eighteenth century, a simple muslin neck tab was worn. It was trimmed with lace or richly embroidered. The *jabot* and *cravat* were the next neckwear forms, consisting of cascades of ruffled lace. These were replaced in 1730 by the neckcloth. It was wrapped about the neck several times and tied in back and a gold stick pin, with a precious gem set in the head, secured the neckcloth layers in front. The military wore black silk neckbands, while civilians wore white silk ones.

neck tab
jabot
cravat

neckcloth

SURTOUT
Men

A heavy, serviceable broadcloth top coat designed much like the justaucorps was worn for travel or country wear. It had a flat collar, functional buttons, and generous pockets with large flaps. It covered the figure to the calf, and was worn with broadcloth knee breeches, woolen hose, and heavy boots. This was the costume of the eighteenth century English squire.

WRAPS
(1700-1795)
Men
balandran
roquelaure

The *balandran* was a heavy full cape used as protection against rain and snow. Two side slits served as armholes. Serviceable cords tied this cape at the neck. The *roquelaure (rochelaure)* was a large overcoat designed by the Duke of Roquelaure. This garment was a large bell-shaped wrap created as a garment of warmth exclusively. Other warm outer garments included: an overcoat with a shoulder cape, deep pockets on the skirt fronts; a long wheel-shaped cloak with a shoulder cape and tie fastenings at the neck; and an overcoat that was thigh length and was designed with an elbow-length cape, high collar, and long sleeves with deep cuffs. The redingote worn by men was a greatcoat, as was the *hangreline*. This garment had full sleeves, with a button trim on the edges of the turned-back cuffs and two flat collars. Made with an amply proportioned body section, it was used for travel and sportswear. It was later worn with formal attire as an overcoat. The *retonne* was a lighter weight version of these overcoats. The *wrap rascal*, yet another overcoat of the eighteenth century, was designed with a large double collar, voluminous body section, huge sleeves but no buttons. Instead the wrap rascal was closed with

redingote
hangreline

retonne

wrap rascal

Roquelaure

tabarrino

bands buckled across the front. The *tabarrino*, a knee-length cape, as well as these other wraps was often worn with scarfs and a variety of hoods by the lower classes.

ACCESSORIES
(1700-1795)
**Men and
Women
    headwear
        tricorn
        chapeau-
        bas
        macaronie**

calash

**gauzier
Thérèse
capeauz
bonnet**

Men of the late Baroque and Rococo eras wore the flat-crowned *tricorn*. The brim was cocked into three points and was often trimmed with gold or silver braid or plumes. The feather-edged brim was an early fashion. The *chapeau-bas* was carried rather than worn, for it was in fashion during the period of the high *vergette à la chinoise* wig. The rather silly small tricorn called the *macaronie* was worn perched high atop the more pointed wigs, and worn by young dandies and fops. The precarious tilt of these ridiculously small hats made the wearers appear all the more outlandish and they became the butt of much ridicule because of their garish and flamboyant costumes. Women, because of their enormous coiffures during much of this period, seldom wore hats as such. The fan-fold hood or *calash* was made of a transparent fabric structured over a collapsible frame that folded like a fan. The *gauzier* was another hood made in a similar fashion. It was also called the *Thérèse*. The *capeauz* and bonnet were considered less formal types of headcoverings and were nothing more than a circle of filmy fabric gathered into a huge puff at the head-band with a face-framing ruffle. These large round caps were fancifully decorated with bows, flower garlands and feathers. The puff bonnets sometimes had a straw brim, but were generally made with a gathered self brim. When the bonnet was made with a straw brim it was trimmed with plumes. The softer ribbon-decorated versions were worn indoors and were popular with older ladies well into the next century. Eventually the bonnets decreased in size and were acceptable headwear for formal occasions, perched atop the towering coifs that had become the mode of the

Redingote and tricorn (1730)

Redingote with retonne, queue wig, and tricorn

leghorn

tricorn

footwear

pumps

shoes

mules

jockey boots

splatter dashes

jewelry
chokers
earrings

late eighteenth century. Floppy straw leghorns with the crowns piled high with feathers, flowers, and huge bows were a late hat style. These were worn for garden parties and for spring and summer wear. Silken ribbons, quite broad, with long trailing ends, were tied under the chin, either over or under the brim. Women too wore small beaver tricorns, tipped forward over the right eye. Feathers and braid were used as trimming for this masculine type of hat, worn while riding to the hounds or other activities on horseback.

High-heeled slippers made of brocade, kid, and velvet in light hues were the foot fashion for much of the early and middle period of this century. These delicate shoes were often embroidered with gold and silver thread. Buckles of gold and silver set with paste imitation or precious gems were attached to the instep. Satin pumps with high spool heels and very pointed toes were a mid-century style of female footwear. Shoes became increasingly simpler, however. The ribbon rosettes and the paste gems disappeared from the large instep buckles, the large bows and satin ribbon ties of the A-strap slippers were eliminated, as were the higher heels. Plain kid or satin mules with rounder toes and lower heels became the dominant shoe forms for women. Men wore a closed toe and heel soft leather shoe that covered much of the foot, the long tongue over the instep disappeared. Boots that were calf-high were introduced in the 1770s. Dandies in tight-fitting chamois breeches, le gilet, long coat and chapeau-bas (the large tricorn with erect brim) continued to wear metal buckles on low-heeled foot-encasing leather shoes. Toward the end of the century the jockey boot came into fashion. These knee-high boots were tightly fitted to the leg, made with dark colored leathers and a buff-colored lining. The tops were turned down, forming a cuff of contrasting color. *Splatter dashes* were puttees or leggings that were buttoned on the inside of the leg and worn to protect silk hose during inclement weather. Shoe forms for both men and women during this period were made in a wide variety of styles that included: the spool-heeled pump, the buckled pump, the brocade or kid mule, the high shoe, and the jockey boot. Late in the century women began to wear an adaptation of the Grecian sandal.

Jewelry, while elegant, was used sparingly as a personal adornment. Chokers of rubies and diamonds, pear-shaped pearl drop earrings, gold

watches
neck
ruffles

watches with enameled cases, and brooches covered with precious gems were common. The neck ruffle, while not jewelry as such, and a wide throat-encircling ribbon replaced gold and jewel neckwear. The preference was for an expanse of white skin exposed by the deep neckline bordered with

tatez-y

tatez-y (touch here) or pleated ruffles.

hand held
accessories
masks
bauta
moretta

Oval and circular masks were an essential accessory early in the century. The *bauta*, white half mask, and the *moretta*, black round mask, were the most common forms. These were often decorated with ruching and attached to a slender dowel, gilded, and encrusted with paste gems. They were hand held or tied around the head by delicate cords. By 1750 the mask was discarded by most Europeans except the Italians, who continued the fad of both masks and patches for some time.

fans

Fans were an important part of female activity patterns through much of this era. Wafting a fan coyly and with grace was an accomplishment and a sign of the user's artfulness and sophistication. Eighteenth century fans were beautifully crafted. They were pleated half circles with ivory or gilded spokes inlaid with mother-of-pearl. The pleated section was made of silk or parchment and intricately painted with romantic pastoral scenes. The complexity of these delicate paintings is remarkable.

muffs

Muffs were huge puffs carried by both ladies and gentlemen. People of this age had a passion for small and unique animals, and grand and sophisticated ladies often carried toy-sized dogs, "dressed" in a neck ruffle, in their muffs, which were made of fur or velvet and lined with satin. Men occasionally slipped the muff loops (ribbon handles) over the top button of their justaucorps, letting the muff dangle there when not in use.

canes
parasols

Thin canes and decorative parasols were very necessary to the posturing and posing manners of eighteenth century society. Both had long slender handles and were carried point down at arm's length in an affected gesture. The parasol did have more purpose than the cane, for the flounce-trimmed shade section did afford some protection

umbrella

from the sun. The umbrella, on the other hand, although it was a more functional protective device, was scarcely used, due to the belief that the person using it thereby indicated that he could not afford to own a carriage or to hire one. Men and women preferred to be drenched by a rainstorm rather than have this thought of them. Jonas Hanaway, an inhabitant of damp London, not worrying about what others thought, persevered, using an umbrella he had brought from China. In 1780, this was a daring act, for cabbies and small lads of the streets ridiculed him as they had done earlier in 1772 to John McDonald. The latter had brought a large black umbrella from Spain and upon carrying it through London's streets one stormy night caused a near riot, frightening horses and having cabbies and urchins hurl epithets and stones at him. The sense of using an umbrella was finally realized, however, and they became popular for all classes. They were sold in Paris streets by vendors for fifteen or twenty francs each. Walking

walking sticks

sticks became so fashionable that they provided a source of revenue when their owners were taxed for the privilege of using them. To carry one of these elegant sticks, a petition had to be submitted which was in turn reviewed by the Censor. At his discretion a "license of use" was granted and the stipulated fee paid. It was not uncommon for dandies and prigs and arrogant young fops to have their requests denied or their cane use restricted to certain days of the week. A copy of the *Tatler*, dated 1702, related the particulars of one such case in which the request was denied. By the middle of the 1700s, canes became a symbol of status. Doctors could easily be identified by the form of their canes. The general design of canes became more and more elaborate, the handles and the stick sections were elegantly decorated. The handles were formed in the shape of a reclining S made of gold and encrusted with jewels set perpendicular to the ivory, ebony, and even glass stick section. Slender daggers or stilettos were often concealed in the stick. Men of wealth were possessors of as many as forty walking sticks, the total value in excess of £1,500 or $7,000.00

handker- chief

The handkerchief was another gesturing accessory in this posturing elegant age. Handkerchiefs were made of fine linen in a variety of shapes including ovals, circles, and rectangles and trimmed with deep lace edges. The square handkerchief of modern times is the result of Marie Antoinette's frustration over such a wide variety of shapes from which to choose. Her accommodating husband, ruler that he was, made one of his more lasting decrees—that from then onward all handkerchiefs, to be legal, must be square.

gloves

Silk gloves and silk mitts replaced the large cuffed gauntlets of the previous century. Red kid gloves were used for travel while everyday gloves matched the costume coloring, or complemented.it by contrasting in color.

purses

A purse formed by gathering a circle of fabric with a drawstring was elevated to an elegant position as an accessory by adding needlepoint decorations.

HAIR STYLES
(1700-1795)
**Men and
Women**

Women's hair between 1700 and 1740 was for the most part brushed back from the forehead and gathered into a small twist in back. There were slight variations which included puffing the hair at

Lady in a combing jacket having a towering coif created by two hairdressers wearing justaucorps and vergette à la chinoise wig

the sides of the brow, then drawing it to the back in large sausage curls. Both were decorated with small bunches of imitation roses or tiny velvet bows. As more elaborately arranged and higher pompadour coifs came into fashion, powder was used extensively on the hair. The high pompadours were at first pulled taut from the brows and temples and secured high, over wads and pads. Much of the hair in back was false, with only that in front being natural. The back was arranged into many small roll curls, large tubular curls or a combination of all of these with a large bun at the nape of the neck. After 1770 the hair was piled even higher and was supported by wire frames. Coiffures of this period were so elaborately dressed that their height and complex decorations took hours in arranging. Hairdressers used ladders to properly attend to the decorations on top of or tucked into the hair. These unique embellishments often included ships in full sail, horses, or carriages with passengers and footmen. Each trim of this sort had a name: *cheveaux à la conseillère* (historic events); *coiffure à la flore* (baskets of flowers); *à la victoire* (laurel or oak leaf wreaths); *parterres galantus* (heroic events); and *chiens couchants* (few decorations but the hair formed into an inverted pyramidal pompadour). Because of the time-consuming task of having these coifs created, once done, they were left for weeks with only minor touching up and repowdering. This, of course, was not the most sanitary way of caring for the hair, and vermin quite frequently established healthy colonies in a lady's hairdo.

Hair was brushed and pomades used extravagantly so that the powder (white, blue, grey, buff, or pink) would adhere. Many contraptions were devised for powdering. One complex invention involved a large shaker under which the person sat, swathed in a voluminous combing jacket, a cone held tightly over the face to keep the billowing talc out of the eyes and nose. Simple bellows puffed talc on the hair, but the cone was used even when this elementary system was employed if for no other reason than to keep from destroying the carefully applied cosmetics. For a time it was perfectly acceptable to have hair powder on the suit coat or gown. It signified that the hair had been freshly done. With the turn of the century the large periwig was relegated to ceremonial status or to judges of the court. The campaign wig had demonstrated the need and desire for more practical hair styling for men. At first this

cheveaux à la conseillère à la flore à la victoire parterres galantus chiens couchants

wigs

Little boy's housecoat, bag wig hair fashion with ribbon fastening bag tied about the neck (1735)

pigtail wig

queue wig

Ramilie wig
club wig (catogan)
bag wig (le capaud)

toupet
pigeon wings (ailes de pigeon)

vergette à la chinoise

resulted in the hair being drawn back into a pigtail and tied with a wide black silk ribbon. Both natural hair and wig styles were created this way. Wigs and natural hair were next pulled back from the forehead and temples and held tightly in place by braiding the hair in a queue in back. The queue was lengthened by being tied at the head and again at the end of the long braid with rather large black ribbons, forming the *Ramilie* wig. Other wig styles included: loose short curls in back, tied at the head with a bow; club wig or *catogan* wig, hair in back folded under and tied; *le capaud* or bag wig, hair in back stuffed into a drawstring pouch, the ends of the drawstring tied in back and then brought to the front and pinned with a brooch or cameo pin; and the *toupet*, hair tufted out over the ears with a queue in back. The *ailes de pigeon* (pigeon wings) style included the queue in back with the hair cut to ear length and brushed into a triangular shape over the ears. In 1790 the hair was rolled back from the forehead and sausage curls arranged in front of the ears. The rolls on the top of the head were next arranged into a point, or *vergette à la chinoise* as it was called, because it resembled a Chinese dusting brush used at the time. Commoners of both sexes copied these styles but dusted their own hair with powder rather than wearing wigs.

The story is related that the talc used for dusting or powdering the hair was discovered quite by accident. It seems that a certain rather prosperous young man was out riding to hounds and became separated from the rest of the hunters. He was a guest, and did not know his way and was trying first one route back, then another. On one of his misturns, his horse crashed through a thicket and suddenly floundered in a white powdery patch of ground. The young man, dismounting to survey his plight, tested the soft earth to see if it were possible to go on. He realized that this earth would make good hair powder, for it was white, pure and very light, a much better substance than the wheat flour then in use. Being of such quick wit and seeing the possibilities for the commercial value of the earth, this young man not long afterward founded a commercial enterprise upon the white earth, talc.

BODY AND SKIRT SUPPORTS

For the most part the upper female figure was supported by the boned bodice of the gown. Corseting, an integral part of this garment, was made

Women
busc
pièce d'es-
tomac

wasp waist
corseting

of whalebone staves about the rib cage and a whalebone or wooden busc (busk) in the pièce d'estomac. It was worn to "keep the body straight," according to one writer of the period, "a plated or quilted thing." Late in the eighteenth century the wasp waist and flat chest reached exaggerated proportions. The desire of all ladies of fashion was to span their waists with "their own two dainty hands" and to achieve, by corseting, a flat narrow bosom in a "whalebone prison of littleness."

farthingale

le bout-en train
la culanta

panier

gueredon
à coupole

elbow panier

à bourselets

à gondales

criardes

dans les pouches
chemise

sattana

The farthingale skirt supports reappeared briefly during the middle of the Rococo period. At this time the band and tape device was used, formed into a hooped skirt. The bands of *le bout-en train* or *la culanta* increased in number as the skirt styles changed. Ultimately they were extended and held out the skirts in an ever enlarging circular bell, from the hips to the hems. In time, as their form changed, they became known as paniers or "hen baskets." Specific names were attached to each type of panier construction which included: *gueredon*, a funnel form, narrow at the waist and wide at the hem; *à coupole*, dome-shaped, curving from waist over hips, falling straight from the hip socket level; elbow paniers, flat in front, semi-curved in back (constructed to fold up under the arms to make coach travel more comfortable—this style projected in a horizontal line from the waist); *paniers à bourselets*, round barrel form, extending in a straight line from the waist-high panier to the hem at the sides, with puffs at the hips created by the overskirt; *panier à gondales*, extending two or three feet beyond the body at the hips, flat in front and back or projecting only slightly in back; *criardes* paniers, using the same shape as à gondales, but covered with oil cloth and called "screechers" because of the squeaking noise they made when the wearer walked; and *dans les pouches*, puffs and panier forms created by tucking the overskirt into pockets or skirt slits. The chemise or simple floor-length shirt was worn beneath the paniers. It had long or three-quarter sleeves that were often visible below the elbow-length bodice sleeves. Men wore a similar undershirt, or waist-length tunic, the *sattana*.

Additional pictorial resources

1. painting—"Mrs. Siddons," Gainsborough—(spencer, coif and bonnet), 1785, National Gallery, London

2. painting—"Elizabeth, Lady Taylor," Reynolds—(gown, fichu, and straw hat), 1785-1786, Metropolitan Museum of Art, Frick Collection, New York City

3. painting—"Family Group," Zaffany—(adult and children's general costuming, pièce d'estomac and fontanges), 1783, National Gallery, London

4. painting—"Queen Charlotte and the Prince Royal," West—(paniers, fichu, pièce d'estomac, petticoat and coif with mob cap), 1778, Hampton Court, London

5. painting—"Lady Elizabeth, Delmi and Children," Reynolds—(coif, fichu, gown—female; long breeches, shirt and jacket—male), 1777-1778, National Gallery, Washington, D.C.

6. painting—"George Wm. Coventry," Ramsey—(waistcoat, knee breeches, hose, pigeon wing wig and shirt), 1750, National Gallery, London

7. painting—"Farmer's Return," Zaffany—(commoner's clothing), 1762, Kenilworth Collection, Kenilworth

Fur-edged bavadere and palatine scarf worn over sheath gown (British: 1790, permission The Metropolitan Museum of Art, Bequest of Edward S. Harkness, 1940)

Chapter 14

CLOTHING FORMS OF THE FRENCH REVOLUTION

D URING the second half of the eighteenth century a series of social revolutions had radically changed the culture of Europe. Opposition to the privileged aristocracy had stirred in England as early as 1688 and reached idealistic proportions in America, where it sparked the successful revolution of 1775-1783. The most disruptive changes were brought about by the French Revolution. Beginning in 1789 and ending when Napoleon Bonaparte became First Consul in 1799, it was the culmination of previous uprisings by the masses, who were suffering deprivation of civil rights and social privileges and were burdened with heavy taxation and a precarious existence. The French Revolution was a bloody, violent, and often senseless civil war, but was felt to be both necessary and just by its instigators. Its beginnings were liberal and sound and the reforms demanded reasonable, but as the civil war progressed power fell into the hands of fanatics, resulting in the destruction of the country's economy, the dissolution of the monarchy, and the demise of all the grandeur of France. The political upheaval caused many French aristocrats to emigrate to England. Countless others, including Louis XVI, his queen, Marie Antoinette, and most of the royal family, were guillotined. In 1792 the proletariat seized the reins of government from the bourgeoisie. After a series of governmental convulsions, Napoleon Bonaparte established himself as dictator.

Chemise à l'anglaise

The Neoclassical and Romantic periods in art continued to run almost side by side and were not without their effect on clothing styles. When the revolt began in France most of Europe was enjoying a period of prosperity. The Rhineland, northern Italy, and Belgium were particularly affluent. Verviers was an important cloth manufacturing center. Ghent, Lyons, and Rouen produced fine laces for fashionable Parisians. But with the call of "Liberty, Fraternity, Equality" luxurious materials and elaborate clothing became the hated symbols of all that the citizens found detestable. Many of the aristocrats fled their homeland, and those who remained discarded their elegant costumes, partly as a means of disguising their identity. With the disappearance of knee breeches, tapestry and brocade pourpoints, silk hose, and lavishly trimmed gowns, social distinctions disappeared. These shifts in costume styles had an important effect upon the economic stability of some of the French luxury-producing areas. This was particularly true where the lace industry and silk mills were located. The depression which overtook these towns and villages was eventually to be a factor in the attempts to rebuild France.

While France was unsettled, the rest of Europe advanced economically. War profiteering, as well as the capture of markets once supplied by France, aided this growth. Fashion houses once located in Paris moved to England, where a supremacy in men's clothing was established which was maintained for generations. The English are credited with the introduction of women's gowns patterned after the Greek chiton. During the eighteenth century many people took an active interest in the governmental organization of ancient Greece and research into this subject led to the rediscovery of other facets of this culture. Meanwhile, England had developed the weaving of cotton fibers into a cloth so fine that it almost rivaled silk in texture and appearance. This new, readily marketable cloth lent itself to the draping characteristic of Greek and Roman clothing. Other themes of antiquity were copied in sleeves, necklines, and decorations. At the time of the revival of the Greek chiton women were attempting to copy as closely as possible the appearance of ancient sculptures. In order to achieve a maximum likeness they drenched themselves with water so that their garments would cling to the body. Men soaked their chamois trousers to achieve a similar effect and wore copies of the Roman toga or the Greek himation over these skintight trousers. However, so many people caught severe colds and pneumonia from going around soaked to the skin that after a number of deaths had occurred the government intervened, declaring it illegal to wear soaked clothing.

After the Reign of Terror had passed, interest in appearance revived. Marie Antoinette's designer, Rose Bertin, returned from exile, as did André Scheling. They became the dictators of men's and women's fashions. As eventually happens in all ages, social stratification began to be identified through clothing.

BASIC GARMENTS OF THE FRENCH REVOLUTION

TUNIC DRESS
(1789)

The tunic dress of the late eighteenth century had many forms. The most basic was a simple flowing

Women

tunic à la romaine

Chemise à la romaine

gown. There were two side seams in the body of the garment, which was gathered to a round neckline or a small circular yoke. The neckline was often trimmed with a double band of decorative braid. The tunic dress was sometimes worn without a belt, but at other times was girdled by a wide sash or apron around the waist. The *tunic à la romaine* was described by an author of the period as "the garment that best suits nudity." It was made of the sheerest tulle worn over a transparent undertunic. Though the lady's nudity was covered with two layers of cloth garments, her figure could easily be seen through them as could her hose-supporting garters. The flowing lines of this dress were gathered about the figure by a ribbon sash, placed around the figure just below the bust. The tunic à la romaine was sleeveless and had a deep oval neckline. The most daring version of this eighteenth century imitation of the chiton was created by A. Duval for Mme Tallien to wear to a theatrical performance. This particular custom-made costume was knee-length, sleeveless, and cut from a most revealing gossamer fabric. To further establish an identity with the Greek ladies of the past, Mme Tallien wore sandals that had ribbon straps cross laced over the feet and up the calf of the leg to the knees. It was this style of tunic which was water-doused to establish the sculptural illusion desired. While many wearing preferences were developed, A. Duval's design initiated the wearing of a thigh-length undertunic and a floor-length transparent à la romaine that revealed sandal-clad feet.

negligée à la patriot

The *negligée à la patriot* was a simple style that identified the wearer as a supporter of the Revolution. Always made of white cotton fabric, it had tight sleeves, a tight short-waisted bodice, full skirt and round neckline. The neck was trimmed with a red and white striped collar. This costume was worn with a blue redingote, carrying out the tricolor theme of the revolutionaries.

à la vestale à la Diane

Both the tunic *à la vestale* and tunic *à la Diane* were introduced in 1790 as replicas of the chiton. They had small inset sleeves, deep oval necklines, and were left open on the right seams of the tunic so that they might more closely resemble the open sides of the Greek chiton. The Diane and vestale tunic dresses were worn over flesh-colored tights. Posturing in which the right leg was extended from the side slit was a part of the wearer's technique of looking fascinatingly feminine. Toe rings and sandals with crossed ribbon lacings were other antiquity-related items. For convenience women wore a purse or buskin suspended from a high-waisted belt. This was an embroidered rectangular pouch hung on the left side from a wide decorative cloth band.

Sheath dress

sheath dress The sheath dress and the chemise dress were more conventional gowns with high waists, round necklines and puffed sleeves. The sheath had rather full skirts and a wide sash tied under the bust. Its sleeves were either three-quarter length or long. A calico ruffle or muslin kerchief were neckline trims. **chemise dress** The chemise had more slender skirts with many hemline variations including scalloping or a deep center front slit with curved edges. Tiered skirts were also characteristic of these dresses. The puffed sleeves had no standard size, varying from small cap sleeve puffs to large puffs that covered half of the upper arm. Skirt and **iphegeneia** sleeve trim included ribbons and *iphegeneia*, or garlands of flowers. Both of these dress styles were introduced in 1797 and were made with separate bodice and skirt sewn together at the high waistline. The *constitution*, *camelle*, *indienne* dress, and **constitution** **camelle** **indienne** **chemise** **grecque** *chemise grecque* were all chemise dresses with distinctive decorations. Rosettes, a wide fringed sash, and hem embroidery were some of the trims used.

Chemise à la grecque

JACKETS and SKIRTS
(1790-1799)
Women

Chemise à la grecque and spencer jacket (1799-1800)

waistcoat

ecrouel-lique

caraco

coureur

spencer

The skirts of the early revolutionary period were rather full and gathered to a waistband. They were worn by most women with a simple blouse or mannish shirt. Later the skirts were a wraparound style, trimmed on the open edge with braid. Braid also edged the hem, and braid frogs were used to conceal or outline the darts in the skirt front. A white waistcoat was often worn with the wrap around skirt as a blouse. It had center front button closings, high winged collar and a wrapped white cravat. The *ecrouellique*, or lady's cravat, was the only neck trim. The waistcoat sleeves were rather snug fitting and wrist length. The *caraco*, also worn with the wraparound skirt, was the feminine version of the frock coat. It was made from an intricate pattern and fitted the figure to reveal the female form. The back was snug across the upper torso and flared into a half peplum, formed by deep pleats or shirring. The sleeves of the caraco were tight and wrist-length and a fichu was worn about the neck, filling in the deep neckline. The caraco was often made of tricolor striped fabric with the stripes arranged horizontally across the diaphragm and vertically from shoulder to bust; sometimes different fabrics were used for the back and the sleeves, contrasting either in color or texture with the front. If this jacket wrap was worn with a long-sleeved sheath, the ruffle cuffs of the latter were allowed to show below the caraco cuffs. The *coureur* was a little jacket similar to the caraco. It was designed in two styles, one with a high standing collar and wide crisp revers, and was very tailored and masculine. The other was softly feminine with bow and satin trimming. The more severe style, which gave the wearer a military air, had long tight sleeves with cuffs of contrasting color, matching the buttondown revers. The feminine frill style had three-quarter sleeves with lace cuffs and a fichu at the neck. Both styles had a peplum in back. This style was usually worn with dresses while the other was worn with a bell-shaped skirt. The spencer jacket was hardly more than a pair of sleeves held together in back by a band that barely covered the shoulder blades. The scant front consisted of two bust-encircling lapels. Derived from the longer caraco, some of these brief jackets had a minute peplum in back. What the shorter spencer lacked in length and body covering potential, it made up in the sleeves, which were amply cut, often puffed at the shoulder, and knuckle length. The curved cuff extended over the greater part of the back of the hand but the palm and finger tips were exposed.

WRAPS
Women
palatine scarf
bavadere scarf

The *palatine* scarf was the most common lightweight wrap. It was made of swansdown and was worn casually around the neck and shoulders with one end trailing down the front. The *bavadere* scarf, a late eighteenth century version of the Greek himation or Roman palla, was hardly a good facsimile, being rather small, made of striped silk fabric and decorated with fringe. It was worn high on the shoulders in the manner of a kerchief or fichu. The only coat worn by women in the last decade of the eighteenth century was the redingote.

redingote

Just prior to the turn of the century it was a slim high-waisted garment with snug fitting sleeves, often trimmed with velvet cuffs that extended slightly over the hands. A matching, rather deep band collar stood up around the neck. Frog closings were used, bringing each front together without overlapping the left and right sides. Other details of the redingote during this period were a small capelette that was lined with velvet to match the cuffs and tall straight collar and a velvet belt gathering the short bodice snugly under the bust. This was not a full-length coat, for it was about twelve inches shorter than the skirt or dress hem. This outer wrap remained in style from 1790 to 1800. Capes, shawls, and other wraps of the past that had enveloped and hidden the figure were almost never worn in France, but women of other countries, not engulfed by a national social struggle, continued to wear them for added warmth.

capes

TROUSERS
(1790-1799)
Men

Trousers, often loose fitting and quite short, replaced the silken knee breeches favored by the court. The little more than calf-length leg was slit up from the hem for four or five inches, and the front closing was usually a wide flap buttoned on either side at the waistband. They were made of a fabric called "king cashmere" as well as other types of cloth. The *sansculottes* worn by the working class were baggy trousers with wide loose calf-length legs. Made of rough red and blue striped material, these pants were the badge of the wearer's status and his political affiliation.

sansculottes

casimir breeches

Casimir breeches were a transitional style. Although the revolution had brought about these drastic changes in France, men in other countries had no reason to radically change their fashion preferences. They continued to wear knee breeches or adopted this new, slightly modified style of trouser.

Bicorn, sansculottes, and carmagnole (1795)

Casimir breeches retained the knee length but became very tight in both the body section and the legs. A drawstring tape was used to hold the leg down firmly below the knee. The waistband was very deep and decorated with the three buttons that fastened the center front. By 1798 some trousers were cut to fit the legs "skin tight," while others were modified and styled with somewhat larger or wider legs. The looser types were bound twice around the ankles with ribbon and tied securely. They were usually worn with low cut slippers and white hose. The very close-fitting trousers were worn with knee-high jockey boots.

WAISTCOAT
(1795-1799)
Men
hussard
buttonholes

The waistcoat of this period was also designed as a close fitting garment. The tight fit was accentuated by deep lapels trimmed with braid or piping. Corded braid fastenings, called *hussard* buttonholes by some authorities, closed the coat. Waistcoats were made of king (also Kingfisher) cashmere, the major garment cloth for male attire of the period. This material may have been a rough woolen twill.

FRAC
Men

The frac as reintroduced by Robespierre toward the end of the century was a sleeveless, double-breasted vest, made of white material, with wide pointed lapels but no tails. When a revolutionary wore a frac each button in the double row would often carry an engraving of the guillotine. An angle closing with an intricate button arrangement was also introduced as an alternate styling detail at this time.

A l'anglaise breeches, waistcoat, ecrouelliques, and en bateau (1798)

COATS
(1795-1799)
Men
demi-converti

The *demi-converti* was an outer coat that was worn either with the fronts buttoned back or closed in a double-breasted style. It had a tall doubled-over collar, sleeves that were slightly puffed at the shoulder, and slim coattails that extended well below the knees. The front of the coat was waist length and straight at the hem. The tails originated at the side seam and were tapered in a gentle diagonal to their ends. Many men wore the simple loose fitting *carmagnole* or workmen's coats. This shapeless boxy coat with large lapels, a broad collar, and a double row of buttons, could be fastened snugly around the neck. The crossed redingote was a long double-breasted overcoat, buttoned down the front to a point several inches below the waist. Here a small straight horizontal notch separated the coat skirt fronts. These were slightly rounded, or cut away, leaving the legs exposed through an eighteen or twenty inches wide opening at the hemline. The sleeves were narrow but had a slight trace of a puff at the shoulder. The sleeve cuffs were held back with a button-trimmed tab. Because this was a double-breasted style, the fronts could be folded back, creating rather deep revers. The crossed redingote collar was modestly proportioned but stood up framing the neck. The excesses of the late eighteenth century dandy can be recognized in the *Incroyable* coat. This garment had an eccentric cut with every detail exaggerated. It was basically patterned after the demi-converti, but the lapels were excessively wide, the points extending four or five inches beyond the figure. The cuffless sleeves covered most of the hands, only the last joints of the fingers being visible below them. The left front of the coat waist was cut to a point, and buttoned at the waist. Lapel facings were made of patterned material and their borders were edged with braid. The tails of the Incroyable extended almost to the ankles.

carmagnole

crossed redingote

Incroyable coat

spencer

The velvet or king cashmere spencer, a waist-length jacket, had an accidental beginning. Lord Spencer, an inveterate horseman, was galloping over the fields in pursuit of a fox when suddenly he and his horse had a slight accident. Neither was hurt, but the tails of the lord's riding coat were partially torn off when they were caught on brambles and branches as he fell. Half in anger and half because he could not continue the hunt in comfort, Lord Spencer ripped off the dangling detail and proceded on his way. He was so pleased with the comfort of the coat without tails that he had several made, both for riding and for casual

Incroyable costume. Brutus haircut (1799)

at-home wear. He was greatly admired by many gentlemen of the time and they too adopted his newly originated jacket fashion. It was designed to fit the figure easily, with rather loose sleeves, wide lapels and high round neck with or without a collar. Other details included cuffless sleeves with a seam slit at the wrist, nonfunctional button trim, and tab-trimmed pockets set rather high on the jacket fronts.

tunic coat

The French, in an attempt to re-create costumes of antiquity, wore a loose fitting tunic coat with a wide sash belt. Over this was worn a square cape which was draped around the figure after the fashion of the toga or male himation. Both of these outer wraps were worn with long stockings made of coarse yarn, thigh-length tight breeches and boots much like the Roman crepida or jockey boots. They also wore a short jacket tunic, floppy breeches, and high shoes.

UNDERWEAR
(1795-1799)
Women
  tights
  undervest
  undertunic

  corset

  hose

While Greek and Roman styles were in vogue, women wore tights made of flesh-colored lisle yarn in order to achieve the desired figure-revealing effect. These knit tights covered the lower half of the body and the legs, while the upper part was clad in a cotton undervest. A sleeveless thigh or floor-length undertunic was worn beneath the chemise or à la grecque. These undergarments were made of finely woven cotton fabric. In England lisle hose were held up by suspenders (garters) attached to an unboned corset. In this fashion phase the body was not restricted. The new corset encircled the figure below the waist and functioned only as a support for the knit lisle hose.

ACCESSORIES
(1795-1799)
Men and
Women
  footwear
  slippers
  sandals à la
  grecque

Low-cut slippers replaced high-heeled pumps during the last years of the eighteenth century. Men's slippers were made of soft black leather or striped fabric. Ladies' slippers were little more than leather shells laced over the instep and up the leg to the calf. Sandals à la grecque were worn by women with their pseudo-grecian gowns. These sandals consisted of a leather sole with crossed thongs of leather or ribbon laces. The thong arrangement was attached to the sole at the big toe, then passed between the first and second toe and across the instep. The heel was closed and in some instances a drawstring was passed through a hem made at the top of the heel closing. This was then tied to the instep thong on the top of the foot. The sandal sole was slightly longer than the foot and came to a modified point at the toe.

jockey boots

Men continued to wear jockey boots that had first been introduced in the 1780s. These fold-top boots reached to just below the knees when the cuff was turned down. They were lined with different colors, and when turned down became a colorful footwear accent. Many boot styles came into vogue at the very end of the century; they were decorated with tassels at the front and fringe tabs on the sides, and the fronts were cut, curving to a lower point at the back of the calf.

headwear

bicorns

tricorns

Men's hats were designed with low crowns and large brims. During and after the French Revolution cocked hats were worn. Bicorns, with the brims folded up front and back, were set squarely on the head and decorated with a colorful cockade—usually tricolored in France. In other cases pleated rosettes in matching or contrasting colors placed in front just below the topmost curve of the brim were used as hat trimmings. The Incroyables, or outlandish dressers of the day, wore wide-brimmed bicorns or large hats cocked into tricorns, which were worn with one point in back and all three points decorated with tassels. Men also wore tall-crowned beaver hats with wide headbands, cockades, and feather trims.

turbans

toques

mob caps

cordey caps

bonnets

casque

The individualism characteristic of the period was reflected in the wide variety of hat shapes for both men and women. Turbans and toques were worn by both sexes. They were prewound and decorated in front with a feather brush. Women's turbans were made with a filmy layer of tulle over the crown and trimmed with a large ostrich plume in front. Women also wore large caps, or mob caps both indoors and out; *cordey* caps with large puff crown and wide lace brim trimmed with cockades or ribbon bows; and bonnets made of straw with tall crowns and wide deep brims set well back on the head. Bonnets had falling plumes and standing aigrettes (esprites) as decorations. The casque was a puff crowned bonnet with a long bill visor, also feather trimmed.

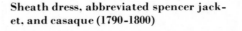

Sheath dress, abbreviated spencer jacket, and casaque (1790–1800)

jewelry

During the Revolution, Republic, and Directoire periods, jewelry was scarce and very simple. The repudiation of the French aristrocracy was symbolized by discarding these forms of personal adornment. Brooches functioned as fastenings and patriotic buttons engraved with the images of revolutionary figures or the guillotine or enameled with the tricolor were worn as decorations and as badges of loyalty to the new order. Ribbons were

neck
ribbons

tied around the neck instead of gem or pearl necklaces. Red ribbons were worn by French citizens as a gleeful commentary and in celebration of the number of artistocrats who had been beheaded. In contrast, the upper classes wore black neck ribbons in mourning for those of their number who had met death during the Reign of Terror. The one jewelry excess was the use of toe and finger

rings
toe rings
ankle
bracelets
watches

rings. Ankle bracelets were a brief fad as well, particularly in France. Watches were a prominent fashion accessory in countries not torn by civil strife. They were made in many shapes and were both key and stem wound. These timepieces were usually skillfully designed with hinged face covers that were painted or decorated with enameled designs.

hand held
accessories
buskin
balantine

The *buskin* or *balantine* was a rectangular purse. It was sometimes called a "work bag," perhaps the revolutionaries' version of the "keep" carried by Roman matrons to hold the household keys. This purse was worn suspended by a woven band from a belt placed around the figure above the waist. It and the suspending devices were elaborately decorated in contrast to the simplicity of the tunic dress.

gloves
mitts

Long gloves of kid or satin were replaced by half gloves of cotton net or lace, and knit mitts (gloves without full fingers) were worn for warmth. The mitts may well have been symbolic, representing the worn, tattered, and fingerless gloves of the poorer classes. With the introduction of the dresses with cap puffed sleeves, longer arm-covering gloves became fashionable once again.

HAIR STYLES
(1795-1799)
**Men and
Women**

This was a period when a casual appearance was popular as well as a time of revolt against all things related to formal conduct. The short curled bobs of the ancient Greeks inspired some styles, while others were merely untended snarled messes. These attested to the disgust the revolutionaries felt toward the elaborately cared-for and created coiffures of the immediate past. Women's styles

dog ears

titus
caracalla
infanta

included; dog ears, a pair of tangled puffs at the sides of the head and an unkept pug in back, the side pieces looking like two dog ears; *titus*, shaved neck with short curls covering the head; *caracalla*, crimped curls; and *infanta*, closely cropped, shaggy, uncombed coif typical of the Directoire. Men's hair was equally unruly. Powdering and wigs were abandoned swiftly and though men tied their hair in back, it was untidy and the hair came loose from the ribbon or string and fell over the face. The major hair style change was in the cut. The hair was snipped into uneven lengths and arranged into ragged tufts in front with longer shaggy hair straggling over the shoulders or around the neck.

Demiconverti, neckband, ecrouelliques; dogear haircut (1801)

Additional pictorial resources

1. drawing—"Indoor Dress of a French Citizen," David—(tunic coat, sash, toga and coarse woolen stockings), 1793, Bibliothèque Nationale, Paris

2. painting—"The Younger de Gassicourt," Prud'hon—(spencer, beaver hat, and chamois breeches), 1791, Musée Jacquemart-André, Paris

3. print—English outdoor costumes, (anon.)—(spencer, chemise dress, muff, bonnet), 1795, *Gallery of Fashions*, Heideloff, New York Public Library, New York

4. painting—"Dona Tadea de Enriques," Goya—(coif and gown), 1793-94, Prado, Madrid

5. painting—"Family Portrait," Francois Sablet—(tunic dress—female; frac, breeches, waistcoat and tall crowned hat—male), 1794, Musée Cantonal des Beaux-Arts, Lausanne

6. painting—"Mme Barbier-Walbonne," Gérard—(sheath dress), 1796, Louvre, Paris

7. painting—"Mlle Bailly," Berjon—(feather trimmed bonnet and sheath dress), 1799, Lyons Museum, Lyons

Chapter 15

ELEGANCE RETURNS
WITH THE EMPIRE

*H*OPES *for peace, personal freedom, and reconciliation of church and state in the wake of the French Revolution were not to be realized. The Republic collapsed, to be replaced by the Directoire, which in turn gave way to the Consulate. The wars precipitated by the French Revolution eventually encompassed all of Europe and presented Napoleon Bonaparte with a unique opportunity to seize power. As Emperor of the French he unified France, reorganized the government, codified French law, established a national system of education, re-established Roman Catholicism as the national religion of France, and*

167

rebuilt Paris into a magnificent city. He gave the French a national pride in their cultural achievements that persisted well into the twentieth century.

In spite of being engaged in military conquests ranging from Egypt to Russia, and perhaps because of their economic impact, Napoleon found time to issue pronouncements on fashion. The elegance of the Roi Soleil was reestablished at his court. The designer Leroy was commissioned to establish fashion with a definite emphasis on sumptuous attire—he was specifically instructed to use rich fabrics, velvets, heavy silks and brocades, with laces and precious metal embroideries. All of these materials were to be French-produced so that regions economically dependent on fashion-related industries could have an opportunity to recover. To ensure that heavier fabrics would be used Napoleon ordered that all fireplaces in the palaces frequented by his court were to be bricked up. Since nature cooperated ladies were forced to order gowns made of velvet and other warm fabrics—a series of extremely cold winters followed the mild ones of previous years, and gossamer gowns were totally inadequate.

In France the art of this period was led and dominated by David. Géricaut romanticized such catastrophes as the sinking of the Medusa in dynamic curvilinear compositions, while David painted in an ordered austere Neoclassical style. Greek forms were copied lamely in the sculptures of Canova and Latrob. It was not yet the time for individually motivated creativity. But Delacroix, Ingres, Corot, Millet, Daumier, and others were to come who would jar the ear and eye out of their accustomed patterns of sights and sounds. Meanwhile in Spain Goya was painting portraits of the royal family, charming paintings of ladies, and powerful compositions using laborers as subjects. The musical geniuses of the romantic period, Schumann and Brahms, were also on the horizon. The great writers who had influenced the political action of the age just past, such as Rousseau and Voltaire, gave place to Sir Walter Scott and Victor Hugo and, in America, Charles Brockden Brown, James Fennimore Cooper, and Washington Irving.

BASIC GARMENTS OF THE FRENCH EMPIRE (1800—1815)

Gala gown (with train cape). Tiara on "à la grecque" coif (1804)

GOWNS
(1800-1815)
Women

Leroy gown

Leroy, commissioned by Napoleon to design elegant female costumes, created gowns bearing his own name. They were made with bust-length bodices and either small puffed sleeves or long hand-covering tight sleeves. The neckline of a Leroy gown was square and very low in front with a deep round curve in back. The waist seam was hidden by fringe. The skirt fell straight over the front and created a conical silhouette with a slight flare at the hem. A padded roll was added at the hemline to hold the skirt out in the required form. A drape that became a modestly

gala gown

mantle train

sheath

proportioned train in back was also characteristic of this gown. The gala gown or gala dress was designed exclusively for wear at Napoleon's court. It was a richly embroidered chemise with small cap puffed sleeves, low bust-revealing neckline, and a slender floor-length skirt. This court gown was designed with a mantle train of heavy velvet and platinum thread embroidery. The platinum thread was used rather than silver because these dresses were ceremonial garments, seldom worn, and silver or gold embroidery would have tarnished when they were not in use. The mantle train was separate from the gown and tied around the figure just below the bust with heavy silk cords that had decorative tassels on the ends. The term "sheath" was applied to all gowns made of heavy fabrics. The typical high-waisted bodice, slender skirt, and puffed sleeves of various lengths comprised the major elements of the sheath. The high waist was marked by a slender ribbon belt tied in a crisp bow. The square neckline had an extreme decolletage, revealing the upper half of the breasts.

Sheath and under-petticoat (permission The Metropolitan Museum of Art. The Mr. and Mrs. Isaac D. Fletcher Collection. Bequest of Isaac D. Fletcher. 1917)

Morning dress of washable cotton (1820)

mamelouk sleeve

à l'anglaise sleeve

theater gown

tunic à la grecque

chemise

tunic

tunic à la mamelouk

tunic à la juive

apron gown

The skirt had some gentle fullness in the front, with greater fullness in back. The sleeves were generally an elbow-length draped form or full-length sleeves in *mamelouk* styling. The mamelouk sleeve consisted of several puffs from the shoulder to the wrist created by tying ribbons at several places along the arm. In many instances this type of sleeve treatment was reminiscent of the puffs and slashes of the Renaissance sleeve style. Elbow-length sleeves were often buttoned into graceful drapes and were called *à l'anglaise* sleeves. An elegant variation of the sheath and the chemise was a formal theater gown in which the bodice and skirt were cut together. A design imitating the high-waisted styles of the period was achieved by diagonal darts starting at the point of the bust and slanting to the side seams. These darts were held in position at the seams by four or five small covered buttons to maintain the desired short bodice effect. The darts merged into unpressed pleats that originated below the last button on either side of the skirt and extended to the floor-length hem. This rolled pleat added fullness at the hemline to an otherwise slender skirt silhouette. These handsomely designed gowns were made from brocade or patterned taffeta fabrics. In some cases small fur pieces of ermine or marten were worn following the decolletage of the neckline.

The tunic *à la grecque* was in fashion briefly during the nineteenth century. It, like the chemise, was made of transparent material and used as summer wear. It had a low ruffle-trimmed neckline and puffed sleeves laced on the upper arm. Two thin belts bound around the figure created a high-waisted dress with a clinging skirt. The skirt was often caught up in front with a brooch. This draped opening extended from the knee to the hem, exposing the sandaled feet. The chemise retained the typical lines of all dresses of this period except that about 1804 a larger fuller skirt was added. This was to develop into a rather long train that extended the skirt six to fourteen feet in back. More simple in general styling, the chemise was worn over a taffeta petticoat. Velvet tunic dresses with contrasting mamelouk sleeves or short puffed sleeves were open from the high waist to the hem. They were an overdress usually worn with the chemise. The tunic with the longer more complex sleeves was called tunic *à la mamelouk*, while the short puffed sleeve style was known as tunic *à la juive*. Yet another style of tunic evolved into an apron gown. It had a full skirt open down the back from a point originating at the base of the high-waisted bodice. More elaborate decorations

Gown with Medici collar and mamelouk sleeves (nineteenth century, permission The Metropolitan Museum of Art, gift of George A. Hearn, 1906)

Tunic gown with mamelouk sleeves
(1810)

classical gown

began to appear about 1804, and the apron gown was trimmed with an embroidered border around the hem and along the edges of the back opening. The classical gown was a simplified chemise with draped or puffed sleeves. The skirt was smooth in front and full in back. Weights were used to keep the skirt straight and vertical. Fringe or a pleated ruffle were used around the hem as simple trims.

betsey collerettes

Other gown details included *betseys*, and *collerettes*. They were basically neckline trims. The betsey was an English innovation imitative of the Renaissance ruff. It was composed of a ruching or small ruffle and a slender gathering cord, and worn tied under the chin. The collerettes were made in two styles, one a high standing pleated and starched collar that nearly obscured the head, the other

à la Cyrus cherusse cherusque

the *à la Cyrus* style that was somewhat flatter and attached to the neckline of the dress. The corrupted names for these neck trims became *cherusse* and *cherusque*.

WRAPS
Women
overcloak

A velvet overcloak made with silver embroidery on silver brocade and ermine lining was the wrap worn at Napoleon's court. It was a large cape fastened on the left shoulder with a brooch and on the right hip by bringing the back left edge across the front and securing it at the hip with another brooch. Variations of this overcloak were many, including a difference in lining and the addition of puffed sleeves that covered only the upper arms.

witzchoura
witchoura

redingote

The first fur coats appeared in 1808 and are believed to have been introduced by the Russians. Two names were used for this garment, each discribing the use made of the fur. If the exterior was fur and the lining silk, the coat was called the *witzchoura* and was of Russian origin. However, when spelled *witchoura* it was of Polish design and was a heavy woolen coat with a fur lining. In both instances this warm outer garment was styled like a redingote. The redingote had for some time been considered as a warm woolen gown worn for walking excursions. In 1808 the redingote became distinctly an outer wrap, a coat, to be worn over sheath or chemise dresses. It was made of worsted fabric, retaining its long sleeves that were lengthened to cover the hand to the first knuckle in a fan-shaped cuff. This coat was shortened to three-quarter length but retained the extremely short bodice and cape trim around the neck and shoulder area. The redingote was single-breasted and fastened by frogs in the center front. Another name given to this coat late in the period was *capotes*, but its design elements were the same, including the semiflared skirt gathered slightly to the high-waisted bodice.

capotes

palatine
canezou
guimp

spencer

Other female wraps of the period included: the *palatine*, a small cape; the *canezou*, a version of the spencer, without sleeves but with a tall collar, that slipped on over the head; the *guimp*, of similar cut with short tippets (extending from the collar) worn tucked into the belt; and the *spencer*. This latter jacket was extremely short. It had long sleeves with the characteristic curved, hand-covering cuffs of the period. Although very similar to the canezou, it differed somewhat in that it no longer had the small peplum in back. Many of these smaller wraps had details adapted from Renaissance styles, such as crescent puffs at the point of the shoulder, ruffle trim around the bustline hem, and variations of the puffed and slashed mamelouk sleeves.

Marino redingote, bonnet, slippers with Greek sandal lacing (1813)

HABITS
(1800-1815)
Men

breeches

Men's clothing appeared to be settling into a pattern forecasting the suits of modern times. The *habit* consisted of trousers, waistcoat, and coat, and was made of woolen cloth in dark blues, greens, and browns with trims of pea green and tobacco brown. Trousers of this period were lengthened but remained slim. If worn with low cut shoes they were crushed over the instep. The nineteenth century trousers were made of many different types of fabric, including fine cotton, usually striped; stockinet, an elastic material; buckskin; and nankeen, a fabric with a soft sheen imported from Nanking, China. Nankeen trousers were usually buff or yellow. Diagonal pockets as well as side seam pockets and a slightly crossed-over center closing were details typical of these trousers. Breeches (or britches) were again in style. They were somewhat longer than knee length and were fastened around the calves with deep cuffs with scalloped trim around the button-holes. Breeches also had a center front closing, slash pockets, and were worn over knee-length stockings or hose with either boots or slippers.

Male habit (suit) including coat, trousers, ruffled shirt with neckcloth, cravat, and shell slippers (1801)

claw hammer coat

waistcoat

shirt

neckcloth

cravat

col-cravat

royal cravat

Coat, double-breasted waistcoat, breeches, and jockey boots (1804)

WRAPS
(1800-1815)
Men
redingote

Coats were waist length in front with tails in back. The claw hammer coat introduced in 1811 was typical of suit coats at this time; the name described the shape and styling of the tails. They were cut rather straight with only a slight curve where the tail joined the coat bodice at the side seam. They were square cut at the tail hem, and extended from the waist to mid-thigh. The body of the claw hammer coat was cut to fit the figure easily and was designed with either a deep V-neckline and shawl collar and a double row of buttons arranged in a triangle forming a double-breasted style; or a single-breasted design, with a rolled collar that rose to the ears, and no lapels. The suit coat sleeves were long, with deep folded-back cuffs, and were slightly puffed at the armhole. Waistcoats became an important and decorative part of the habit. Styles varied because of the many collar treatments, which included the shawl collar and the high standing collar with deep lapels. The front of the waistcoat was lengthened and cut straight. The back and fronts were made of different materials, the finer, more decorative fabric being used for the fronts. This "vest" was usually double-breasted, sleeveless, and made of white pique, colored percale, or patterned fabrics which were often quilted. Shirts were made of linen with a modestly full body section, a yoke, and large sleeves. The shirt opened down the front and trimmed with flat pleating or ruching on the edge. Shirt collars were high with pointed tabs, worn flat against the cheeks. A neckcloth was wrapped around the throat, sometimes so high that the chin was hidden. A cravat (often two, one white and one black) was wrapped over the neckcloth and knotted once. Madras and foulard silk were customarily used for cravats. The col-cravat of the Empire period was attached to a collar that could be put on top of the shirt collar and fastened in place with a button or spring pin. The royal cravat was trimmed with cascades of Alencon lace and was worn without a collar.

The male redingote during the Consulate and Empire became a narrower garment, though it continued to be of double-breasted design. Russian frogs made of braid were used as fastenings and as trim. The back was made of four sections with a slit in the center of the coat skirt. A two-button decoration marked the waist on the curved seams. The collar (only one collar instead of the two of the previous style), pocket flaps and sleeve cuffs were of a contrasting color to that of the main body of this garment. Buttoned bands were

Waistcoat and frilled shirt (Spanish:
1820, permission The Metropolitan Museum of Art, The Theodore M. Davis
Collection. Bequest of Theodore M.
Davis, 1915)

**cossack
greatcoat
carrick**

an alternate sleeve trim. Sleeves were slightly puffed at the armhole. This top coat was also called the *cossack* or greatcoat. The *carrick*, styled after the livery of coachmen, was a large, long, full, ankle-length coat. It had a double-tiered cape, double collars worn high around the neck (almost obscuring the face in profile), and long cuffless sleeves. Some carrick coats had two high pockets, in the form of vertical slits, placed well above the waist. These were trimmed with an inverted scalloped and buttoned-down flap. The carrick was generally made of heavy woolen cloth in somber colors.

UNDERWEAR
(1800-1815)
**Women
petticoat
braces**

pantalet

Undergarments reappeared after the fads of revealing the figure and imitating antiquity had gone out of style. The petticoat, or gathered half-slip, trimmed with lace, was worn beneath chemise, sheath or tunic, and held up by knitted braces or suspenders. Pantalets, two tubes formed into shapeless underdrawers, made of flesh-colored cotton, were worn by some women. The pantalet legs were tied below the knee with ribbons, and they were gathered around the waist with a drawstring. Lace occasionally trimmed the legs, but not much attention was given to this garment, for it was thought by many to be indecent for any woman to wear a form of trouser. Also, the ribbons binding the pantalets to the legs often came loose, dropping them below the skirts. This was embarrassing to many and it was not until after 1830 that they became an acceptable item of underwear.

**slip chemise
smock
under-
petticoat**

bandeau

braces

corsets

Other pieces of underclothing included a slip, slip chemise, smock, and underpetticoat. Basically these garments were simple tubes of cloth with a variety of shoulder straps. They were made of cotton or silk taffeta and worn next to the body, singly or in multiple layers depending on the weather and the modesty of the wearer. The bandeau held the bust firm and flat. It was knitted in a stitch that created an elastic quality and was worn over the chemise slip. Braces used to support the half-slip or petticoat were made of material using the elastic knitting stitch. After some years of freedom from body binding corsets, they were reintroduced in 1804. This figure-controlling garment was a linen bodice that covered the body from the shoulders to below the bust. In 1806 a busk and some boning was added, and by 1808 the corset was extended to cover the stomach and hips as well as the breasts. All of the corset variations were laced tight by crossed lacings slipped over hooks in the back of the garment. The corset *à la Ninon* used during the latter part of 1808 was less rigidly boned and the busk was eliminated.

à la Ninon

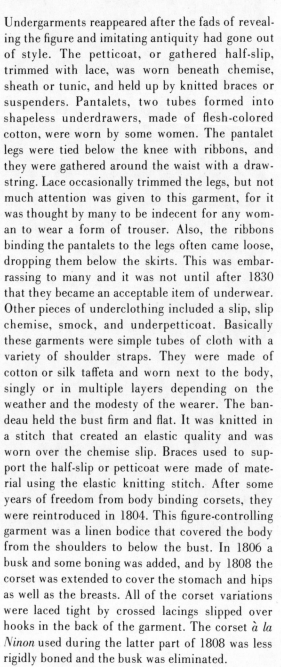

Undergarments: bandeau, pantalet, chemise (1810)

garters

Up to the time of the development of the elastic knit stitch, hose had been tied up with ribbons. In 1811 knitted garters replaced the ribbon ties and were used not only as hose supports but also to hold long gloves up firmly on the arms.

ACCESSORIES
(1800-1815)
**Men and
Women
    headwear
        à l'invisible
        bonnet
        pamela
        capote**

Women's bonnets and hats changed many times between 1800 and 1815. Bonnets with large face-hiding brims *(à l'invisible)* and tall crowns were tied under the chin with wide ribbons. The *pamelas* were smaller bonnets also tied with ribbon streamers into huge bows under the chins of their wearers. Straw variations of these bonnets were called *capotes* and were first introduced in 1806. The capote, with a much shallower crown than

Triangular scarf or cornette (1800)

Children's clothes: (left) bonnet, sheath, shawl and mitts, (right) sheath, shawl, bonnet and gloves (1815)

that of the other bonnet forms, was tied on with a triangular kerchief arranged over the top and tied under the chin.

stovepipe
boat brim

scoop brim

Stovepipe hats, often made of beaver with tall slightly flared crowns and rolled brims; boat brim hats with the brim rolled, scooping forward and back; and tall crowned hats with a conical shape, a dip in the top, and a modestly scooped brim were typical of male headgear.

footwear
English
boots
Hussars

slippers
shoes

gaiters

escarpins
pumps
slippers

hose

Boots of several styles were in fashion for men: the snug fitting English boot with turned-down cuff; the jockey boot, that was looser fitting over the leg; and *Hussars (Hessians* or *Souvaroff)*, knee-high in front curving to a point in back below the knee. Low-cut shell slippers with no heel were also used. These shoes later were styled with higher tops that covered much of the foot over the instep. Gaiters were worn with the slipper shoes to protect the upper part of the feet and the legs. These stout canvas leg coverings were fastened by laces on the outside of the leg. Women's shoe styles included *escarpins* (pumps cut very low, with slender toes and a slight heel); and simple cross-laced heelless slippers. Both were made of soft leather or a striped fabric. A small rosette or slender bow decorated this slight slipper at the side of the foot. Both men and women wore stockings of white silk or wool. Women's hose were often made with decorative openwork over the instep or with horizontal stripes and a random pattern of rosebuds.

jewelry

Jewelry fashions at this time included toe rings, earrings set with tiny watches, finger rings, ankle bracelets, wrist bracelets, and long pendant ear-rings. Men often wore two watches, each with a fancy fob. In the courts of Europe diamond tiaras and heavy necklaces made of precious gems covered the deep decolletage of the court gown.

hand held
accessories
walking
sticks

Bamboo walking sticks and riding crops replaced the slender stiletto-concealing canes and swords which had been carried by men of the previous period. Women adopted the drawstring bag, in which they carried so many articles that it soon became the butt of many jokes and much ridicule, hence the name "reticule." These rather small bags were decoratively embroidered and often had a small tassel dangling from the bottom. The drawstring served as a handle. Men used umbrellas and women parasols, trimmed with small ruffles, for protection from sun and rain.

HAIR STYLES
(1800-1815)
Men and Women Brutus

During the early part of the nineteenth century, men wore a tousled hair style called the Brutus cut. Many styled the hair in an effort to look like a Roman general, with waves over the forehead, rather long (even bushy) sideburns and long locks brushing the tops of their high collars.

Children's clothing: spencer jacket, trousers, and chemise dress with pantalet (British, permission The Metropolitan Museum of Art. Bequest of Mary Stillman Harkness, 1950)

à la Titus

en porc-épic

à la caracalla

cashefolies

snood

kerchief

Women also wore more casual hair styles. Basically they were cut much like those worn by ancient Greek males. They acquired many picturesque names, including *à la Titus, en porc-épic, à la caracalla,* and others, some of which were retained from the immediate past. False switches called *cashefolies* were also used in an attempt to recreate the coifs of ancient Greece. Snoods were used to hold these wigs or switches in place, but no attempt was made to match the cashefolies to the natural hair color, often with startling effects. Triangular kerchiefs made of transparent materials were also tied over the hair and knotted loosely under the chin.

Additional pictorial resources

1. painting—"Isaline Fi," Massot—(ostrich trimmed bonnet, betsey), 1810, private collection

2. painting—"Portrait of a Lady," Gérard—(sheath), 1806, Nancy Museum, Nancy

3. painting—"Comtesse Walther," Lafevre—(tunic overgown, sheath, slippers), 1811, private collection

4. painting—"The Billet-doux," van der Koot—(trousers, spencer, neckcloth and cravat—male; sheath with draped sleeves—female), 1808, Fries Museum, Leeuwarden

The masterful paintings of David are perhaps the best resource for this period and are contained in many public and private collections here and abroad.

Ringlet curl coif; gown with V slit overskirt, lace, and multidetail trims of ruching, braid, and ruffles

Chapter 16
FASHIONS OF A ROMANTIC PERIOD

*W*ITH *Napoleon Bonaparte defeated and in exile, a reaction set in. At the Congress of Vienna Metternich repudiated the two great principles of the eighteenth century, democracy and nationalism. "Sovereigns alone are entitled to guide the destinies of their people . . .," he said.*

During the period between the Battle of Waterloo and the end of the American Civil War, political and social forces again took new directions and reshaped western civilization. Revolutions broke out in Poland, France, Germany, Austria, Hungary, Bohemia, Italy, and Greece, with the participation of Lord Byron and other politically-oriented writers and

181

artists. Liberals were impatient and indignant at their leaders' delay in establishing some form of constitutional government, a tardiness due at least in part to the early pronouncements of radical agitators who declared that crimes against existing forms of government, even the assassination of leaders, were justified in order to bring about the changes they felt to be necessary. Count Metternich, foreign minister to the Austrian Emperor, formulated a policy that allied England, Russia, Prussia, and Austria with their one-time foe, France, to counter these revolts. Victoria, who ascended to the throne of the United Kingdom in 1837, ruled "by the grace of God" as Queen of Great Britain and Empress of India during a period in which a screen of Romanticism concealed the violent military struggles which were taking place—the Crimean War, the Austro-Prussian wars, and the American Civil War among them. Rulers like Bismarck, Napoleon III, and Francis Joseph controlled the directions, political and social, of their countries.

In America, expansion westwards began with settlements in Ohio, Kentucky, Wisconsin, and Minnesota. The Gold Rush in California sent hundreds still farther west. Industrialization appeared early in the century and soon created a division between the agricultural South and the industrial North. Industry depended upon cheap labor and coal for fuel. The poor factory worker and coal miner, the business tycoon coming up out of the middle class—all helped to shape the nineteenth century.

In the midst of these political and social struggles, writers, musicians, and artists were evolving new forms of expression. In music Beethoven broke with tradition, as did Chopin and Tchaikovsky, creating romantic sounds. Then Wagner arrived to startle the musical world. In the visual arts, Daumier, Constable, Turner, Millet and others effected changes that would radically influence and reshape imagery and aesthetic values.

Frock coat with high standing collar and straight cutaway front (1850)

Scientific advances, discoveries, and inventions abounded in a hitherto unparalleled profusion, beginning before the century reached the half-way stage. Watt's steam engine, Morse's telegraph, the cotton gin, the spanning of the American continent by the railroad, Fulton's steamboat, all brought about changes in manufacturing, travel, and communication. Fashion was modified and reshaped swiftly as the life of the average person underwent rapid changes. As early as 1820 there were signs of boredom with classical revivals in costume. Women renounced the participation in political affairs which they had enjoyed during the post-revolutionary period, devoting themselves instead to literature, art and music. Once again they established a society interested in the romantic and gay pastimes of balls, parties, operas, and theater-going. New fortunes were being made and the wealthy families became the taste-setters of the nineteenth century. An international clothing style developed among the members of the newly affluent society throughout the western world. The number of fashion periodicals designed to inform people interested in the changing face of costume grew.

During the first half of the nineteenth century, fashion designers discarded the flowing vertical silhouette of the French Empire in favor of billowing skirts, huge puffed sleeves, and gowns overembellished with garlands of flowers, lace flounces, and gathered ruffles. Men shed their "peacock habits" for suits which were soon to develop into somber, conservative costumes. The elegance displayed by one section of society was furnished by the hard labor of seamstresses in the couture shops of Paris. It was an age of extremes, of deep decolletages, bouffant skirts, and multilayer pettiskirts. It was a time of proscribed behavior. It was a time of reaction against libertine activities, simplicity in dress, and of the assertion of free men's right to choose their own destiny.

BASIC GARMENTS OF A ROMANTIC PERIOD (1816—1870)

GOWNS
(1816-1840)
Women

Ladies' gowns or dresses ceased to be named and classified by exotic terms, but were instead grouped as morning dresses, walking dresses, afternoon gowns, ball gowns, and bridal gowns. The high-waisted silhouette continued in vogue until about 1830. Skirts became somewhat fuller and were held out into a gently swelling bell shape by several petticoats and the padded roll at the hem that had been introduced by the designer Leroy. The most significant change in gown design took place in the size and complexity of sleeve

mamelouk   treatment. The mamelouk sleeve and the full-length tubular sleeve with cap puff remained in fashion through the 1820s. It was then that great breadth was added to the upper part of the figure

à l'embicile   by huge puffed sleeves called: *à l'embicile*, tapering from a large puff to a tight cuff buckled about the

balloon   wrist; *balloon*, a great round puff from the dropped

**Visiting dress and formal gown (1860:
from author's print collection)**

**beret
elephant ear**

jockey

Gown with elephant ear sleeves (1836)

shoulder to wrist; *beret*, or elephant ear, a large flattened puff covering only the upper arm, or a longer style combining the flat puff and a tight tubular section that extended to the wrist; and the *jockey* sleeve, a complex combination of puffed cap sleeve with tight lower arm section covered with a full balloon sleeve made of transparent fabric. All of these sleeves were attached to a very low shoulder line. The breadth across the figure was further exaggerated by a large collar or huge full ruffles sewn around the armholes of elephant ear or beret sleeves.

Waistlines were lowered and rounded bodices, puffed slightly, replaced the snug fitting high-waisted silhouette of the French Empire. Skirts of the 1830s were very bouffant for formal balls but were a bell shape for daytime wear. They were ankle-length, revealing slipper toes, crossed laces, and insteps. Gowns for evening wear were slightly longer, showing only toe tips as the ladies walked. Skirts were gathered with more fullness on the sides and in back. The total frontal silhouette resembled two triangles with the apexes joined at the waist, for gowns were buckled snugly with wide firm belts. Bodice necklines varied from wide "boat" shapes that were very shallow but left the top of the shoulders bare to deep wide V-lines extending from the tip of one shoulder to the other. Flat *fichu* drapes, the *chemisette* bodice, and decorative *collarette* often filled in the deeper neck-lines. The modest high round necks of daytime and walking dresses were trimmed with small flat collars. Floral cotton prints, heavy silks or velvets, and striped or plain satins were used for these dresses and gowns.

**fichu drapes
chemisette
bodice
collarette**

Carriage dress and child's dress (1845: from author's print collection)

Toward the end of the 1830s and during the early 1840s, the bodice lost its cocoonlike appearance and was cut in several pieces to fit the feminine form more snugly. The waistline was dropped even further in front, forming a point, much like the bodice silhouette of the High Renaissance. Sleeves continued to be bulky, but the wider girth was shifted to the area of the lower arm or wrist. Skirts became fuller for daytime wear and were either gathered or pleated with deep box pleats. The flounced or ruffled skirt was introduced as a design variation. The edges of each ruffled tier were often scalloped, or trimmed with fringe, or both.

In the 1850s, while the general proportions of the gowns and dresses remained the same, a new

à la jardinière

bertha collar

sleeve form was introduced. Called *à la jardinière* or jug sleeve, it was designed with a tight upper arm and a puff encircling the lower arm. It was attached to a deep yoke that was the major styling innovation of the bodice. *Bertha* collars, flat bands of lace, came into fashion as neck trims during this same decade.

double skirt gown

The double skirt gown continued in fashion. This dress style was copied from the eighteenth century gown and consisted of an overskirt that was open in the front to show the matching pettiskirt beneath. Both overgown and pettiskirt were decorated with flounces, garlands of flowers, ruching, and lace ruffles. The sleeves were somewhat more slender, with some made in the pagoda style. These were often three-quarter length with soft full bishop sleeves of the chemisette showing below them.

morning dress walking dress redingote dress

While more formal gowns were made with bodice and skirt attached, morning and walking dresses were usually two-piece garments. The redingote dress returned to fashion as a dress rather than as an outer wrap. The inverted V-opening of the double skirt dress adapted easily to this dress style. Ladies wore less decorative dresses at home during the 1850s and the redingote style was described by a fashion reporter of the time as a dress "of sober cut." Darker tones of blues and browns as well as black were the colors selected for these daytime costumes. The fabrics were plain, checked or striped. Formal gowns were made of velvets, fine cottons, crepes, taffetas, and delicately woven silk gauzes. The formal robes, as they were often called, were elaborately decorated with linen hand embroidery, lace, and ruching. Ruffles at the hem and midskirt were other typical detailing features.

bloomer dress

The excessive bulk of the huge full skirts supported by many petticoats irritated some women because they hampered their activities. Mrs. Bloomer invented a costume, giving it her name, which she hoped would revolutionize women's clothing. This costume consisted of a loose-fitting knee-length dress and full gathered ankle-length trousers. The trousers were fastened around the ankle by small buttoned cuffs and gathered at the waist by a band. The sleeves of the bodice were only slightly puffed and inset to a deep yoke. Very tight cuffs held the sleeves firmly around the wrists. A more daring hip-length jacket and full trouser costume was introduced in Italy and was perhaps the style worn by George Sand, the au-

trouser suit

thoress. Its trousers had very wide legs and were

Afternoon dress with balloon sleeves and gathered skirt without crinoline support (1840-1843)

Bloomer dress (1851)

gathered at the waist. The jacket was worn over a mannish shirt with a ruching-trimmed neck and cuffs. Both of these innovative styles, though startlingly incorporating trousers, were very modest, covering the female form from their snug high necklines to the ankles. Of the two, the bloomer dress was the least attractive, for its proportions were quite awkward and ugly. Neither gained wide acceptance, though some venturesome women were still trying to establish bloomer dresses for everyday wear as late as the 1870s. Few authorities mention this long struggle, but from a family story it is known that about 1875 in Viroqua, Wisconsin, a woman appeared in a bloomer dress. Her fate was less than happy. Rumors spread that she was a member of an unorthodox religious cult or was crazy or both. In any event, she and her family became the victims of ridicule and finally moved from the town, she, it was reliably reported, still wearing the costume that caused all of the adverse criticism. As a radical reformer of women's outer garments, Mrs. Bloomer failed, but the term "bloomer" in reference to gym clothes and female underpants lasted for years.

turkey back

train

town gown

The dresses of the 1860s took on a slightly different side silhouette. Skirts were still overloaded with decorations, but there was greater fullness in the back (turkey back) and a short train was added. Braid replaced ruffles on the town gown. Sleeves were reduced in size and were less puffed. Town gowns were made in two pieces, a snug fitting bodice and a full skirt that was made with less gathering or pleating in front than in back. The braid trim circled the round collarless neck and extended down the center front opening. Braid, applied in the same pattern that decorated the bodice, bordered the hem. The toothed design of the Gothic period and flat scallops were also used on the hems of bodice jacket and skirt. The jacket was lengthened by a hip-length peplum that was attached at the nipped-in waist. Cords and tassels were added as additional decorations on shoulders, cuffs, and upper sleeves.

Ladies' fashions of the 1860s (from author's print collection)

ball gowns

Gowns for formal balls and cotillions were designed with off-the-shoulder, very deep necklines. The bodice, sleeves, and skirt were trimmed with multiple rows of lace ruffles, bands of patterned fabrics inset above the hem forming a geometric border, and fringe. Bands of ribbon encircled the skirt at several points; multiruffled skirts with scalloped edges and ribbon bows were also lavishly added to ball gowns to make them more elegant. The general shoulder-revealing neckline shape was that of an inverted heart, a deep U or wide angle V. A long sash edged with ruching and with beagle ear tabs was tied in back, adding to the bulk of the skirt.

tunic dress

The tunic dress was introduced about 1865. This was an overdress that was draped to expose a decorative petticoat. There were buttons at the waist and buttonholes or tab loops on the tunic hem so that it might be fastened up, creating a draped effect. This costume was said to have been inspired by the French couturier, Worth, who became prominent as a designer for the very wealthy in the 1860s. Mr. Worth, an English immigrant to Paris, had been a clerk in a fabric house. After his marriage, his wife encouraged him to design clothes. His first creations were made for the Empress of France, but in time most ladies of wealth on the continent and in America wore his gowns. The great reputation he established lasted for decades, and the House of Worth became synonymous with elegant clothes, chic and innovative.

basque bodice and skirt

The skirt and *basque* bodice, cut like a man's jacket with several gored and shaped pieces, became a popular costume during the decade of the 1860s. The jacket was quite long, often slit in several places around the deep peplum. The sleeves were amply cut but not full nor puffed, and hit the arm just above the wrist. These suits, for they were the forerunner of women's suits, were made of heavy fabrics such as velvet and wool. They were less lavishly trimmed, but were by no means undecorated. The snug fitting jackets had round high necklines with or without collars, making them snug and warm for winter wear.

princess gown

The influence of the couturier was strongly felt, and from the 1860s onward dresses, gowns, coats, and sportswear garments were to change radically almost every season. The most important styling difference that was introduced at the close of the sixth decade of the nineteenth century was the *princess* gown. This dress was cut in many sections or gores, but the individual pieces had the skirt and bodice cut together. The lines of the princess gown were slim and much simpler. They created a slender triangular silhouette. The skirt was no longer decorated to excess but formed a smooth, circular shape with slightly more fullness in the back. In 1869, the skirt of the princess gown was pulled up on the hips. This draping was supported by padding or flounces. This was the beginning of the "style tapissier" or upholstered look.

"style tapissier"

WRAPS
(1820-1870)
Women
capelette
canezou

The *capelette*, a gossamer cape that had long tab-shaped fronts, appeared to be a large shawl collar. The tab ends were either square or rounded and were usually worn under the wide buckled belt, so typical of the early 1800s. The *canezou* was another version of this light summer shoulder wrap, a decorative frothy piece that added to the roundness of the bodice. The carrick coat replaced the redingote as a warm outer wrap during the second decade of the nineteenth century. It was intricately cut and fitted the figure smoothly. Double capes covered the shoulders, and it had a double-breasted buttoned closing. The *witchoure*, or fur coat, continued in fashion, though the design of the sleeves, bodice, and skirt was modified to correspond to the changing silhouette of the gowns worn beneath. The spencer bodice was fitted snugly over the rounded fullness of the gown waist and had a low V neckline and multipuffed sleeves. This style of spencer was very short-waisted, appearing to be a bolero with three-quarter sleeves.

carrick

witchoure

spencer jacket

cashmere shawl

After a brief eclipse during the 1830s, the cashmere shawl was again in fashion as a light wrap. It was made in both large and small sizes from a square of fabric that was trimmed with deep fringe. Folded on the diagonal, it was worn either around the shoulders or loosely about the upper arms. The *visite* was another of the many capes used during these decades of full skirts and heavy puffed sleeves. It was a small cape with slit armholes and ruffles arranged in tiers from the neck to the hem. In summer it was made of lawn or tulle, in winter of velvet. Lace trimmed the edges of the summer visite, while fur or braid decorated the velvet version. This little cape was introduced in 1845 and remained in vogue with only slight modifications for nearly forty years. The *pelerine* was a three-tiered capelet with long front tabs that often extended to the knees. This wrap was similar to

visite

pelerine

Morning visiting dress and cape (1840s: from author's print collection)

Formal cape with
weighted ball tassel
trim on sleeve tips
(1830)

Gown with à l'embicile sleeves and canezou (1820)

canezou

pelisse

**double capes
mantles**

the canezou, which in the 1840s and 1850s became a very fussy bodice cape with shirred sleeves, lace and eyelet trim, and many forms of shirred decorations. They were usually made of very lightweight transparent cloth. The voluminous pelisse (or circular cape), with vertical armhole slits returned to fashion as gown skirts increased in size. This formal velvet cape was fur-trimmed at the neck, sleeve slits, hem, and front openings. The pelisse and the huge double capes or mantles of the next decade were designed with many varying details. Crushed astrakhan was used as trimming and for the large flat collars and deep circular yokes to which the flared cape body was attached. Some of the formal evening wraps had great wide sleeves that, if left hanging, extended to the knees. These great figure-enveloping capes swept the floor and often had the three-tiered pelerine effect about the shoulders to create an even more elegant wrap. Embroidery, braid, and balls bound round with silken thread were all used to enrich the appearance of the mantle. Many of these garments had slit panel skirts, so that they might be arranged over the huge hoop-supported skirts of the formal gowns.

Formal attire. Two waistcoats, claw hammer coat, and trousers with pleated hip fullness (1825)

tippet

The tippet was an enormously long furpiece, one pelt wide, that was worn loosely around the neck or shoulders or looped over the arms at the elbows. The tippet was varied slightly as time went on and was designed with a short cape in back, retaining the long slender tippets in front. Marten or the fur of other small animals was used in creating this wrap.

**pardessus
mantelet
zouave
garibaldi
scarf
shawl
Spanish
bolero**

During the 1860s, outer wraps took many forms, each designed to meet the demands of the occasion. The basic styles included: the *pardessus*, a semi-fitted jacket; the *mantelet*, a small cape; *zouave* and *garibaldi*, small tight fitting jackets; scarves, semi-circular in form; and the cashmere shawl, a large square with or without fringed hems. The Spanish bolero replaced the spencer bodice.

fichu

The fichu returned as a neckwear accessory and as a lightweight summer wrap that could be worn over the shoulders and upper arm. Its revival was due to the interest the Empress Eugenie had in Marie Antoinette, her costumes, and her activities. This interest also gave impetus to the reintroduction of the double skirt gown and the longer pointed waistline.

SUITS
(1820-1870)
**Men
trousers**

The most significant change in men's wear after the turn of the eighteenth century was the acceptance of long trousers. The snug-legged pants of the Empire period (made of chamois or knit fabric) were discarded in the 1820s in favor of fuller, longer trousers that covered much of the instep and had a strap under the foot. In 1830 men's trousers were gathered or pleated at the waist and increased the width across the hips. They were made of many different types of fabrics, stripes, or plaids (often very large bold plaids), in a variety of colors. Both plain and patterned materials used for trousers contrasted with those of the coats.

**Claw hammer coat, tucked shirt with
vravat in Valigia knot, and instep strap
trousers (1835)**

breeches

ditto suit

bucksain

coat jacket

suit coat

The legs were cuffless and the pants pockets were either diagonal slashes or half moon cuts, placed on the front of the trousers rather than on the sides. The center flap continued to be used as a trouser closing. For a brief period, during the restoration of the French monarchy, men wore silk knee breeches. As time passed, and in countries other than France, knee breeches were worn primarily for horseback riding, morning wear or in the country, and were made of serviceable fabric. The full style of trousers gradually became narrower until they "fit like a glove" though the general styling characteristics remained constant. They were cuffless and the instep strap helped to keep the trouser legs taut. Some, often more formal styles, were cut away over the instep but fell well below the top of the slipper in back. The cutaway areas revealed the decorative striped stockings worn by many men. Some time later, the trouser legs became quite long and were worn crushed over the tops of boots at the insteps. The instep strap was to continue in style for several decades. During the years just before mid-century, trousers and coats either matched in color and fabric texture or were mix-matched. However, in the 1860s the *ditto* suit was introduced, consisting of matching pants, coat and vest, all made of the same fabric and in the same color. This suit was later called the *sack* suit because of the looser fit of the coat; that is, it hung on the male figure like a sack.

Before the introduction of the ditto and sack suits men wore a variety of jackets and coats. The *bucksain*, a short jacket, was introduced during the period when women's dresses were styled with a full, rounded bodice. It too was a garment with a full bodice section achieved by padding the area over the chest. It had a tight waist and rather full thigh-length skirts that were pleated in back to add fullness at the hips. The bucksain had a single vent in the center back. The sleeves were rather snug, but were slightly puffed at the shoulder. The padded coats and pleated trousers of male clothing during this period reflected silhouette design concepts similar to those applied to female costumes. The coat jacket, a casual wear garment, was also padded in the shoulders and the chest. It was cut with straight, boxlike lines and slightly puffed shoulders. It, like the bucksain, had no tails, but an even, thigh-length hemline. Side vents on the seams added a slight flare to the lower portion of the coat jacket. The suit coat of the early nineteenth century was fitted snugly at the waist

Men's styles (1852: from author's print collection)

basque belt

and had chest padding added to emphasize this silhouette detail. Fashionable gentlemen of the period achieved a smaller waist by wearing a basque belt, worn beneath the shirt and cinched up tightly. Large and rather decorative basques were worn over the shirt. This type extended from the armpits to the waist and was pulled tightly about the figure, to control the shape, with three tab and slip-buckle fastenings. The suit coat had waist-length fronts and thigh-length tails, which in time were elongated to strike the legs just above the back of the knees. The tails sloped from the side seams to the back, ending in a straight hem. Other variations had tails attached slightly over the front and curving toward the back. In this style, padding was inserted between the lining and the coat over the hips. Sleeve styling was similar to that of the coat jacket, though somewhat fuller over the upper arm and with greater fullness of the puff at the shoulder. Shawl collars that rose quite high at the back of the neck were characteristic at this time, though the rolled lapels were narrower than in the previous fashion period.

While trousers and suit coats were either matched or mix-matched, they were considered to make up the suit. Beginning with the 1830s, the coat shoulderline was sloped, though the chest padding and slender waist continued in style. The thin-waisted look was exaggerated by side fullness in the coat skirt, created by pleats or slight padding. The coats of this decade and the next were either single- or double-breasted, with tails or with complete knee-length skirts. The single-breasted style was never buttoned, in fact it was designed to be worn open. The rolled lapels of the single-breasted coat were often velvet or fur and extended almost to the hem of the coat skirt. The shoulder puffing was eliminated and the sleeve was set smoothly into the armhole. Narrow wrist-length cuffs, matching the collars, and a breast pocket, high on the left side, were typical details. Collars of tailed coats were wide and flat and triangular lapels rolled into the back-sweeping line of the square-ended tails.

cutaway

The cutaway and frock coat were introduced in the 1840s. The former was designed with the fronts sloping into a rounded tail in back, a flat collar, and high set lapels. The shoulders sloped into sleeves that were of average width. These had no cuffs, but had a button trim that was characteristic of men's suit coats for many years. The button decorations at the cuffs were added first for a functional purpose at the wrist slits on the outside of the arm. An unsupported tale suggests that sleeve buttons were retained after their usefulness as a fastening had ceased. They remained as trim but also to discourage men from using their sleeves as handkerchiefs. During one phase of men's suit coat fashions, the number of buttons on the cuffs indicated the quality of the suit—the greater the number, the better the suit. This has since been discarded as a quality indicator.

frock coat

The frock coat during the 1840s and 1850s was a snug-fitting coat with the fronts waist length, cut to a point at the side seams. The square-end tails were attached to the body of the frock coat at this point. The back waist section was cut in several parts to make the coat fit the figure more smoothly. A two-button trim at the waist in back, where the tails were pleated toward the deep center slit, was a distinctive feature of this coat, retained to the present. Later, frock coats of the 1860s were designed with knee-length skirts. This style was single-breasted and had two pleats in back to add a flare to the coat hemline. This style of coat remained in fashion for some years with only minor modifications of collars and lapels to coincide with

Bell-shaped dress coat, trousers, low shoes, and alla Byron knotted cravat

changes in these details as they occurred in other suit coats.

waistcoats
Waistcoats became a very flamboyant apparel accessory during the early nineteenth century. They were tailless, with shawl or rolled collars and double- or single-breasted, in the latter case with V-shaped fronts. Waistcoats were made of patterned silks, velvets, or striped pique and two of them were often worn with formal evening suits, one of white pique over one of black velvet. The collar, rolled or shawl, of the black waistcoat was worn over that of the white one. Gold buttons decorated both the single and double-breasted waistcoats for formal or everyday wear. During the 1840s and 1850s the vest replaced the waistcoat.

vest
It too was decorative, double or single-breasted, but the collar was discarded. These garments had a V-neckline and the vest fronts were cut straight. A below-the-waist line accessory to the suit, they were made with decorative fronts and a plain silk back. To ensure smooth fit, a half belt with a slip buckle was attached in back and adjusted to the correct size when worn. During the 1860s the vests were usually double-breasted with small shawl collars or collars with small notched lapels. White vests were worn with the black tailored tailcoat and tight-legged trousers for formal balls.

shirts
Men's shirts of this period were basically a tailored garment, made of fine cambric or imperial cotton. The ruffles on the shirt fronts and around the tight-buttoned cuffs became smaller and smaller. Until the 1860s the shirt collars were large and worn standing up, the points projecting above the chinline. The wide neckcloth was bound around

neckcloth cravat
the throat and a cravat worn on top of it. In 1827 a pamphlet was issued entitled "The Art of Knotting the Tie in Sixteen Lessons" in which thirty-two ways of tying a cravat were carefully illustrated. Each knot was given a name such as: *In Valigia; Alla Colia; Alla Talma; Gastronoma; Sentimentale;* and *Matematica*. The simple looping of the ends and pulling them up to the throat was called the *Americana* while the large floppy bow tie was called *Alla Byron*. The importance of tying styles changed as shirts lost their ruffles. The pointed collars were worn with a standing stock and cravat. The false shirt front or *dickey*

dickey
was first introduced in the 1840s and continued as a male accessory to the shirt until the end of the following decade. It was made of satin and worn with a "practiced crushed" look, in keeping with the romantic and casual air men affected. The dickey was a slender strip of satin, ten or twelve

Deep-tailed frac with rear set pockets (1853)

inches wide, fitted with a neckstrap. Individuality was asserting itself, and men's shirts, during the 1860s, were designed with a wide variety of collars as a means of self-expression. There were high standing, overlapping, flopping, fold-down, winged, and rigid shapes. With each collar style the cravat size and knot changed. Soft loop bows were worn with soft pointed collars left slightly open at the throat. String ties knotted either once or in a long bow; crisp tailored bows that had wide flat knots; and loose, looped, single-knotted ties, chin-hugging or neck-revealing—the cravat knotting was the wearer's choice.

WRAPS
(1820-1870)
Men
topcoat

greatcoat

redingote

raglan
talma
dust-coat

burnous

MacFarlan

Chesterfield

pardessus

During this fifty-year period men wore a wide variety of warm heavy wraps. The double-breasted topcoat, with ankle-length skirts and high fur collar and lapels, was typical of the overcoat styling of this period. The waist of the topcoat was intricately cut in the back and the pleated skirt section added slight hem fullness to an otherwise slender coat. Made of heavy woolens, these coats were usually green, buff, blue, or bronze in color. Between 1820 and 1830 the greatcoat was worn like a cape, though it was double-breasted, styled with a tall fold-over collar, and deep, wide lapels. The male redingote was knee length during the early part of the century. It was double-breasted and had very full skirts. Other wraps included: the *raglan*, a circular cloak; the *talma*, a large semicircular cloak, introduced long before the great actor Talma became popular; the *dust-coat*, a traveling coat of grey alpaca; and the *burnous*, a very full knee-length coat with an attached, tassel-trimmed hood that was more decorative than functional. Shoulder capes on top of coats were a characteristic feature throughout much of this period, and many were trimmed with several of graduated sizes, with piping of contrasting color on the cape hems. The *MacFarlan*, a knee-length wrap, was designed with two side capes. These capes were thigh-length, covering the full sleeves but not the back of the shoulders. They were attached at a point about four inches from the back center seam and on the front about the same distance from the opening. The *Chesterfield* was introduced in the late 1860s, as was the MacFarlan. It was a calf-length, fur-lined greatcoat, with a flat fur collar, lapels, and cuffs. During much of this period men's fashions were established by the dashing Englishman Beau Brummel. The flamboyant manner of this dandy and his followers inspired many elegant costumes and wraps were no exception. The *pardessus*, a

Greatcoat and beaver hat (1820)

large black formal cape, was typical of the elegance of men's evening attire. This large semicircular cape had a deep, broad, sloped shoulder yoke to which the body of the garment was attached. The hem of the cape and deep back vent were edged with braid arranged in a complex series of looped patterns. A wide velvet collar, worn either flat or standing, added flair to this evening wrap. The

opera cape voluminous black opera cape, gathered and smocked beneath its large krimmer or Persian lamb collar, was also an elegant wrap. This cape, which was often lined with the same fur as the collar, covered the full figure to the ankles.

ACCESSORIES Footwear was as varied in types and styles as the
(1820-1870) rest of the costume parts during these years.
Men and Boots, including *Hussars, Hessians,* and *Welling-*
Women *tons;* high shoes for both men and women with
  footwear leather vamps and cloth tops of nankeen; slippers;
  Hussars splatter dashes; and gaiters were some of the
  Hessians available styles. The soft leather slippers had very
  Wellingtons narrow toes with square tips. In the 1830s the

Gown with mamelouk sleeves, female; lounge robe, waistcoat, and trousers, male (1845: from author's print collection)

high shoes
slippers
gaiters
splatter
dashes

high shoes with cloth tops and side lacings on the inside of the foot were replaced by little boots with leather counters and toes and elastic side gussets. This type of footwear was used for daytime wear while leather slippers were worn for formal occasions. By the 1860s women's footwear was created to suit the activity; laced boots and high-topped shoes with side gussets were worn for daily duties while slippers of colored kid or satin were worn with ball gowns. Women's formal footwear had slight spool heels and ruching or bow trims. Men's boots and shoes for daily wear were styled with rather broad square toes, the other construction details remaining constant. Men's

dress
slippers

dress slippers were made of black leather and trimmed with black flat bows or black ribbon rosettes.

headwear
bonnets
turbans
toques
berets

Bonnets became exaggerated versions of à *l'invisible* with taller crowns, vast cheek-hugging brims, and long, wide ribbon ties. The ribbon ties made into great bows under the chin or to the side of the cheek. Turbans, loaded with feathers and toques (à *la russe* and à *l'espagnole*) with satin puffs and lace bunches, added width to the head to counterbalance the large skirts and huge

shawls
veils

sleeves of dresses and gowns. Cashmere shawls and filmy veils were also used as head coverings. The shawls were either plaid or paisley. They were draped over the head and shoulders, and enveloped the figure, wholly or partially, depending on their size. The small square veils were folded diagonally, draped over the head and knotted loosely under the chin. The general hat or bonnet shapes remained the same for some time, but grew somewhat smaller. The poke bonnet, introduced

poke
bonnet

in the 1840s, was made of cloth with a large puffed crown, long neck sheath, deep bill, and matching cloth ties. In the 1860s bonnets were very small, as were hats. Both were richly trimmed with ruching and bunches of rosebuds. The bonnet was worn well back on the head, while the hat was worn tilted over one eye.

beaver hat

Men wore tall, flare-crown beaver hats in white, fawn, or grey or black silk hats of polished beaver. The collapsible high silk top hat was invented in 1823 by M. Gibus and was the prototype for the

opera hat

mat satin opera hat of more recent years. Hat styles for men changed little over the first half of the eighteenth century except that the crown of the beaver hats became taller and they were

stovepipe

called stovepipe hats. Brims were unchanged in size and continued to be rolled, though by the late

bowler
boater
Figaro
cap

1850s many men preferred the flat brim style. The soft, wide-brimmed, round-crowned felt hat was worn by men in rural areas. During the decade after mid-century, many hat forms for men were introduced. These included the bowler, the boater, the Figaro, and the cap. The Figaro was a broad-brimmed hat with a wide, slightly flared, flat crown made of angora rabbit fur. The boater was much the same design but was made of straw. The bowler was aptly named, for it was shaped much like a straight-sided bowl, trimmed with a black hatband, with a rolled brim of very rigid fabric. Flat or pancake style billed caps made with four sections in the crown were worn squarely on the head.

jewelry

Neckwear of the era of extreme decolletage was rather heavy, made of rubies and diamonds and pearls. Necklaces that appeared to be brilliant large gem collars encircled the throat and had pear-shaped jewel pendants suspended from a matched row of gems. Round multigem red rosettes were strung alternately with swags of pearls. During the Empress Eugenie period, the bare decolletage was fashionable and few necklaces cluttered the throat or the exposed shoulders and upper bosom.

brooch

Brooches set with one large jewel surrounded by small diamonds were worn at the peak of the low neckline or were used to fasten a neck ribbon.

neck ribbon earrings

For much of this period, ladies' coifs covered the ears and the need for earrings was minimal. Those that were worn were made of gold and precious gems in a pendant design attached through pierced earlobes.

rings bracelets

Rings, if worn at all, were small, though bracelets were wide gold bands often worn in multiples, many with small gold discs dangling from them.

watches

Men wore pocket watches with gold fobs attached to the timepieces with wide ribbons. Cases were chased gold and had lids over the faces. They were either stem or key-wound. In this age of excessive sentimentality, watchpapers with loving phrases were inserted in the lid beneath a disc of thin glass. Watchmaking was a fine art and often the maker signed a timepiece on these watchpapers as well. The craft of watch repair and making was an honorable occupation, the craftsman taking care of the watches he had made as long as he or their owners lived.

hand held accessories mitts gloves

Mitts of lace and leather or silk gloves continued in fashion. Mitts were worn more often than gloves and lace, silk, or net mitts were even worn indoors while performing sedentary activities such as knitting.

fans

Fans were as decorative as they had been during the eighteenth century, but were made of elegant lace attached to ivory or mother-of-pearl spokes and folded into pleats when not in use. Paper-thin sandalwood segmented fans strung together with tiny ribbons were brought from the Orient. Both styles were held together at the base with a metal ring to which was attached a silk, tassel-trimmed cord or ribbon. Cords or ribbons were slipped around the wrist and the fan when not being used was carried this way.

parasols

Though the industrial revolution was forcing many superembellishments from manufactured goods, the dainty parasol was an exception. It was elaborately trimmed with ruffles and lace stretched over complicated rib constructions.

canes Men carried thin wandlike canes with round knob heads. This male accessory was usually made of ebony, but after mid-century the bamboo cane was introduced for summer use.

HAIR STYLES
Men and
Women

During this age of romantics and dandies who were mimics of Beau Brummel, men's hair styles were casual and often tousled. The Beau himself, however, had three hairdressers, and took fanatical pains with his dressing. He had two valets, one who did little else but wear Brummel's new suits until they had acquired the proper casual look, casualness being such a desirable attribute of male styles. Men wore their hair short, as a general rule, at the turn of the century. However, Giacomo Perollo of Palermo preferred his long and for wearing it that way he was arrested and sentenced. His punishment consisted of being locked into the public stocks while his hair was cut off. Later men's hair was styled in a long bob, parted on the side and slightly curled. Beards were either chinline whiskers, full brush beards, or long flowing ones. By the 1860s men's hair was again short and sideburns and beards were worn.

Interest in the fashions of the past influenced the female coif. Hair was dressed high on the head into large loops by pulling the hair up from the back following the head contour. Puffs and frizzes were arranged on either side at the temples.

puffs
frizzes

à la girafe
à la dona
Marie
à l'anglaise

ferronniere

Asymmetric arrangements of sausage curls and braids piled high on the head were called *à la girafe* or *à la dona Marie*. Hair worn smooth and taut, covering the forehead and lying snugly over the cheeks in front of the ears, *à l'anglaise*, had a triangular part. During the 1830s and 1840s some women affected the Renaissance ferronniere, a fine gold chain worn low on the forehead with a pearl pendant in the center. Flowers, ribbon bows, large decorative combs, and pleated lace ruffles adorned the head when a lady was dressed for a festive ball. In the 1840s the hair was parted in the center, dressed into a tight pug at the back of the head, with long curls, originating at the temples, on either side. During the next two decades the side curls were eliminated and the hair was drawn to the back of the head and gathered at the nape of the neck. Curls cascaded over the shoulders or down the back from this point. The hair at the sides of the cheeks was pulled taut but puffed out low over the ears, forming a pyramidal head silhouette. Large ribbon bows or garlands of flowers, worn like a halo, trimmed these coiffures.

Coif with ferronniere trim over forehead; gown with leg-of-mutton sleeves (1835)

UNDERWEAR
(1816-1870)
Women
  petticoat

As women's skirts became more bouffant, the petticoat, though an undergarment, became an important accessory to the female costume. At first 'a simple half-slip made from a length of material gathered to a tight waistband with a back placket, this gown accessory increased in size and required many yards of material. The petticoat was worn in multiples, sometimes as many as eight or ten, and was trimmed with deep ruffles to further increase the girth of the skirt at the hem. During the popularity of the double skirt gown, the pettiskirt, made much like the petticoat, was worn on top of these many half-slips. The development of the crinoline, a stiff horsehair underskirt, eliminated some of the petticoats. The crinolines were made in a wide range of styles, and while they functioned adequately to support the gown skirt, they often led to rather embarrassing consequences for the ladies who wore them. Because of their stiffness and hooped hem, they were likely to stand straight up when a lady seated herself. They not only obscured her view but, what was worse, they revealed her underwear. These underskirts changed in style each year as the fullness of the skirt shifted from all round to the sides and to the back. Each year a new name was given to them to identify their hooped form, such as: 1857, *The Parisien*, a tiered ruffled circular style; 1858, '*D.D.*' petticoat, with gathered poof bands, open from waist to hem and tied together in the front; and 1865, *Patent Medicis*, flat in front with side and back fullness. Many detested the awkwardness of these skirt supports and Taine said that the ladies at the Court of St. James lacked grace and were outrageously crude in them. Though one group attempted to have them banned, they remained in style but were modified by hoops and finally became hoop skirts only. These were constructed by attaching steel bands, of graduated sizes, together with cotton tapes. The hooped pettiskirt was first patented by Tavernier in 1856, and resembled the eighteenth century farthingale that was used just prior to the introduction of the panier, or hen basket. An articulated version was introduced in 1860 and by late 1867 the hoop skirt consisted of a fabric half-slip with hoops or boning at the hem only. These styles were more easily managed and swayed gracefully, following the movements of the body.

pettiskirt

crinoline

The Parisien
'D.D.'
Patent
Medicis

hoop skirt

pantaloons
pantalettes
bloomers

Pantaloons (pantalettes or bloomers), though not accepted at first, became an important fashion accessory when once in vogue and by 1830 could be seen beneath the full gown skirts as women walked or under little girls' dresses. They were made with wide tube legs, and were trimmed with ruffles and lace. By 1860, however, women's bloomers were again out of sight. They were merely an awkwardly made pair of underdrawers, a calf-length half-slip sewn together across the hem, except for two holes on each side, and fastened below the knees with tight bands.

corsets

basque belt

Corsets, worn over a simple slender undertunic, were less restrictive during the early years of the nineteenth century. A laced belt, or basque belt, sufficed. These were worn to cinch in the waist and were made just like their male counterparts. The boned bodice corset, laced in back, with ribbon or lace trimmed shoulder straps, returned in the 1860s when the wasp waist came into vogue. An oddity, for an age that many consider most prudish, was the fact that the basque belt and the corset were displayed in the windows of department stores. These displays were realistically set up with wax dummies (clad only in undertunics, bloomers, and corsets) modeling the

hose

garments on sale. Hose made of cotton lisle were either white or striped. The feet were not in view, and there was no need for decorative hose.

Additional pictorial resources

1. drawing—"Lady's Toilette," Vernet—(gowns, coifs—female; cravat, neckcloth, suit coat and trousers, and Wellington boots—male), 1814, Bertarelli Collection, Milan

2. painting—"Mrs. Thomas Brewster Harding," Chester Harding—(coif, en touffes, cape, and fur betsey), 1826, Metropolitan Museum of Art, New York City

3. actual garments—(pelisse and visiting dress), 1830, Metropolitan Museum of Art, Costume Institute, New York City

4. painting—"Artist and Family," John Lewis Krimmel—(general apparel, adults' and children's), 1820, Mellon Collection, National Gallery of Art, Washington, D.C.

5. statuette—"Comtesse Greffuhl," (anon.)—(double skirt gown), 1868, Musée des Arts Decoratifs, Paris

6. actual garment—(gown of white silk brocade), 1850—1855, City Museum, Birmingham

7. sketches—crinoline—(styling details, wearing hazards), c. 1850s to 1860s, Bibliothèque Nationale, Paris

8. painting—"The Painter's Mother," Waldmuller—(poke bonnet), 1830. Österreichische Galerie, Vienna

9. actual garment—(redingote), 1820, Rijksmuseum, Amsterdam

10. actual garments—(red silk gown and bonnet), c. 1850, Collection of Don Rocamora, Museo de Arte, Barcelona

Polonaise dress with overdress swept
back to reveal underskirt (1875)

Chapter 17

IMPRESSIONISM AND THE EDWARDIAN ERA

*T*HROUGHOUT *the nineteenth century the British Empire, at its
height the greatest empire of the world, dominated the world
political scene. A succession of able prime ministers from both the
Liberal and Conservative parties (the successors to the Whigs and Tories)
skillfully manipulated international diplomacy. But the leaders of both
Houses of Parliament were unable to cope with the internal problems
which arose as a result of the expanding industrial revolution. During
the American Civil War little cotton fiber was shipped abroad, leading
to unemployment in English cotton mills. Inspired by the example of the*

French, Englishmen began to agitate more aggressively for the right to vote, but reforms were formulated slowly and passed grudgingly, so that it was 1884 before the Third Reform Bill gave the suffrage to the majority of British males. This, however, did not relieve the problem of unemployment. As political power shifted from the Liberal to the Conservative party and back again, Disraeli and Gladstone outshone the other politicians of Queen Victoria's reign.

In America the Reconstruction program begun after the end of the Civil War floundered, for Johnson, the assassinated Lincoln's successor, had neither the wisdom nor the congressional backing to bring it to a successful conclusion. Already before the war the industrialization of the United States had brought about radical changes in the production of food, clothing, and shelter. Handcrafted commodities ceased to contribute to the economic wealth of the country. Transportation and communication methods changed. Agriculture lost its dominant role and young Americans were forced or attracted to the urban and industrial centers. Under the new system the laborer worked for someone else. He did not own his tools. The city shop clerk had no real interest in the retail store in which he worked. Young women flocked to the fabric mills in New England and to the "sweatshops" of the garment industry. Eventually the industrial workers succeeded in arousing interest in their plight and protective legislation was passed and labor unions formed. The public's attention was

Costume styles of the 1870s (from author's print collection)

drawn to the miserable working conditions of the women garment workers by a fire which killed many of them trapped in a New York factory. In England the writings of Charles Dickens had acquainted Queen Victoria with the deplorable condition of child workers. The unions succeeded in making the two political parties in the United States study the need for reform, at least to the point of making promises.

During the reign of Edward VII (1901-1910) international activities were at a quiet ebb. The British Empire now covered one-fourth of the earth. Medicine and scientific research advanced, and some dreaded diseases were eliminated. Education was modified and improved. The American government found itself called upon to regulate railroads and utilities as commercial and industrial frontiers expanded, and to oversee the relationships between business and labor. Oil, steel, coal, and railroad tycoons secured a place in the history of industrial development for themselves and also amassed huge fortunes in the doing. Many fortunes were based on the refinement of inventions of the past and the creation of new ones. Gaslight, followed by electric light, the phonograph, wireless, forced air and steam heat, all changed the living patterns of both rich and poor. Electric trollies provided inexpensive transportation for the many and horseless carriages or "machines" were first playthings and then transportation for the few. Such environmental conveniences as indoor plumbing also served to modernize the living conditions of the American population. In 1909 devices available to free women from heavy household duties included an elementary gasoline-driven washing machine, and the electrically powered vacuum cleaner followed in 1910.

This was a period when the wealthy pursued their pleasures with elegance and grace. American financiers and their wives dressed, acted, and entertained as if they were royalty. Fortunes made in mining gold and silver were spent lavishly duplicating foreign palaces in remote western villages or in small thriving state capitals dependent on the ore from local mines. There were pronounced contrasts between the different economic levels—those struggling for a livelihood, those in the middle income group, and those with great wealth. The decorous genteel behavioral patterns of the social elite filtered down to all economic levels and were admired and emulated. Edward VII, however, while Prince of Wales, seemed indifferent to the restraints placed on behavior during his mother's reign. One of his favorite party diversions, it is said, was to mount a giant silver tray and ride it down the grand staircase at Buckingham Palace. Whether this anecdote is true or not, it is known that his amiable personality helped to establish friendly relations with other nations on the continent.

During the last period of Queen Victoria's reign and that of Edward VII American society was seeking to establish a cultural identity. Small mining towns like Central City, Colorado, and villages like Dickinson,

Princess gown

North Dakota, as well as cities like San Francisco and New York, built opera houses patterned after those of Europe. Many still stand and some, like that in Central City, still function, offering an annual opera season in which internationally famous singers perform to packed houses. Others have vanished, among them the original New York Metropolitan building. This had been built because the original "400" of New York would not sell box subscriptions to the nouveaux riches. On one "Met" opening night a woman entered wearing, suspended from an ankle-length gold chain, an enormous diamond. As she mounted the stairs it was tossed into glittering view with her every step, but once she was seated in her box in the "diamond horseshoe" it was obscured from view. Undaunted, she dangled the gem by its chain over the protective railing, thus giving everybody an opportunity to evaluate her husband's achievements.

Knowledge of and appreciation for the quality of the production were not always the prime motives behind these cultural undertakings. Members of the wealthy class bought art collections to show added proof of their cultural sophistication. The paintings they purchased ranged from portraits by Gainsborough to landscapes of the Barbazon School to the Impressionists and even to the work of young artists who would one day be leaders in the modern movements. In so doing they left a magnificent legacy to commemorate if not their aesthetic awareness (though this did exist in many instances) at least their astute judgment. Corot, Turner, Constable, Manet, Monet, Lautrec, Degas, van Gogh, Gauguin—all these and many more were represented in these collections.

The Impressionists' concern for the effects of light evolved into the Expressionists' concern for self. Ensor, Munch, and many others explored on canvas and in various media the reactions of the inner self to experience. At a time when such dynamically influential painters as Cézanne, Renoir, Matisse, and Picasso were producing their early works, Maurice Denis wrote, "A picture before being a force, a nude form or some story is in essence a flat surface covered with a certain arrangement of colors." This statement summarizes many of the concepts of these artists. The church had lost its power to dictate the pictorial content of a painting. At last choice of subject, color, shapes, and messages was in the hands of the artist.

Meanwhile the vision of the engineer Eiffel, the innovative genius of such architects as Gaudi, and the Prince Consort's conception of the Crystal Palace, with its vast expanse of glass walls and ceilings, were to have an influence on the architecture of the future. In music and literature also there was a break with tradition. Musical innovators included Wagner, Verdi, Moussorgsky, Rachmaninoff, Ravel, and Debussy. The last-named was expelled from the conservatoire because, in the absence of his harmony professor, Délibes, he produced on the piano "such sounds of overwhelming discord and terrifying progressions" that he was thought unfit to continue.

It was an exciting time for those gifted with creativity. Artists, no longer bound to patrons, were making choices. Everyman was striving for the chance to choose. This was the age when it seemed that, led by artists, he might at last achieve this goal.

Town dress (1871-1872)

BASIC GARMENTS OF THE EDWARDIAN ERA (1870 — 1910)

GOWNS
(1870-1910)
Women

The introduction of the princess gown influenced the female silhouette dramatically. Hoop skirts were to disappear entirely during the 1870s. From the Worth atelier came a gown that was responsible for revolutionary changes in ladies' dress styles. This designer, whose previous experience in fabric shops, a London accessory shop, and in a fashionable Parisian boutique had given him an understanding of women's fashion wants, knew a new figure shape was long overdue. His polonaise gown was an immediate success, for he had long been established as a haut couturier after following the advice of his wife (a former vendeuse at Gagelino's) to cater to the whims of wealthy and royal clients.

polonaise

Afternoon dress with elaborately smocked, gathered, and ruching-trimmed skirt (1882-1883)

**turkey
back
pouf
saddle
bustle**

The polonaise gown modified the turkey back by adding a "saddle," an oval-shaped pouf, and draping the sides of the pleated gown skirt. The pouf at first was a low-set pad of horsehair or very full double ruffles. Other polonaise gowns of the 1870s consisted of outer dresses swept up and back over bustle frames, revealing a decorative underskirt. The overskirt was draped in a swag across the front of the figure and shaped into an elongated puff in back, trailing on the ground in a short train. Both overskirts and underskirts were trimmed with frills, ruchings and passementeries.

**princess
gown**

The princess gown of the 1870s was patterned after that of the previous decade. The graceful line of the skirt, created by back draping, was somewhat fuller over the hips than that of the polonaise gown. The profile silhouette with the low-slung pouf was similar to the Worth creation, but the front of the skirt was arranged into a semihobble effect. The twelve-inch ruffle trim of the princess underskirt was an important detail

**Ladies' and gentlemen's costumes of
the 1880s (permission of Whaley family)**

balayeuse

dust ruffle

and was called the *balayeuse* or sweeper. This ruffle was either gathered or accordion pleated, and braid often trimmed the seam where it was attached to the skirt. The dust ruffle, which was not decorative but functional, was sewn inside the skirt hem. It was attached by simple basting stitches so that it could easily be removed and laundered. This ruffle was intended to keep the skirt hem clean and was a slight skirt hem support as well. It was made of coarsely woven cotton and heavily starched. Later versions of this ruffle were made of box pleated buckram about four or five inches deep.

tunic dress

The tunic dress continued in style with the added innovation that it was often styled to create an apron effect. This draped skirt trim was in turn edged with ruching and tiny pleats. Scarves were also worn over the tunic dress, draped across the front, creating a shallow apron, and tied in back with the scarf ends draped over the pouf. The necklines of daytime dresses were round and quite high with small lace or braid-trimmed collars. Evening and ball gowns had an extreme decolletage with bosom emphasis exaggerated by the addition of lace frills and ruching. The heart-shaped neckline exposing the shoulders (or off the shoulder) was a common design characteristic of formal gowns. Ball gowns were styled with no sleeves, but gowns and other dresses had slender elbow or three-quarter length sleeves. All of these dresses, tunic dress, princess gown, and polonaise gown, were overloaded with scarves, braid, ruching, and flounces, with most of the emphasis in back though the bodices were very tight, accentuating the curves of the breasts.

vertical pleats

crinolette

bustle

Women's dresses during the 1880s were modified by the introduction of very narrow vertically pleated skirts. The bustle was eliminated for a brief period and a slim columnlike silhouette was popular. These skirts were so narrow that women had to take mincing birdlike steps. This styling did not last and in 1883 the bustle was again back in vogue. A version of the crinoline skirt replaced the narrower one. This was a short-lived fashion called the *crinolette*. Doucet, a couturier of note and personal elegance, who had a great interest in Watteau paintings and costumes of the eighteenth century, was perhaps responsible for the profusion of laces, frou-frou, and ruffles of this period that continued until the turn of the century. During the 1880s the bustle changed in shape and position on the rear of the figure. It protruded in a line at

Formal gowns (*Peterson's Magazine*, from author's print collection)

Afternoon gowns (Hungarian: 1880s, permission The Metropolitan Museum of Art, Bequest of Mrs. Martha T. Fiske Collord, in memory of Josia M. Fiske, 1908)

right angles to the body at the waist. Poufs and flounces assisted in enlarging this posterior embellishment to excessive proportions. Many yards of material were used in making these dec-

"pipe pleats"
"butterfly
wings"

orative rear appendages called variously "pipe pleats," "butterfly wings," and other descriptive names. These exterior frills and the gown skirt were given added size by the whalebone or wire cage skirt support often called the "dress im-

dress
improver

prover," which changed in shape with each new fashion dictate. The draped gown skirt was often slit in the back so that the poufs on the under-skirt might be seen. These were decorated below their enormous ballooning shape by ribbons and tiered rows of pleated ruffles, ruching, and lace. Seen from the side and back, ladies looked as if they were wearing the tail feathers of an exotic bird.

For the most part dresses and gowns during this decade had very snug-fitting bodices that empha-sized the rounded bustline. The waist was at the normal position and the sleeves were rather tight in daytime dresses, either elbow, three-quarter, or wrist length. Toward the end of this ten year period, the sleeves had added fullness over the upper arm or slight puffs at the shoulders.

Shirts continued snug in front but were length-ened in the back. The resulting train, which be-came quite long in formal or ball gowns, was an added, sometimes separate element, attached at the waist and spread over huge "dress improvers" or bustles.

Simplification of dresses and gowns developed during the 1890s. By 1899 the bustle had com-pletely vanished as a skirt support. Daytime dresses were designed with a graceful flared skirt. The new slim silhouette was a startling innova-tion. The bodice front took on a new shape and the emphasis area shifted from back to bosom. The female bodice of the late nineteenth century resembled the peascod jacket of the male Renais-sance costume. Ample and voluptuous, pulled into a narrow tiny waist somewhat lower than the nor-

mono-bosom
pouter pigeon
bodice

mal position, it was referred to as the mono-bosom or pouter pigeon bodice. The bell form skirt with hemline flare was created by pleating or many gores. Attached to the narrow waist, it lay flat over the front of the figure but had side and hip fullness. In 1895, leg-of-mutton sleeves extended

leg-of-
mutton
sleeves

the shoulder line and raised it. The huge sleeves, tiny waist, and flared skirt established the hour-glass silhouette with a wasp waist.

At home gown and children's costumes
(French: 1890s, permission The Metropolitan Museum of Art, Wolfe Fund,
1907)

**skirt and
shirtwaist**

Skirts and shirtwaists (blouses) with huge sleeves
and high throat-encasing collars—severe in line
yet feminine in trim—were day wear for most
women. The billowing leg-of-mutton sleeves were
given added breadth with the addition of "pinafore wings" which were laid over them, attached
at the armhole, and often extended to the waist.
Tight tube sleeves encased the lower arm and
were trimmed with lace or lace insertion. The high
collars were similarly decorated. Belts held in

belt pin

place around the wasp waist by belt pins were
fastened to the skirt below the waistline and assisted in creating a long bodice look in front.
These belts rose over the normal hipline at the
sides and followed the natural line of the waist in
back.

bell skirt

The lined and interlined bell skirt was worn with the shirtwaist and was quite plain in contrast to the gown and dress skirts. Because of the slender lines of these skirts and the lining, the number of petticoats worn was reduced. The dust ruffle of buckram (used on most of the dresses, gowns and skirts) helped to hold the hemline out to the required silhouette flare. No other skirt support was used.

Gown with pouter pigeon bodice (1904: *La Mode Illustrée*, from author's print collection)

ball gowns

During the two decades between 1890 and 1910, ladies' dresses and gowns maintained an ever increasing simplicity when compared to the costumes of the past. They were by no means plain, and both daytime and formal wear had a variety of carefully placed ruffle, ruching, and lace decorations. Ball gowns were made of elegant heavy satins and velvets. They were styled with large puffed sleeves (with buckram lining) or no sleeves,

Ballgown with princess line and leg-of-mutton sleeves completely devised (1895)

deep heart-shaped or V-necklines, tiny waists and long flowing skirts. The skirts emphasized the hips, fell straight and smoothly in front, and had long graceful elegant trains in back. They were lined with rustling taffeta and made from elegant textiles including delicate sheer fabrics, moiré, damask, figured satin, and tulle. Formal gowns worn after the turn of the century were elaborations of those worn during the day. Deep, square off-the-shoulder necklines trimmed with large bertha collars and a tighter skirt with a knee-to-toe ruffle and train were typical of this period.

By 1907 most female costumes had reedlike silhouettes. The bustline was raised and flattened. The collar remained high and boned, coming well up on the back of the neck, dipping down under the chin. Bishop sleeves and slender tubes replaced the high, shoulder-widening leg-of-mutton style. Jacques Doucet, countering the more masculine styling of women's suits, designed elegant dresses with deep lace yokes and sloping shoulders. The haut couture houses of Worth, Redfern, Doucet, Vionnet, and Poiret were prominent in establishing fashions during the years after the turn of the century.

Ball gowns (1900: permission The Metropolitan Museum of Art. Wolfe Fund, 1927)

Lace insertion trim on ball gowns (Belgian: 1828-1906, permission The Metropolitan Museum of Art, Gift of the Estate of Marie L. Russell, 1946)

Gown and bonnet (1894: *La Revue de la Mode, Gazette de la Famille*, from author's print collection)

SUITS
(1880-1910)
Women

Women's suits, first as lavishly trimmed as the gowns and dresses, were more tailored and less fussy during the 1880s. Braid and fur-trimmed jackets of these suits had tight sleeves and a peplum that was often knee length. Suit skirts were styled much like those of the dresses. In the next decade women's suits were made with matching skirts and jackets and contrasting shirtwaists or blouses. These were made of light delicate fabrics with tucking and lace insertion in the fronts and high collars. Necks as well as the tight, deep cuffs were also lace-trimmed. Voluminous jabots cascaded over the pouter pigeon bosom of the suit blouse. The delicate and lace-decorated blouses introduced by Maison Callot as a reaction to the general severity of the suit started a vogue which influenced many styles of the period. This trend was reversed by the very tailored ladies' suits introduced by Redfern, an English tailor whose designs were to influence the shape of the female form during the first decade of the twentieth century. The curvilinear lines in both suits and dresses were modified, the hips became narrower, but the waist remained small. Short snug jackets, bell skirts, and shirt waists with high, ear-lobe-hugging collars were characteristic of Edwardian suits for women. In 1905 the suit coat was lengthened to well below the knees. Sleeves retained a slight puff at the shoulder, with a snug fit at the wrist. Collars and cuffs were made of colors and textures contrasting with those used for the rest of the suit. The suit coat was single-breasted and cut on princess lines. Suit skirts were smooth in front with slight fullness and a modest train in back. The bolero suit, introduced in 1906, had a high-waisted skirtline and a boxy, short, pleated jacket. The skirt hem was raised and the train eliminated.

WRAPS
(1870-1910)
Women
  jackets
  capes
  pelisse
  paletot

Wraps during these decades were many and varied in design, according to the fashion whim of the year or decade. Capes and jackets with a rear vent that made room for the bustle pouf dominated the 1870s. The floor-length, fur-trimmed pelisse coat had wide sleeves that were designed to create a cape in back. The paletot was another popular coat worn in the next decade. Designed primarily for travel wear, it was floor length with a tight waist, box pleated back and elbow-length cape and small attached hood.

Coats generally reflected the traits of other costumes and in 1900 collars were tall, flared and often made of fur. The coat skirts flared, as did the dress skirts, and were often elaborately decorated with braid or fur trim or both. Lapels and shoulder capes in multiples were the significant coat details of the decade between 1900 and 1910. Evening wraps with deep dolman sleeves made of heavy velvets and lace or fur trimmings were typical. The designer Doucet was the first to treat fur as fabric. He made an otter coat for women that imitated the design of Prussian officers' fur coats. The *charmeus*, a jacket with deep dolman sleeves, was first introduced into the female wardrobe about 1908. This jacket had curving, cutaway fronts sloping to a rounded point in back, and sleeves that were full over the upper arm but snug from elbow to wrist. Marten or similar fur edged this jacket all around the hem, fronts, and neckline.

charmeus

boas
stoles

Boas made huge by fluttering feathers, long fur stoles, astrakhan capes with tall standing collars (calf or floor length) and double capes of velvet with silk fringe and beaded braid trim (made with many intricate sleeve effects) were worn for different occasions.

redingote

The double-breasted redingote, an outer wrap that had been popular for many decades, continued in fashion. It was styled with princess lines, had a snug high collar, ample lapels, and tab pockets. With the advent of the automobile the enveloping **duster** made of white or buff-colored linen was an essential part of the touring costume. This coat was usually unbelted, buttoned from throat to hem and had tight buckled wrist cuffs.

SPORTS COSTUMES
(1890-1910)
Women

As women became more active and participated to a limited extent in sports, special costumes were devised for these pastimes. Tennis dresses, yachting suits and riding habits as well as the rather daring calf-length hunting dress were all part of leisure class ladies' wardrobes. Generally these costumes consisted of severely tailored skirts and shirtwaists worn with short jackets. The shirtwaist, with high mannish collar and tucked bodice front, was the costume usually worn for playing **tennis** tennis—often with a black four-in-hand tie. Yacht-**dresses** ing suits had nautical collars and were trimmed **yachting** with red, white, and blue braid. The correct cos-**suits** tume for horseback riding consisted of an ankle-length wraparound skirt, tailored jacket, and **gym bloomers** shirtwaist with an ascot about the neck. Gym **middie** bloomers and middie blouses with sailor collars **blouses** were used for the more strenuous physical exer-**bathing** cises of lifting dumbbells and Indian clubs. Bath-**dresses** ing dresses were figure-concealing and included long baggy ruffle-cuffed bloomers, worn beneath a calf-length belted dress that had elbow sleeves and a high round neck. The bathing dress was worn with black stockings and high-topped bathing shoes. For individual sports, a women never

Lady's skirt, shirtwaist, and jacket, with leg-of-mutton sleeves: gentleman's sack suit (1895)

hunting dresses

exposed more of her body than face, neck, and forearms to the sun. Most of these sports costumes retained a distinct femininity. The hunting dress was an exception. This costume consisted of a calf-length skirt, much like the Scottish kilt, a tailored blouse, and mannish jacket. Boots, gaiters, and long heavy stockings were worn with this hunting habit, primarily an English woman's style.

UNDER-GARMENTS
(1870-1910)
Women corsets

Petticoats decreased in number and fullness as the skirt silhouette was modified and became narrower. Bloomers, underdrawers, and pantalets were in common use during the 1870s and 1880s. Corsets were mid-bust to waist designs with gussets over the bust and intricate boning and back lacings to mold the figure into the prescribed small-waisted form. By 1905 the corset was restyled; the longer foundation garment was extended to cover the figure from just under the breasts to over the posterior. This style was hooked up the center front with large steel hooks and eyes, and laced in back. Two garter stocking supports were attached near the center front.

umbrella drawers

chemise corset cover

Umbrella drawers, lace-trimmed knee-length underpants with a full flared leg, as well as knee-length bloomers or knickers, gathered tightly at the knee by an elastic band, were worn next to the body beneath the corset. A waist-length chemise with a ruffled front or a corset cover was worn to add fullness to the bust during the period when the pouter pigeon bosom was in vogue. During the colder winter months, lisle or woolen underwear was worn beneath the chemise and umbrella drawers. These shapeless one-piece garments had long legs and cap or long sleeves and were buttoned up the front to a high round or V-neck.

petticoats

A gored petticoat with ruffles, ruching, and lace around the hem was worn singly or in multiples depending on the skirt shape of the dress. A lace insertion gusset was inset from knee to hem to act as a skirt support during the period of the princess gown and flared hem bell skirt. These petticoats were waist-to-ankle length, gathered or sewn to a band that buttoned on the side or in back. The full slip did not appear until some time later.

SUITS
(1870-1910)
Men

Men's suits after the Civil War became standardized and had little or no decorative innovations. Even the one touch of individualism, the waistcoat, was discarded. Younger men, for a time,

Young man's suit; note jacket, watch-chain, and derby (1880s: permission of Whaley family)

wore mix-matched trousers and jackets, but the male suit in general was a somber dark costume consisting of trousers, matching vest, and coat. The only changes, and they were moderate ones, were in the number and position of the coat buttons; the size and shape of the collar and lapels; and the coat length. In the 1870s the lapels and collar were small and braid-trimmed. The coat fronts were slightly curved and the rather narrow trousers were uncreased. In the 1880s the more formal and rather distinctive **lounge suit** was introduced. This was a single-breasted suit with a hip length coat that had sloping shoulders, fuller sleeves and was buttoned quite high on the chest. It was later to become a less formal suit than the swallowtailed morning suit, and was made up of a black coat, grey striped trousers and vest or double-breasted grey waistcoat. The **ditto suit**, with the coat jacket following the general lines of the male figure, dominated the men's fashion scene.

Male suits and neckwear styles (1900: permission of Whaley family)

Until the mid-1890s older men continued to wear the longer **Prince Albert** or **frock coat**s. The **cutaway** and **swallowtail**ed coats, styled with collars and lapels to correspond to the detailing in the **sack suit**s, were in time relegated to Sunday morning wear or morning formal functions. These coats were patterned after the suit coats of the 1830s, with waist-length fronts, cut straight, diagonally downward to the back or in deep curved lines to the back. They were usually worn with black and grey striped trousers.

Garments of everyday wear (1904: permission of Schmidt family)

Norfolk jacket, knickers, gaiters, cuffed woolen argyle stockings, and billed cap (1900)

trousers

Trousers, full and creaseless in the 1870s, became more and more slender and were finally pressed with a center leg crease after the turn of the century. Two side pockets, two hip pockets and a small waistband watch pocket were characteristic details. One of the hip pockets was usually buttoned with a small tab. The fly front trouser closing was fastened by concealed buttons. The instep strap was discarded by the end of the 1870s and cuffs on the trouser legs were added a little before the turn of the century.

knickers

Norfolk

Knickers, an adaptation of the knee britches of the eighteenth and nineteenth centuries, worn with a sack suit jacket for spectator sports, continued in vogue for many years. The Norfolk jacket was designed especially to be worn with knickers, primarily as a country or hunting costume. This jacket was quite long, as were all men's suit coats, at the time of its introduction in 1890. The Norfolk was belted, hipbone length, with one narrow inverted box pleat in the center back that acted as a belt guide. Later this sporting jacket had two such pleats, front and back. They continued to act as belt guides. Men wore white flannel trousers with striped or plain blazers for boating, tennis, and other summer activities from 1890 through 1920. These blazers, like the sack suit coat, were styled with a loose fit, larger sleeves, lower set button closings, and slightly larger lapels by 1910.

blazers

formal suits

Formal attire for men developed into a selective number of costumes, depending on the hour of the day and the type of function. The tailed coat, black (opera or ball) costume worn with braid or satin sideseam-trimmed trousers, "boiled shirt" and white waistcoat, was the most formal. In the 1890s the trousers of this costume were very narrow and the tailcoat lapels narrow and shallow. The waistcoat was made of white pique or linen to match the white tie. Stiff winged collars or stiff tall collars and deep stiffly starched cuffs were details of the formal shirt. The center front of the shirt was very stiffly starched (hence "boiled shirt"); later, a heavily starched U-shaped dickey, held in place with a diamond stud, was worn to give a full-chested masculine silhouette. Morning suits composed of swallowtailed coats, gray and black striped trousers, and gray waistcoats were worn with soft white shirts. These had winged collars and were worn with an ascot about the neck. The least formal of morning clothes was the lounge suit. This semiformal costume was made up of a black sack coat, striped trousers, and gray double-breasted

morning suits

lounge suit

Morning dress and business suit (1908)

tuxedo suit

waistcoat. It was also worn with a soft white shirt (fold-down collar) and a four-in-hand tie. The tuxedo was first introduced in the 1880s. The sack suit coat was made more elegant with the addition of quilted lapels and collar. It was usually double-breasted and worn with braid-trimmed trousers. The tuxedo costume was completed with the black silk tie worn around the stiff-necked collar of the tucked front white shirt. The tailless evening coat was an innovation for evening wear.

shirts

Men's shirts were altered in design about 1880 to resemble the basic cut of more modern shirts. They had a shoulder yoke, modestly proportioned sleeves and either curved cuffs or French cuffs fastened with large swivel shank links. Generally collars were detachable and heavily starched. Rounded or pointed collars, at the turn of the century, were white, matching the shirt cuffs. The bodies of the shirts were either white, plain colors or striped. There were many collar styles, ranging from winged collars and high straight standing

collars
cravats
ascots
four-in-hand

collars to stiff tall fold-over collars that were worn with ascots, string ties with large loop bows, big bow ties, and the more modern four-in-hand. These were made of silk with small patterns or diagonal stripes.

Sack suit, shirt with detachable collar and cravat

WRAPS
(1870-1910)
Men
  Chesterfield

During this forty-year time span many kinds of topcoats and overcoats were worn. The Chesterfield was modified and was styled with a flyfront and a concealed button, single-breasted closing. The body of the coat was usually heavy black wool with a black velvet collar. It was most popular after 1880 and designed with straight boxy masculine lines, amply cut to fit easily over the sack or ditto suit. Great ankle-length coats of buffalo fur or beaver were worn during the 1870s and 1880s. These straight line coats had rather large cuffed sleeves, flat wide collars, and were single-breasted. The Inverness coat was one of the more unusual top coats of this period. It was introduced in the 1880s and was sleeveless, mid-calf length, and had an elbow-length cape attached beneath the collar. The Inverness was worn firmly belted at the waist. The collar was a tall "square." When worn unbelted, it seemed more a buttoned cape than an overcoat. Considered a lightweight wrap, it was usually made of fabric with a shepherd's plaid weave. Some call this wrap the Sherlock Holmes coat.

  buffalo skin
  overcoat

  Inverness

  walking coat

The walking coat, a knee-length garment with large flapped pockets, was often worn with matching cuffless trousers. It was usually worn in the country and made of tweed materials or other rustic fabrics. The knee-length skirt was sewn to the waist section at the normal waist. This seam acted as a belt or waist demarcation, as well as trim, for it was a prominent welted seam. As the masculine image became more sturdy the length of the coat skirts became shorter. Raglan sleeves and less bulky coat bodies came into fashion. The male overcoat was suddenly a serviceable garment with few flamboyant details. The shoulder capes and braid trims disappeared. Double and single-breasted knee-length coats of heavy woolen in a limited range of colors of buff, tan, brown, and black were worn. Greatcoats with fur collars and cuffs were worn by wealthier men, but topcoats were usually conservative garments, cut with collars and lapels adapted to the suit coat modifications of these details.

  raglan-
  sleeved
  overcoat

  greatcoats

ACCESSORIES
(1870-1910)
Men and
Women
  headwear

Women's hats during the years between 1870 and 1910 underwent yearly styling changes. The brimmed bonnets of the years before totally disappeared and were replaced by small felt or straw hats elaborately trimmed. These were perched forward, their tilted and rolled brims loaded with ruffles, bows, and curled plumes. In keeping with the back interest created on gowns, these hats

Ladies' suits (second from right with
polonaise skirt treatment); hats, small
and tall (*Peterson's Magazine*, from
author's print collection)

were more intricately decorated in the rear. By
the middle of the decade and continuing through
the 1880s, hats began to gain height and were
worn farther back on the head. Throughout the
next years and continuing until after the new
century, hats were structured into towering forms
of flowers, feathers, lace, and ribbons. Hat frames
were purchased at a millinery shop from which
the decorations were also bought. A lady, called a
"trimmer," would hold the bits of lace, feathers,
or flowers in different places on the hat frame as
the lady purchaser sat before a mirror giving ap-
proval of the suggested arrangement of the decorations. The hat was then left in the shop for the
trimmer to secure the desired frills in place. In
the 1890s hats became somewhat lower and broad-
chapeau   er. The *chapeau paré*, or small bonnet with wide
paré   sashes that covered the ears and tied under the
                 chin, was introduced. Major styling trends dic-
                 tated a narrow swooping brim, a shallow crown
                 trimmed with whole stuffed, spreadwing birds
round hat   perched on top. The round hat was a more tailored

style worn in the morning or for informal occasions. It had a wide flat crown, round brim, and was often trimmed with a circlet of gathered silk under the brim. The **tam-o-shanter**, a wide flat beret with a puff tassel on top, was worn either pancake style or pulled down over the ears to protect them in very cold weather. This was also the reason for the use of the wide ear-covering streamer ties on the chapeau paré.

The flamboyant hats introduced after the turn of the century were monumental in size and trim. Flowers, feathers, and veils covered the wide swooping brims and large crowns. The face veil of the 1890s all but disappeared. These hats were worn high on the pompadoured coif. A bandeau on the underside of the brim helped raise the hat and functioned as the area through which the long stiletto hatpins were thrust. These huge fanciful chapeaus, often called **Gainsborough** hats, demanded that ladies stand erect in a haughty pose. They achieved their maximum size in 1907 and were decorated with heron feathers, bird of paradise plumes, and tied "flues." The **automobile bonnet** was a large brimmed hat with a net or tulle scarf tied over the top and under the chin. The brim was stiff, and the scarf made a gossamer triangle from the huge chin bow to the hat brim edge. **Straw sailor hats** were worn for tennis matches, bicycling, and croquette games. These were flat-crowned, round-brimmed hats with wide grosgrain ribbon hatbands trimmed with bows on the sides.

Men's hats included: the bowler, the derby, the felt fedora, the homburg, the cap, and the straw boater. These hat styles for daytime and sports wear continued in style throughout this forty-year period. The tall silk hat, the collapsible opera hat, and the gray top hat were used for formal wear.

Shoes for ladies were rather serviceable for day wear. They were high-topped, either fabric or leather, with leather toes and counters, buttoned on the side or laced over the instep. During the 1870s toes, though pointed, were squared at the tips, and the heels, while raised, were not high and rather thick. Tops and counters were often made of contrasting colored leathers and as the turn of the century approached, toes became more pointed. Formal shoes and dressy shoes for daytime wear were made in a variety of **pump** styles with bows and rosette trims. In the 1890s, the low shoe or laced **oxford** was introduced. These were

Margin notes:

tam-o-shanter

Gainsborough chapeau

automobile bonnet

straw sailors hats

footwear
high shoes

pumps

oxfords

often worn with gaiters during colder weather or for sporting activities.

boots
high shoes

oxfords

tennis shoes
formal slippers

Shoes and boots for men continued to be made in approximately the same styles for some years. The changing shape of the toes was the only variable. These were square tipped in the 1870s, rounded during the 1880s and 1890s, growing more pointed after the turn of the century. Tie oxfords, two-toned or plain, replaced the high-topped male shoes in the 1890s. Rubber-soled low shoes, the forerunner of the tennis shoe, with canvas tops and rubber soles, were also introduced in the same year. Pumps with flat bows or rosettes were made of black patent leather and were correct formal footwear.

jewelry
necklaces

dog collars

watches

watch chains

rings

pocket watch

cufflinks
rings
stickpins

Pearl necklaces, drop earrings, and gold bar pins with chased designs were the popular pieces of jewelry worn by women. Diamonds, garnets, and pearls as well as semiprecious stones were mounted in gold pin settings. These pieces were not large, but the filigree settings were often intricate. Between 1900 and 1910, long pearl rope necklaces, pearl chokers, and diamond, ruby, or emerald sets mounted in gold or platinum made into throat-encasing dog collars were popular neckwear. The first earrings with screw fastenings were introduced in this decade. Up to that time all earrings had been worn through pierced ears. Women's watches were rather large circular shapes and had covered faces. They were either gold with chased designs or decorated with enameled patterns and were worn suspended from a pin fastened on the bosom, or from a rather heavy watch-chain (with a small decorative chain guide) worn around the neck. When worn with the chain, they were often tucked into the snug-fitting skirt belt. The chain with its guide could also be arranged into a variety of draped swags with the watch pinned to the chest. Rings were usually single set gems in gold mountings. Wedding rings were simple gold bands and engagement rings had sunken diamond settings or the raised Tiffany type. Men's jewelry included pocket watches with closed or open faces (though the former went out of style before the turn of the century) worn in the vest pocket. These were attached to a heavy gold chain strung through the vest buttonhole and anchored in the opposite lower vest pocket with a gold case penknife. Gold cufflinks, stickpins with gem heads, and gem or signet rings were popular pieces of jewelry worn by men. The stickpin (a stiletto with a crooked-over head) was used to keep the tie inside the vest as well as a decoration. In addition to precious or semiprecious gems, unique mounts, emblems of fraternal orders, oval discs with the wearer's initials, and even images of small insects —flies, ladybugs, and the like—often served as pin heads. The jewelry wardrobe of the man of fashion also included diamond shirt studs and gold collar-buttons.

hand held accessories fans

Hand-painted folding fans, fans with incised ivory segments, and circular or semicircular printed paper fans were widely used. The literature and art of the period depict coquettes flirting with their fans. Fans were also used to revive ladies suffering from the "vapors." During the 1880s little velvet bags with strap handles and a semicircular snap-closing metal frame were used as purses. Fitted leather purses were designed with a number of small compartments, each with a snap fastening. They usually had leather strap handles. The pocketbook, introduced in 1910, styled in the Empire mode and carried for afternoon social functions, was a sacklike pouch with a drawstring closing or a small pouch attached to an arched metal frame with snap fastening.

purses

pocket-book

gloves

Short wrist-length gloves of kid or cloth with radiating tucks on the backs and buttons at the wrists were used for daytime wear. Long kid gloves that covered the entire arm, which had small pearl or covered buttons on the under side of the wrist to make them fit snugly above the hand, were worn with formal gowns.

HAIR STYLES
(1870-1910)
Men and Women

Throughout these years of rapidly changing fashions, hair styles were modified many times. Women's coiffures, for the most part, were pulled up off of the neck and arranged in curls, frizzes, bangs, and bouffant pompadours in front. Small head shapes with face-framing small curls were typical during the 1870s and 1880s. Frizzed bangs, curls over the ears, and twisted knots of hair on the crown were popular during the latter part of the 1880s and into the 1890s. The next coif fashion added breadth at the temples created by soft waves. After the turn of the century, coif height was attained by combing the hair over "pads" or "rats." A chignon was sometimes worn at the nape of the neck or the hair was upswept, held in place by decorative tortoiseshell combs set with rhinestone brilliants. Men's hair gradually became shorter and faces were clean-shaven except for flat sideburns and mustaches. The hair was combed

from a side part, a center part, or in a slight pompadour. Mustaches ranged from thick walrus styles to neatly cared-for waxed mustaches. By the turn of the century sideburns and mustaches were completely out of style and men's hair was clipped short in back and worn parted on the side.

**Shirtwaist, gored skirt; little girl's dress
(permission of Whaley family)**

Additional pictorial resources

1. painting—"Festivities Aboard Ship," J. Tisset—(women's gowns showing a variety of bustle styles), 1874, Tate Gallery, London

2. painting—"Evening Party," J. Béraud—(formal attire), 1878, Comtesse d'Avricourt Collection

3. painting—"Portrait of Mme Valtesse de la Begne," Gerves—(gown with hobble skirt, low set oval bustle, chapeau paré), 1889, Louvre, Paris

4. painting—"Francisque Sarcey with his Daughter," Baschet—(male attire; lady's gown with leg-of-mutton sleeves and coif), 1893, Versailles Museum, Versailles

5. painting—"Place de la Concorde," Béraud—(town suit, shoes and gaiters), 1895, Musée Carnavalet, Paris

6. painting—"Mrs. White," Sargent—(formal visiting gown), 1883, Corcoran Gallery of Art, Washington, D.C.

7. painting—"Bar at the Folies Bergère," Bettini—(hats, ladies' suits and shirt waists), 1907, Museum of Modern Art, Paris

8. painting—"Portrait of Count Robert de Montesquieu," Boldini—(gentlemen's suit, double-breasted waistcoat, shirt with winged collar and French cuffs), 1910, Museum of Modern Art, Paris

9. painting—"Portrait of the Duchess of Montellano," Boldini—(formal gown, pearl rope necklace, coif), 1910, Duke of Montellano Collection, Madrid

10. painting—"Jardin de Paris, Night of Beauties," Béraud—(general costuming of the period), 1905, Musée Carnavalet, Paris

11. painting—"Le Trottin," Beraud—(lady's suit, shoes, gaiters, hat, and coif), 1906, Musée Carnavalet, Paris

Elegance of the early twentieth century (c. 1912, permission The Metropolitan Museum of Art, Gift of Consuelo Vanderbilt Balsan, 1946)

Chapter 18

COSTUMES OF THE MODERN AGE OF CHANGE

*C*HANGE *is an integral part of every period of the history of mankind, but at no time did so many or such dynamic changes occur as between the early 1900s and the great depression of 1929-1933.*

During the period following the death of Edward VII new, hitherto unexplored humanitarian philosophies developed. Activist social reformers sought to promote a higher standard of living, better physical and mental health, and a consciousness of the plight of minority groups through educational and legislative measures. Economists, sociologists, and politi-

232

cal scientists drew attention to the inadequacies of the social structure in the United States and in most European countries. After the Civil War America had developed under a burgeoning plutocracy. The country's vast expanses of open country, its rich oil and mineral deposits, as well as the revenues from the many labor-saving, employment-creating devices which had just been invented, produced great wealth which fell into the hands of a few families, while at the same time the labor force was swelled by the arrival of immigrants who worked long hours in crowded factories, often with unsafe equipment, and lived in squalid tenements owned by absentee landlords, whose number included some of the wealthier established churches. Many would-be reformers felt that these wealthy families were obstructing the restructuring of the living conditions and patterns of the greater mass of the population. Lester Ward, Anna G. Spencer, and others believed that the government should be responsible for regulating congested conditions in the urban slums and factories and for controlling the spread of contagious diseases. They felt that in order for living standards to be measurably altered it was necessary for the negative factors contributing to many of the intolerable conditions to be first recognized and then eliminated. Others attempted to improve the lot of the poorer members of society by a different route. Carry Nation, convinced that she was divinely appointed, went round smashing up saloons and agitating for temperance. As a result of her activities and those of her followers the Eighteenth Amendment was added to the United States Constitution. The effect of prohibition and of the strict Volstead Act was, however, to increase rather than eliminate the use of alcoholic beverages, and from the time of the amendment's ratification until its repeal in 1933 it did more harm than good.

As early as 1815 a Quaker lady, Lucretia Coffin Mott, had begun to work for women's rights. Margaret Fuller, Clara Barton, Susan B. Anthony, and Isabella Beecher were among the nineteenth-century feminists who promoted her free-thinking attitudes. Their work was continued in the twentieth century by such firebrands for women's suffrage as Victoria Woodhull and Emmeline Pankhurst, who organized parades, published magazines, and enlisted the aid of influential and wealthy backers. In 1920 women in the United States were finally given the right to vote, although in some states and some overseas countries they had received it somewhat earlier. Margaret Sanger sought to raise living standards by organizing the birth control movement. She established the first clinics in the United States in 1921 and held the first international conference on birth control in 1925.

Many of these social reforms took place against a background of war and revolution. Touched off by the assassination of Archduke Francis Ferdinand of Austria at Sarajevo in June, 1914, World War I erupted in August of that year and eventually involved almost all of the countries of Europe as well as Japan. In 1917 the Bolsheviks seized power in Russia after the "October Revolution" and in 1922 the Union of Soviet Socialist Republics was born. Meanwhile the Great War had come to an end and the Treaty of Versailles, signed between the Allies and defeated Germany, ushered in twenty years of troubled peace.

Lace insertion on summer dress bodice (1912: permission of Whaley family)

A wave of enthusiasm for "life" swept across the world, and a concern for self rather than social reform characterized the immediate postwar period. *In the United States business, money, and pleasure were the gods that men worshiped. Blocks of stock were bought and sold with little or no real backing. Paper wealth for some meant dire poverty for others, and the Veterans' March on Washington in May, 1932 gave expression to the feelings of despair and frustration which persisted in America.*

In Ireland Home Rule had been granted in 1914, only to be suspended for the duration of the war. The Irish Free State was set up in 1921, but a period of bloody civil war followed before De Valera established the sovereign country of Eire as part of the British Commonwealth of Nations in 1932. Postwar Germany was plagued by inflation and England by labor strikes. In September, 1929 the New York Stock Exchange went on a selling rampage and prices fell to record lows. No one was able to withstand the force of the financial catastrophe. Businesses failed, banks closed, and the worst depression since the 1830s enveloped the entire United States and Europe.

The changing international scene was reflected in the world of the arts. Expressionism, cubism, dadaism, fauvism followed one another in swift succession, culminating in the famous New York Armory Show. Both serious and popular music developed new thematic tonal systems and rhythmic beats. Moving pictures represented a new creative form. Inexpensive home entertainment was provided by the radio. These two new media, at first regarded as experimental novelties, had the effect not only of creating new theater art forms, but also of bridging distances. The Bauhaus in Germany gave impetus to innovations in architecture, which was stripped of its excessive ornamentation and became direct and functional. Miës van der Rohe, Frank Lloyd Wright, and Walter Gropius led the way in this field. In painting Picasso, Braque, and Matisse were the innovators, while Schönberg, Bartok, Berlin, and Gershwin created new sounds for concert halls and the new mass medium, radio.

Persian draped tunic; Castle style hat and baby Louis pump (1913)

BASIC GARMENTS OF THE MODERN AGE OF CHANGE (1910—1940)

DRESSES
(1913-1939)
Women
flounced
frock
lampshade
tunic

Persian
drape tunic

After 1910 women's dress styles seemed to change more radically from season to season than they had in the past. The innovation of 1913 was the flounced skirt frock, a derivation from the eighteenth century panier skirt treatment. In the same year, Poiret introduced the lampshade tunic. This dress was designed with a thigh or knee-length tunic over a pencil-slim, ankle-length skirt. The tunic was supported by a wire in the hem to hold it out away from the figure, and was often trimmed with a plisse frill, a circular flounce, or ruffle. The Persian drape tunic was another dress style popular during this year. These dresses were designed with soft full lines in the bodices and slender, draped skirts. They were patterned after the

Peg-top dress with kimona sleeve (1910)

kimona sleeve dress

peg-top dress

hobble skirt dress

Empire gown

kimona sleeve dresses that had been in vogue in 1910. Frocks that year and for several years thereafter were designed with rather loose, bloused bodices and skirts that became increasingly narrower. The smaller girth at the hemline first appeared in 1911 as a band trimming that drew in the skirt at the hem, creating a peg-top silhouette. The hipline fullness was achieved by slanted pleats originating at the waist and draped in a curved line to the sides. The hobble skirt dress resulted from decreasing the hemline circumference to ridiculously small proportions. Small hem-to-midcalf slits were cut in the skirts so that women might walk rather than hop. Just prior to World War I hemlines were raised and the foot and leg to the ankle were revealed.

Another silhouette modification introduced in 1911 was the raising of the waist. Empire gowns with high wide waists and shallow bodices eliminated the corseted, longer waisted lines of the gowns of the preceding decades. Ladies' costumes were more comfortable, designed with loose-fitting kimona or dolman sleeves and V or oval necklines. The fan collar, echoing the late Renaissance neck treatment, was attached at the shoulder seam and stood up in back, flaring slightly and framing the head. Large wide belts accented the high waistline. Hip and thigh width was created by skirt draping. Peplum and tunic skirt effects, lace and ribbon trims, and bands or piping of sharply contrasting colors were characteristic details of the frocks of this period.

afternoon frocks

The afternoon frocks of 1916 used fabrics with interesting textural combinations. Velvet and georgette crepe were the most popular of these combinations, but chiffon broadcloth, crepe de chine, dovetyne, suede cloth, and soft twill gaberdine were also used extensively. The skirt, shortened first by the designer Lanvin in 1914, continued to have hemlines eight inches from the floor.

chemise frock

slip dress

The chemise frock introduced in 1915 was the result of some designers' interest in medieval costumes. It was designed with a long, straight, sleeved blouse worn over a slender "slip" dress. The loose tunic blouse was gradually lengthened and worn with a belt placed low on or below the hips. The under, or slip dress was designed with a straight skirt attached to a sleeveless bodice.

tonneau silhouette dress

A short-lived figure form called the *tonneau* silhouette was proposed in 1917. This was a barrel shape with great fullness in the skirt between the waist and the knees. Tonneau silhouette dresses were never generally accepted, though bulky coats styled with these lines were.

tea gowns

handkerchief frock

The tea gowns of 1919 were short-sleeved frocks with a wide girdle or sash. They were originally designed by Vionnet as a simple tubular dress made to fit the figure comfortably with the sash as the accenting detail. The handkerchief frock of the same year was a variation of the Vionnet gown. It was styled with the same simple tubular one-piece dress with an overskirt made from squares of soft fabric sewn to the gown by the points. This arrangement created a series of free hanging panels, the lower points extending below the gown hem in an uneven line. A fashion periodical of September 1919 suggested that the feminine silhouette should have a softness "not the curves of restriction but the softly rounded curves of the natural figure trained to emphasize its feminine roundness rather than its boyish slimness." Young ladies' fashions of this year listed frocks with such lyric names as: Minette, Elice, Cordia, and Azure. These dresses had loose-fitting bodices, rather full skirts, and a waistline slightly lower than the normal waist. Trimmed with a large sash, the Cordia, for example, had a straight line, bloused bodice, long slender sleeves, and an accordion pleated skirt. The necklines of these frocks were generally modest, usually round and trimmed with neat small round collars.

**Minette
Elice
Cordia
Azure**

Asymmetry was a typical skirt design theme during the 1920s. The handkerchief frock had initiated the uneven hemline, and this became a typical trait of dresses of this decade. One fanciful dress of the frivolous postwar period designed by Cheruit, the *Broderie anglaise*, was created with a round-necked bodice, lampshade sleeves of chiffon and crepe, a crepe underskirt, and ruffle-trimmed chiffon poof overpanels. During the first half of the 1920s dresses were styled with rather shapeless long-waisted bodices, pleated or straight ankle-length skirts, and long straight or lampshade sleeves. Two fabrics of contrasting textures and colors were used in making the sleeves and as skirt swags, draped skirt panels, and hanging vertical ruffles on the bodice. Throughout this period the straight trim lines introduced in the creations designed by Chanel influenced all costumes. Three-quarter jackets and slender skirts, often with side pleating as a skirt detail, emphasized the asymmetric design theme of this decade.

Broderie anglaise

Chanel dress

Cordia frock (1919)

Tea frock (1922)

Chanel jersey suit and cloche (1920s)

The clothes and the mood of this period were summed up by a leading fashion magazine editor who noted that the 1920s "was scarcely an age of nostalgic charm" but one which was hectic, lacked poise, and was full of "slap-happy optimism" and that the chemise frock had irresistible charm only in retrospect. The extremely short skirts for which this era is noted were first presented in the 1925 fashion shows. In that year women's frocks were styled with a slim, shapeless, boyish silhouette. Hemlines were knee length, necklines were either low V-shapes or high turtle necks. Blouses of dresses were created with long wrist-length sleeves for the winter season and no sleeves for summer. The long-waisted chemise was extremely plain and trimmed with subtle refined details at the neckline, cuffs, and waist.

The bubble (the irresponsible era of the twenties characterized by the "flapper" with her bobbed hair and daringly short chemise frock) burst after the financial crash of 1929. The basic silhouette changes that appeared in the 1930s were the lower hemline, the raised waist and, last in the decade, the addition of width across the shoulders. Costumes reflected the somber economic conditions of the world. Designers such as Schiaparelli, Molyneux, Balenciaga, Paquin, and Mainbocher dominated the coutoure scene. It was they who reintroduced puffed sleeves, the leg-of-mutton sleeve, and, late in the 1930s, created another silhouette change—the raised, divided, and rounded bustline. Costumes were designed for all occasions and met the demands of many different activity patterns. Tea frocks, cocktail dresses, beach pajamas, shorts with halter tops, day time frocks and evening gowns, all became necessary items in the feminine wardrobe. As the political parties exchanged places in the White House, people looked forward to "happy days" and became involved in more lighthearted pastimes.

summer frocks

During the decade of the 1930s, summer frocks were made of light printed chiffons with full circular skirts, loose-fitting bodices, and no sleeves. Squares of fabric were attached at the shoulders as sleeve substitutes. Skirts, which continued long for some time, became quite slender in 1931, as did the entire figure outline. Necklines were round and modestly proportioned. Complex geometric designs were used as skirt and blouse decorations. Bows made of the dress fabric were tied in a tailored manner and trimmed both blouses and skirts. Soft gathers or pleats on one side of the skirt added some fullness to the skirts. The generally restrained appearance of dresses during the early thirties was heightened by the use of long sleeves and simple necklines with a variety of collars and narrow, tied or buckled, belts. By 1935 more flair in dress design was introduced. Bishop sleeves, uneven hemlines, modestly raised and puffed shoulders, and side draping created more imaginative costumes. Pleating, minute tucks, and diamond smocking were typical detail features of blouses worn over slip-top skirts.

blouse and slip-top skirt

run-about dress

Made of wool jersey for winter, silk or cotton for summer, the run-about dress of 1939 was designed in a shirtmaker style. A simple pointed collar, V-neck, center-front button closing, and long, short, or three-quarter sleeves were the basic styling traits of this casual frock. The shoulder line was given added breadth by a variation of the leg-of-mutton sleeve. The raised puff of the sleeve was eliminated and a smooth, squared pleat at the sleeve top extended the line across the shoulders well beyond the normal contours of the figure. The "basic black dress" became an integral part of the female wardrobe toward the end of the 1930s. Designed with simple lines, this frock was suitable for daytime, cocktail, or theater wear. It had short or cap sleeves, a full-busted bodice, and a slightly flared, gored skirt. The thin "wafer waist" accented the broad shoulders, full bust, and flare of the skirt. Some of the dresses of this period were designed with back skirt fullness reminiscent of the 1890 bustles. This skirt effect was created by unpressed pleats placed in the center back. Braid and bead braid was often used to trim the neckline or sleeves. Late in 1939, shoulder padding replaced the puffed and flat pleat sleeves as a means of extending the shoulder line. This construction innovation was used in the basic black dress (which remained in vogue for several years), daytime dresses, suits, and coats. With the introduction of the shoulder padding, bodices were cut with a longer shoulder seam. Sleeve puffs were completely eliminated and the sleeves were inset flat and flush. The added bodice fullness was slightly draped, placing emphasis on the bust and creating an extremely feminine silhouette. Skirts at this time were draped, soft and flowing.

basic black dress

formal gowns

Formal gowns of the 1920s carried out the figure themes of daytime dresses. The easy uncorseted look persisted. Extreme decolletage marked the difference between day and evening wear. An extremely simple formal gown usually consisted of a

Short evening gown (1925)

straight long-waisted chemise with thin shoulder straps, deep V-shaped armholes, and plunging V-neckline front and back. Swag sashes, side puffs falling into a train, uneven hemlines (short in front and dipping to the floor in back), or handkerchief skirts were detail characteristics of evening gowns of the early twenties.

short formal

The most significant change in formal gowns was the introduction of the short formal. The hemline was raised first to the calf of the leg and then to the knee. A deep V-shaped back neckline and a draped girdle placed low on the hips and tied into a loose bow behind, with the sash ends trailing down to the ankle, drew attention to the new emphasis area of these gowns—the back. This was the fashion during 1929. The designer Paquin is credited with originating this styling, which also included softly fluted skirts. Informal dinner dresses worn during the summer of 1929 had large capes with ruffled trimming. The gowns were simple and floor length. They were worn with small hats.

informal dinner dresses

formal dinner gowns

Many costumes during the 1930s were influenced by the female stars of the cinema. The dinner gowns of 1935 were no exception, and they imitated masculine formal attire preferred by one of the popular movie "queens." These dinner costumes were designed with a jacket with wide lapels, sometimes faced with satin, and a pencil-slim floor-length skirt. They were usually made of black crepe, severely tailored and extremely simple.

bolero jacket evening dresses

A semiformal, floor-length gown, often worn at informal country club dinner parties, was styled with an elbow-length bolero jacket. When worn without the jacket, this bare-shouldered gown was appropriate for informal dances. The bodice was intricately cut with a gathered bust, snugly fitted over the rib cage, and had ribbon shoulder straps. The floor-length skirt flared gently at the hemline. Many of these informal evening gowns were patterned after the polonaise gown of the 1880s. A draped apron effect was created between the waist and thigh, curving back and upward to the center back. The softly fluted skirt was attached to this pseudoapron. Both the gown and the bolero jacket were often trimmed with rather deep ruching.

polonaise skirt

bare midriff formal

The influence of the halter top, originally designed to be worn with sportswear, was applied to the design of formal gowns. There were several variations of this styling, including: a backless bodice with two fitted panels over the bust; an elaborately fitted brassiere form that fastened around the neck and the rib cage, leaving the midriff bare; and a short bodice, with or without sleeves, that covered the figure from the shoulders to just under the bustline. These various bare midriff tops were worn with a separate flared skirt that extended from the normal waistline to the floor.

dinner suit

A more formal dinner suit was first introduced in 1939. It was composed of a high-necked jacket with long tight sleeves, slightly puffed at the shoulder, and a pencil-slim skirt that had a modest flare at the hem. This was a floor-length costume which was often designed with a bustle treatment created by large soft puffs in back below the waistline. There was, throughout the 1930s, an interest in classical Greek costumes resulting in an increased use of skirt draping. Gradually the styling trends capitalized on the turn-of-the-century silhouette. The transition from soft, smoothly flowing lines to more rigidly controlled and contrived shapes took place during the third decade of the twentieth century.

WRAPS
(1910-1940)
Women fur coats

Large dolman sleeves, creating fullness above the hips and around the waist, dominated the coat fashion of the period between 1910 and 1920. Fur coats, often made of two furs with contrasting textures, had the sloped shoulder and middle figure bulk of the cloth coat styles. Russian sable and Hudson Bay seal were the most popular furs

Coat (1937)

Coat, cloche (1925)

dolman coat

**redingote
Empire coat**

princess coat

fur coats

of this period. Fabric coats were often trimmed with elegant furs at the neck, cuffs, and hem. Dolman sleeves, bloused back, long waist, and a huge high collar were typical coat design features well into the 1920s. A trim straight coat design, accented with a large collar and cuffs, a revival of the redingote coat, and a style patterned after the double-breasted Empire coat were also in fashion during this decade.

During the depression years, American designers dominated the fashion scene in the United States. The consequences of the 1929 financial debacle affected and controlled the import of French couture designs. Adrian, Fogarty, Mainbocher, Greer, Golones, Zuckerman, and Simpson designs became the sought-after creations of the 1930s. There was less discrepancy between social and economic strata. Good styling was available inexpensively because of technical improvements in garment-making machines and refinements in production methods. A leveling of the social strata and the generally poor economic situation resulted in fewer marked design changes each season. The subdued depression years were given visual expression in clothing, with coats in particular reflecting social and economic conditions. Tweed coats had simple princess lines while black and other dark dull colors were used for making single or double-breasted cloth coats. Puffed sleeves, fitted bodices, and gently flared skirts were the basic characteristics of coats during the early 1930s. By 1937, however, a certain confidence in the recovery programs developed and this mood was reflected in all garment designs. More imaginative use of textured materials, lighter and somewhat brighter colors, plus more originally designed details appeared for coats of that year. The slope-shouldered, full-bodied coat with lantern sleeves was introduced in contrast to the conservative coats of the previous years. Large bell-shaped sleeves were a typical detail of coats created with a full bodice, tightly belted waist, and full, circular, calf-length skirts. Gored coats with tailored puffed sleeves and bell cuffs in colorful tweed were popular casual coats in the late 1930s.

Monkey fur capes, coats of sable, mink, chinchilla, baum marten, broadtail, and Persian lamb were worn as the countries of the world recovered from their economic slump. Lesser furs such as dressed goat and lambskin were also considered chic. Leopard, beaver, and plucked muskrat skins were used in creating casual and sports coats. These

Suit, hat, and muff (1914)

coats were often styled with a straight-line, almost boxy silhouette. Collars that could be turned up for warmth or left lying flat over the single button closing at the neck, and sleeves that echoed the general styling trends of the season were details of fur coats during this period.

formal wraps Velvet and sable in combination were used for formal wraps. Similar in design to the Victorian coats, evening wraps in 1939 were designed with huge leg-of-mutton sleeves, long floor-length skirts with back fullness, and amply cut bodices. They were trimmed with shawl collars and deep sleeve cuffs.

SUITS
(1910-1940)
Women

The more comfortably fitting costumes of the late 1910s continued in vogue and suits were designed with the same silhouettes, styled with a tailored, masculine overall design but very feminine detailing. Suit skirts were ankle length and the jackets echoed many of the styling traits that were typical of a particular season's fashion. There were cutaway jackets, lampshade jackets, snug-fitting thigh-length coats, and high-waisted jackets following the Empire style. Chanel, who greatly influenced women's fashions of the 1920s, introduced

dressmaker suit the jersey chemise and dressmaker suit in 1918. This costume had straight lines with a loose fitting bodice, wider waist, and slim skirt that created a

Suit (early 1920s)

town blouse

seven-eighth suit

ensemble

Ensemble, jacket, skirt, and cape (1932)

SPORTSWEAR
(1910-1940)
Women

exercise suit

beach pajamas

pajama suit

boyish silhouette. Major detailing features included georgette embroidery, beads, and metal brocade, gold and silver fringe, and grosgrain ribbon. The town blouse often worn with women's suits during the late teens and early twenties, was a long overtunic with a very low V-neckline and short sleeves. Some of these blouses had a deep V-neckline formed by crossing one front over the other and buttoning it at a point on the hipbone. During the early 1920s, suit jackets were knee length and called the seven-eighths coat. They had masculine detailing, such as large notched lapels of double-breasted jackets with button and braid trims. These suits had slender skirts and were worn with blouses designed with high standing collars. Suits of the thirties were made of men's wear flannel or tweed and designed with hip-length jackets. They fit the body snugly, were nipped in at the waist, and were designed with slightly puffed sleeves. The three-piece suit (or ensemble) was introduced in 1932 and consisted of a skirt and jacket and matching cape or three-quarter length coat. Late in this decade blouses became an important suit accessory and were styled with bow-tie necks that softened an otherwise tailored costume. Insets of two or three colors were used in the making of intricately cut suit jackets as the general styling trends in women's costumes became more complex. The skirts of these suits were plain and straight, with a box kick pleat in the back. Like most women's daytime costumes, they were calf length.

For some time the conservative "covered up" active, participation sports clothes persisted in fashion. Seaside suits, while sleeveless, still consisted of an overdress and knee-length bloomers. As the emancipated woman of the 1920s found the excitement of her new freedom, she engaged in a number of different outdoor sports. These active women created a demand for more comfortable and practical sports costumes. The exercise suit which replaced the old-fashioned and bulky black bloomer and middie blouse sports costume of previous years consisted of a sleeveless middie blouse and knee-length shorts designed with a deep center pleat. These shorts had the appearance of a very short skirt. Beach pajamas were another sports or casual wear innovation of the 1930s. This costume was designed first as a one-piece pants outfit. The trousers had large flared legs and the bodice was loose-fitting with shoulder straps that were tied into large knots or bows. The pajama suit, forerunner of the very tailored and mas-

Slacks suit (1939)

slacks suits

bathing suits

**tennis dresses
slack suits
snow suits
culottes**

Swimming costumes (1910)

ACCESSORIES
(1910-1940)
**Women
hats
Castle hat**

culine looking slack suit, was introduced in 1929. These suits had "bell bottom" trousers and a matching blouse that was often designed with a sailor collar. Tri-colored pajama costumes with flared leg slacks, a matching blouse, and boxy jacket, became the fashion as casual outdoor or patio entertaining became popular. During the 1930s and into the 1940s, very tailored woolen slack suits were designed with single or double-breasted jackets. The trousers of these suits had somewhat slender legs with deep cuffs, wide waistbands, and a fly front zipper closing.

Bathing suits were radically altered in 1922. They were one-piece knitted woolen costumes with thigh-length tight-fitting shorts, covered with a shorter tight skirt. The tops of these suits had deep oval or V-necklines and thin shoulder straps. They were thought by many to indecently expose the female body and plainclothes women (police) were stationed on some eastern beaches to measure the depth of ladies' bathing suit necklines to see if they met the code of decency. This style of swim suit replaced the earlier two-piece suit with a sweater top and knee-length shorts. By 1929, the necklines of swim suits exposed the back through a deep U-shaped opening. Midriff suits in a variety of halter styles were popular throughout the 1930s. Suits were made in a wide range of gay colors rather than the earlier black or dark blues with contrasting red or white bands on the skirt hems or around the bust. Short shorts with halter or blouse tops were worn for patio lounging or sunbathing during this decade. Tennis dresses, slack suits, snow suits with tight ankle bands holding the amply cut legs snugly, and culottes were some of the many casual wear and sports costumes adapted to specific activities. Golf, skiing, tennis, bowling, boating, and badminton were the popular sports, and costumes were created specifically for them.

Hats took their shape from the line design demands of the major costume styles. They remained large until 1913, when smaller, head-hugging shapes were introduced. The famous dancer, Irene Castle, popularized a hat that was given her name. It had a crushed crown, an asymmetric tilted brim, and was trimmed with "numedie feather fancy" on one side for a perky decoration. Feathers such as ostrich or egrette were eliminated as hat trims when the Audubon Society forced the passage of legislation protecting "rare birds from careless and indiscriminate killing." Bandeau beehive

beehive hat

crown hats of velvet with ostrich plumes plucked from live birds replaced the exotic feather decorations of previous styles. These hats with their turban shapes were worn squarely on the head and quite low over the brow.

cloche

The cloche emphasized the small head look introduced by the boyish bob coif. These hats had very deep crowns and small brims that framed the face. They were worn pulled well down on the head, obscuring the forehead and the cheeks. During the 1930s, hats were styled with shallow crowns, snap brims, and severely tailored bows. They were worn slightly tilted over the right eye. Toward the end of this decade a style attributed to Schiaparelli evolved when the designer "clapped a stocking on her head." This "corkscrew turban" had a towering crown and was usually made of decorative printed fabric. Hats with tall crowns and snap brims were derivatives of this creation. The floppy brimmed round-crowned hat of the twenties, worn usually to garden parties, was modified until it resembled a gentleman's felt fedora. Other hat styles of the 1930s included: the skullcap; the pancake beret; the Schiaparelli knotted cap; turbans; and small brimmed bonnets (inspired by the movie version of *Gone with the Wind*) similar to those worn during the American Civil War.

corkscrew turban

footwear

Shoes became a significant costume accessory as skirts became shorter. Minor changes that appeared during the first decades of the twentieth century included: mules of white kid and strictly tailored satin bows; pumps with "little Louis" heels; and oxfords for summer, high shoes for winter wear. Tweedies, or gaiters, were a winter fashion fad in 1916. The most radical changes in female footwear occured during the twenties. The T-strap sandal with high, thick heels, the dress oxford with eyelet cutouts arranged in decorative swirl patterns, two-toned spectator pumps originating in the twenties, were modified slightly during the 1930s, but remained the basic daytime styles for several years. Playshoes, made of colorful heavy canvas fabrics and "wedgie soles," were introduced to be worn with the wide variety of casual costumes available.

mules
pumps
oxfords
high top shoes
tweedies
"T" strap sandal
dress oxford
spectator pump
playshoes
wedgies

jewelry

The basic jewelry items remained constant for several years. The ladies' wrist watch had been the most startling innovation until the introduction, by Chanel, of inexpensive costume jewelry. During the 1920s great ropes of glass beads and plastic bracelets were the most common types of neck and arm decorations. Long drop earrings were also popular during this decade. During the depression, inconspicuous strings of beads were worn in keeping with the somber mood of the times. Women's wrist watches changed from small round shapes to small oblongs and were made much smaller. Costume jewelry was given wide acceptance and one fashion magazine wrote, "... to a girl with a born-to-the-purple feeling and a pinched pocket book ... wear fake jewelry."

hand held accessories

Leather, fabric, or beaded bags and functional leather pocket books persisted throughout the 1920s. More serviceable forms were carried in the thirties and were made of leather with hinge-snap closings and leather strap handles. When women entered the business world they discarded the more fanciful and decorative purses for fitted leather pocket books. The tapestry, beaded, and embroidered small bags were used for evening.

UNDERWEAR
(1910-1940)
Women
  camisole
  envelope
  combination
  combination
  with knickers

  step-in

  vanity
  thora
  vest chemise
  slips

Some of the most radical changes made in women's apparel were introduced in female underwear. Corset covers, camisoles, and petticoats were replaced by "envelope combinations," a one-piece undergarment with ribbon shoulder straps, drawstring neckline and front buttoning. The combination with knickers had gathered legs rather than the loose style of the envelope combination. Both of these 1915 underwear innovations were discarded for the step-in. This one-piece undergarof the 1920s was advertised as "comfy as brother's." They were given a variety of names with each minor design difference, such as: thora, vanity, vest chemise, and combination. Underslips with slender bodies and ribbon shoulder straps were worn instead of petticoats.

corsets

scandal belt

foundation garments

bras

Because of the more loosely fitting dresses and suits, figure-controlling garments were seldom worn during the 1920s. The scandal belt, or simple below-the-waist band with elastic garter supports, was introduced first in 1933. Later in the thirties, when bust and slender waists were in style, the foundation garment was developed as a firm figure support. These were designed in a variety of ways, often combining corset and brassiere into one garment. Tight bust-flattening brassieres were worn when the boyish silhouette was in vogue, but with the return of emphasis on feminine curves, bras were designed to raise and separate the breasts. By the end of the 1930s, women's underwear included some form of gartered corset, a brassiere, underpants (long-legged or very scant) and a slip.

At this period they were usually very tailored garments, the only decoration being a lace trim on the slip hem.

HAIR STYLES
(1910-1940)
Women

The large bouffant pompadours of the Edwardian period were flattened and pushed well down over the forehead. The hair remained long until the 1920s when the first short bobs for women became the style. These boyish bobs were daringly short, combed from a center part with "spit curls" framing the cheekbone. At first they were the same length sides and back, but during the flapper era the hair was shingled (shaped to the head) in back. During the thirties the marcel wave and then the permanent wave brought back longer hair and feminine curls. The invention of the permanent wave machine made it possible for women who wished to suffer through the long electrically "cooked" hair treatment to have curls that would last. This eliminated rolling up the hair in curl papers or curling rags or using the heated curling irons of the past. Hair was arranged to follow the natural contours of the head, with waves falling from a side or a center part. A small roll of sausage curls controlled the hair at the back of the neck, while that in front was pulled off the face and up over the ears. Late in the 1930s the pageboy bob was introduced. This was a shoulder-length style with the ends of the hair rolled under and allowed to hang free or caught up on either side over the ears. There was a variety of acceptable and fashionable ways of wearing the hair at this time, and women went to the beauty shops to have their hair styled to suit features, faces and personalities.

SUITS
(1910-1940)
Men
sack suit

peg-top
trousers
business
suit

The sack suit maintained the general design characteristics that had been established before the turn of the century. The concave shoulder line with the padded chest and "spider silhouette" of the teens disappeared totally by the 1920s. A looser coat with emphasis on broader shoulders and greater chest girth was introduced. About 1927 suit trousers were styled with a high waistband and rather full legs. The trouser cuff was deepened. The trouser waistband returned to a normal size and position in 1934, but front pleating was introduced, creating a peg-top effect. The double-breasted business suit of the early 1930s consisted of a modestly proportioned coat, trousers with waist pleats and large legs, and a matching vest. Handpicking, small detail stitches, replaced machine-made detailing along the edges of the flat collar and notched lapels. Two side pock-

Suits (1919)

Sack Suit (1930s: permission of Whaley family)

ets on the coat fronts and a breast pocket on the left were typical functional trims of the business suit coat. A vent in the center back, buttons on the sleeve cuffs, and a buttonhole on the left lapel were also major styling features of these suits. Gabardines, flannels, Harris tweeds and serges in pinstripe patterns or plain dark blues, browns, grays, and light browns were used to make most men's suits during this decade. Summer weight fabrics such as seersucker were used for the first time in the late 1920s and early 1930s. The summer seersucker suit was the same style as the sack suit or included a pair of trousers and a jacket with a belt in the back and deep center or side back pleats.

seersucker suit

golf suit plus-fours

In 1927, the golf suit consisted of a Norfolk jacket and plus-fours. These trousers or britches were a variation of the designs used for sports knickers and knickerbockers. They were called "plus-fours" because the legs were lengthened to extend four inches below the knees. These baggy pants were worn with argyle socks covering the lower leg. In addition to the plus fours and jacket, the properly clad golfer wore a shirt and sweater and topped off this costume with a crushed fedora or billed cap.

sports slacks
peg-tops
Oxford bags
bell bottoms

sport jackets

bathing suits
swim trunks

Other male casual garments included: sports slacks, which in the twenties had a wide, high waistband; peg-tops; Oxford bags, with a high waistband and wide legs trimmed with deep cuffs; and bell bottom trousers with huge flared cuffs that were often two to two and a half feet in diameter. Casual sport coats or jackets with a half belt in the back were worn with the various styles of casual trousers. These jackets were generally made of tweed fabrics. The long-legged two-piece bathing suits of the 1900s were replaced, in the 1920s, by thigh-length trunks and sleeveless shirts with deep armholes and U-shaped necklines. One-piece suits designed with large necklines, armholes and two oval cuts on the side in the area of the rib cage were popular male swim attire late in the twenties. Bathing trunks, or knitted shorts, worn with nothing covering the upper figure, were first introduced in the 1930s. Woolen knitted swimming apparel persisted until the 1940s for both men and women.

formal suits
dress sack
suit
lounge suit
tuxedo
evening
suit

mess jacket

cummer-
bund
dinner
jacket

Evening clothes *(en règle)* of black or dark blue included: the formal dress sack suit; the formal lounge suit with black coat and grey and black striped trousers; the tuxedo, black coat with satin lapels and trousers with satin band seam trim; and the formal evening suit with black tail coat, white waistcoat, trousers with satin band seam trim. The formal evening suit was worn with a white shirt that was stiffly starched in the front or with a stiff white dickey. Winged collars and white ties were other formal attire accessories. The height of the collar was an indication of the period. It was very high during the years just after the turn of the century, getting gradually lower during the late 1930s. The mess jacket, styled after the cut of formal military jackets, was introduced in 1930. This jacket was waist length, tailless, and cut with a deep V across the back hem. It had rather large lapels (which had no satin facings) and was buttoned below them with shank buttons. The mess jacket was worn with a cummerbund (a wide horizontally pleated sashlike belt that was buckled in the back) rather than a waistcoat. The white dinner jacket, patterned after either the single-breasted sack suit coat or the double-breasted business suit coat, replaced the mess jacket in the mid-1930s and was worn with tuxedo trousers, as a summer or informal evening costume. The lapels were modified in size and shape to conform to the prevailing design traits of these details used on daytime suit coats. They were faced with satin and were rather large during the 1920s, gradually growing smaller during the 1930s.

WRAPS
(1910-1940)
Men

Men's overcoats such as the Inverness, Ulster, and Chesterfield continued in popularity until the 1920s. The Chesterfield was reserved for more formal occasions, replacing the large opera cape. It was a single-breasted straight coat with a black velvet collar. The huge, bulky raccoon coat, popular with university and college men, was introduced in 1928. The long polo coat of camel's hair, the double-breasted, knee-length trench coat, and the topcoat with raglan sleeves were all belted. They were typical overcoat styles of the 1930s.

Trench coat, Chesterfield, and topper (1916: permission of Whaley family)

UNDERWEAR
(1920-1930)
Men
B.V.D.

The long-legged union suit of wool (winter) or cotton lisle (summer) was discarded in favor of the one-piece B.V.D., a one-piece sleeveless vest and thigh-length shorts. This in turn was replaced by the sleeveless lisle undershirt and broadcloth shorts.

ACCESSORIES
Men
hats

Men's headwear from 1910 to 1940 continued to include the fedora, boater, and homburg. Brims and crowns were large and the fedora crown was "pinched" into a three-cornered shape or creased on the top. The straw panama and the straw boater were worn for the summer. Until the middle of the 1920s, caps were popular for younger men. Height of crown and width of brim were modestly proportioned during the 1930s.

shoes

Shoe styles changed only slightly during these decades. Most men wore plain or two-toned Oxfords. Toes of men's shoes were more rounded, with a straight "cap," stitched or perforated trimming, and large shallow heel lifts. Sport shoes were styled with "wing tips," a fringed flap covering the laces, or with intricately designed perforations on the toe tops. Black patent leather pumps with flat grosgrain ribbon bows were worn for formal occasions.

belts
ties
shirts

Suit and shirt accessories included belts (rather wide leather belts and large buckles during the 1930s); elastic suspenders or thin light leather braces; detachable shirt collars (discarded by 1930); and plain, diagonally striped, or patterned ties, worn with tiepins or tieclips with spring hinges which could be fastened over the tie and under the front opening of the shirt. After 1930 shirts were made with soft fold-down collars, shallow shoulder yokes, rather straight sleeves with rounded cuffs, and plain buttoned fronts. Hose were silk or cotton lisle, about calf-length and supported by garters. In the 1930s ankle socks with elastic ribbed cuffs were introduced.

spats

Spats, which were worn as a shoe accessory until the end of the 1920s, covered the tops of the feet and the ankles, with button fastenings on the outside and instep straps to hold them in place under the foot. They were white, gray, or buff.

HAIR STYLES
(1910-1940)
Men

In 1910, male hair styles included side parts, pompadours, and ear-length hair combed from a center part. During the 1920s, men's hair was styled with a "patent leather look" created by using brilliantine and combing the hair flat against the head from a center or side part or back from the brow. During the thirties, the hair was combed back, parted on the side and cut quite short, trimmed in back to follow the contour of the head. For the most part throughout this period men were clean-shaven, though some during the 1920s wore rather long straight sideburns and pencil line mustaches.

Additional pictorial resources

Fashion periodicals for the years 1910 to 1940, such as *Vanity Fair, Town and Country, Vogue,* and *Harper's Bazaar* are the best visual resources available. Bound copies of these magazines are usually included in the libraries of the larger metropolitan cities. Historical societies of some cities will have photographic collections and family photographs will also give a generalized version of styling trends for these decades.

Formal gown (1969)

Chapter 19

COSTUME REVOLUTIONS OF THE RECENT PAST

*T*HE *postwar "boom and bust" mood had ended in an uncontrollable inflationary situation in Germany. The mark was valueless, and the German government inept. From the conflict which developed between socialists and communists emerged a fanatical Austrian house painter, Adolf Hitler, who became dictator of Germany. Russia was still experiencing the aftermath of its traumatic revolution, while England and France were barely recovering from the effects of the protracted depression that had begun with the stock market collapse. Franklin D. Roosevelt enacted his New Deal legislation after his inauguration* in 1933 and by 1940 the United States, under his forceful and imaginative leadership, at last appeared to be achieving economic stability.

While the first world war had ostensibly been fought to end all wars, the "peaceful" 1930s had in fact witnessed many conflicts. In 1935 Italy invaded Ethiopia; the Spanish Civil War broke out in 1936; in 1937 Japan invaded northern China, and in 1939 Russian troops crossed the border with Finland. By the end of the 1930s Hitler had totally reorganized Germany and was now ready to expand its territory. His "peace in our time" meeting with the British prime minister, Chamberlain, was swiftly followed by the occupation of Czechoslovakia and the beginning of Germany's relentless march across Europe. The League of Nations, created as a world peace-keeping and arbitration organization to fulfill the dream of the American president during World War I, Woodrow Wilson, had proved powerless to act in solving international disputes. Europe was once again caught up in a great war as the Axis powers of Germany, Italy, and Japan strove to control the world. At first Britain and France battled alone on many fronts in their attempt to halt the apparently invincible Axis armies.

The United States, going through a period of isolationism, had managed to avoid direct involvements in these conflicts (although it was helping the Allies with "Lend-Lease" materials) until the Japanese attack on Pearl Harbor on December 7, 1941, brought it into the war. A series of global battles was fought on the African and European fronts and in the Pacific. After Germany invaded the territory of its former ally, Russia, the tide began to turn. Finally Germany surrendered in May, 1945, and in August of the same year Japan capitulated after atomic bombs had been dropped on Hiroshima and Nagasaki. The United Nations Charter was signed by fifty nations at San Francisco in that same year.

The peace found Europe in ruins. The United States furnished financial aid to allies and enemies alike in order to help them rebuild. The Marshall Plan, the brainchild of President Truman's Secretary of State, George C. Marshall, was successful in restoring the economy of the European countries. Most of Eastern Europe found itself under Russian domination. In the United States the Republicans, under Dwight D. Eisenhower, who had led the allied armies in the war and become a national hero, in 1953 succeeded in ousting the Democrats after twenty years in power. A tenuous armistice was negotiated in Korea (where fighting had broken out in 1951 between the North Koreans, supported by China, on the one hand and the more democratically oriented South Koreans, supported by the United Nations, on the other). Emerging nations, freed from the colonial control of Britain, France, Belgium, and the Netherlands, struggled with the problems of independence. The newly constituted State of Israel and the Arab nations alternated between border skirmishes and outright war. Russia and the Western Powers were confronted with tribulations of the "Cold War."

There were many indications of the need for new social reforms, and minority groups were now able to make themselves heard. As a first step the Supreme Court in 1954 ordered desegregation in the public schools. As the civil rights movement gained impetus the antagonism which had developed between northern liberals and southern conservatives increased.

The New Look suit (1947)

American involvement in the Far East, in particular in the struggle between North and South Vietnam, as well as disappointment with the pace of civil rights reforms, resulted in riots, demonstration marches, strikes, and sit-ins on college and university campuses both in America and in other countries. A highly paid and skilled work force had produced an economic boom reminiscent of that following the end of World War I. Material comfort and pleasure were pursued, but at the same time America's affluence was attacked by dedicated and youthful social reformers who denounced the establishment for its conservatism and expressed their opposition to violence either by rioting or by "escaping" through the use of drugs.

It was a science-oriented age, but there was also increased interest in cultural pursuits. Both Russia and the United States began the exploration of space which led to the first moon landing. New museums and centers for the performing arts were established in many cities, while existing ones were added to or rebuilt. Artists explored the visual philosophies of surrealism, abstractionism, abstract expressionism, nonart, pop art, op art, happenings, constructivism, and minimal art. In the early 1960s many artists looked backward to the work of Blake, Art Nouveau, and the newspaper funnies cartoonists of the 1930s. Television offered the public programs ranging from significant cultural offerings to mediocre entertainment, and through this medium people around the world were able to watch such events as the coronation of Elizabeth II of England, the investiture of the Prince of Wales, man's first steps on the moon, and the funerals of a president, senator, and civil rights leader of the United States, all three of them victims of an assassin's bullet.

It was a dynamic age, full of social concern, an age which was impatient for change and glorified its zestful, activist youth. Moral attitudes were in a state of flux, and many old taboos were discarded. Old liturgies were modified as religion struggled to be relevant and the clergy worked actively for social reforms. Astrological mysticism, witchcraft, and back-to-nature cults all found followers. Socially aware artists carried out their own individualistically motivated explorations of music, art, theater, cinema, and literature, and nonart, the "theater of the absurd," underground movies, and "four-letter-word" poetry were accepted as significant creative acts of expression. Many attempted to be involved and relevant, but few offered viable solutions.

As in earlier times, costumes reflected the period. They became symbolic of membership of a specific group—establishment, reformers, or escapists—none of which understood, or wanted to understand, the others. There were many who were ready to exploit these divisions, and the streams of love, hate, and apathy flowed together in a jumbled and chaotic life pattern.

BASIC GARMENTS OF THE RECENT PAST (1940—1969)

DRESSES
(1940-1969)

During the 1940s women's costumes were greatly affected by the Second World War. Paris, although

Women

**street
dresses**

invaded and subdued, maintained, for a time, its traditional position as the fashion leader. Drawings of the latest styles were allowed past the censors and were reproduced in leading American fashion magazines. René Willaumez's sketches of Alix, Creed, and Balenciaga designs indicated the major silhouette and detailing trends. Large white areas were used as trims, bold decorations that served a good purpose during the pitch dark nights of the "blackouts." Fashion magazine editors rationalized their continued interest in chic styles in a policy statement that suggested handsome fashions lifted women's spirits and helped them to carry on. The couturiers carried on also, sometimes under grave handicaps. Many left Paris and, in self-imposed exile, created costume designs for the war-oriented society. Many of the dresses of the 1940s were very tailored, with broad shawl collars, broad, padded shoulders and short slender skirts. Shirtmaker-styled bodices with V necklines trimmed with pointed and notched collars were common. The straight skirts were given width at the hemlines by deep kick pleats. Cap sleeves, three-quarter sleeves, and long, slender sleeves similar to those of men's shirts were typical sleeve treatments of casual daytime dresses. Street dresses were plain with a masculine simplicity and austere detailing. The shoulder line increased in

Double-breasted business suit and spring frock (1943: permission of Schmidt family)

**afternoon
frocks
dressy
dresses**

width, accenting the full bust, small waist, and narrow hips. Afternoon frocks and dressy dresses for semiformal evening wear accentuated the full bosom. These frocks were made with intricately cut bodices that had gathers radiating from a center seam and cap or three-quarter length sleeves. Waists were small, and the short skirts were slightly draped over the hips. Slit side pockets were also used to add to the hip emphasis. The deep V necklines were trimmed with sequins, as were the sleeves, bodices, and skirts around the hips. By 1944, skirts of afternoon dresses were flared at the hem. Front skirt fullness was retained but the back was smooth, creating a slender silhouette.

**new look
dresses**

"A-line"

The most startling development of postwar fashions was the "New Look" introduced by the couturier Dior in the spring of 1947. The costumes he designed had narrow sloping shoulders, nipped-in waists, rounded bodices, and—the season's surprise—the lowered hemline. Skirt hems plunged from knee length (the standard length throughout the war) to within twelve inches from the floor. Skirts were not only long but also rather full. One fashion editor reported these costume innovations as "seemingly new," a lovely look that had polished rounded lines but no effect of heaviness. The female silhouette changed from the stiff masculine triangular shape set on its apex to completely feminine forms. The influence of the New Look "A-line" silhouette dominated women's fashions for several years. Dresses with long full skirts, tight waists, and full bodices remained in vogue until 1953. New man-made fibers and interest in fabrics with interesting weaves contributed to the design characteristics of women's garments. Fabric, rather than involved and contrasting shapes of bodice and skirt, hinted at a renewed interest in the straight-line silhouette of the 1920s. Simple straight dresses with bodices slightly bloused over a low waistline, straight sleeves, and much shorter skirts, were known variously as sack dresses, sheath dresses, and chemise dresses.

**sack dresses
sheath
chemise**

mini-dress

The straight-line dresses continued to grow in popularity and were made interesting and exciting by a wide variety of textured fabrics and startling color combinations. Exterior influences such as the interest in space science, Pop and Op art, and renewed attention to Art Nouveau contributed to the development of elaborately curvilinear and strictly geometric detailing. Decolletage was broad, with standing circular collars. Sleeves were modified bell-shapes, straight three-quarter sleeves, or elbow-length straight sleeves. Skirts became startlingly short, most hems were knee length or above, with the mini-skirt reaching only to the mid-thigh. Simple waistless and sleeveless mini-dresses were decorated with contrasting horizontal and vertical bands, echoing the perpendicular linear themes of Mondrian paintings or projecting space travel costume stylings. During the late 1960s a number of skirt lengths were proposed including the midi, maxi, and mod hemlines. The midi length touched the leg at mid-calf while the maxi-dress hemline touched the floor. Only the very young, or young in heart, wore extremely short or extremely long skirts. Late in 1968, there was a nostalgic look backward to the fluff and lace beruffled Edwardian period. The severely plain silhouette made elegant by intricately cut patterns, however, dominated the styles of the 1960s. Fashions for casual wear, tea parties, and formal occasions were all styled along the same lines.

midi-dress
maxi-dress

SUITS
Women

During the 1940s women's suits imitated the severe tailoring of men's clothing. They had short pencil-slim skirts and jackets with broad shoulders, flat collars, and notched lapels. Suit jackets were nipped in at the waist and smooth and narrow around the hips. They were quite long and made in single- or double-breasted styles. Dressy suits were made with intricate diamond-shaped insets that emphasized the bustline of the jackets. These were often collarless and worn with decorative blouses. The New Look suit was designed with a long full skirt and a short jacket. The deep dolman sleeves of suits of the early 1940s were replaced by straight, more slender sleeves. Suits of the late 1940s and early 1950s retained the "A" silhouette and were styled with figure-fitting peplum jackets and full gored skirts. Gradually the silhouette was modified to a more slender outline. Short, waist-length jackets and shorter, narrower skirts became the dominant styling features. By the middle of the 1960s suits were quite bulky and made from heavy textured fabrics. Short boxy jackets with large, away-from-the-throat collars were combined with straight-line skirts with slight fullness below the waist in front. Double knit suits became extremely popular in the late 1960s. These were handsomely tailored costumes consisting of a jacket, skirt, and matching blouse. They were either plain-colored or two-toned, and sometimes trimmed with large, oversized zipper fastenings, big brass hooks, or cleverly designed metal chain and button closings.

New Look
suit

"A" sil-
houette

double knit
suits

Grey flannel suit and cloche (1946: permission of Schmidt family)

Softly feminine suit (1952)

Bulky suit of the 1950s

pants suits

Pants suits for women were introduced in the late 1960s. These were styled from a variety of fabrics including velvet, wool, double knit, orlon, or quilted cotton prints. The more elegant velvet pants suits were styled with jackets patterned after the eighteenth century justaucorps and worn with lace-trimmed white blouses. Those of wool or woollike man-made fibers were designed with Nehru jackets and were very masculine. The pants were at first very tailored with extremely slender legs. Later these were modified to flared leg or bell bottom styles. Pants suits were worn for both formal and casual occasions.

Pants suit (mid 1960s)

Young lady's jacket and velvet knickers (1969)

FORMAL GOWNS
Women
dinner dresses
ball gowns

cocktail dresses

During the war years of the 1940s women's formal gowns were designed with softly flowing or full bouffant skirts. Floor-length dinner dresses and ball gowns were styled with the typical bust emphasis of daytime costumes. Bodice backs were sometimes slit from the high round necklines to the waists. Dinner dresses had full-length dolman sleeves, cap or three-quarter length sleeves, slightly flared skirts, and small round necklines. Ballgowns had a single shoulder strap, two thin shoulder straps, or no strap at all. Necklines of some formal gowns were deep V shapes while others were small round shapes. Cocktail dresses duplicated these bodices and neckline treatments, but were made with street-length skirts. The feminine curves typical of the New Look were used in the designs for formal costumes of the late 1940s and 1950s. Hemlines of these gowns

Elegance of form gown achieved by complex draping (late 1940s)

Formal pants suit with detachable skirt trim and fur hat (1960s)

ballerina formals

see through formal

formal jumpsuit

were often styled to reveal the feet in front but dipped low in back, giving the appearance of short trains. The ballerina-length formal was designed with a slightly above-the-ankle skirt, a wasp waist, and a variety of sleeves. During the late 1950s and early 1960s formal gowns were designed with intricately cut bodices, often trimmed with huge bows with wide streamers reaching to the floor-length hem. Tulip or lily-shaped collars, loose hanging panels and large shoulder puffs added elegance to the slim floor-length formal sheaths of these years. Late in the 1960s, the "see through" costume was introduced for formal evening wear. This consisted of a long-sleeved blouse with a deep decolletage made from gossamer fabric (worn without concealing undergarments) and a slim, floor-length skirt. Other formal gowns were designed with plunging necklines that extended below the navel, sleeveless bodices, and tight skirts slit from knee to hem. At home formal costumes were designed with full transparent harem pants (worn at hipbone level) and elegantly bejeweled gold brassieres. Late in 1969, a one-piece jumpsuit with bell bottom trousers, Empire waistline marked with a wide belt, and bust-outlining bodice with long bishop sleeves, was introduced. This too was a formal at-home costume made of "lunar white" crepe. A variety of novelty cocktail dresses were suggested for the holiday season of 1968. Some of these were made with several shapes of silver tabs hinged together to form a metal sheath or mini-dress. Another unique cocktail dress proposed for that season was decorated with battery-operated lights, which when switched on declared provocative, one-word answers to spoken or implied questions.

Metal tab cocktail dress, mini-skirt length (late 1950s)

SPORT CLOTHES
(1940-1969)
Women
pedal-pushers
stretch pants
Bermuda shorts
hip huggers
pants dresses
swim suits

slacks

elephant ear pants
bell bottoms

ski costume

car coat

Sport clothes for women were supplied in a wide variety of shapes and styles. Slacks, swim suits and shorts dominated the scene until the 1950s. During the next two decades of ever-increasing casual living, there were developed: pedal-pushers, calf-length tight pants; stretch pants, long pants with instep straps made of form-fitting bonded knit fabric; Bermuda shorts, thigh-length tight-legged shorts; hip huggers, pants dresses, culottes, and skimmer dresses. Swim suits made of cotton were designed like short-skirted dresses or as bikini suits with narrow breastbands and minute pants. Knit suits were much like those of the 1920s, two-piece suits consisting of modest top and short trunks worn low on the hips, worn with a delicate gold chain around the waist and a solitaire pearl dangling from it in an appropriate position in front. Slacks changed radically during the late 1960s, particularly in leg proportions. At first they were form-fitting and tight from waist to ankles. Toward the end of 1968, the flared cuff was introduced. These slacks were called elephant ear pants, if very large and floppy, or bell bottoms, if only modestly flared. Slacks were no longer simply a female version of male trousers, but were often trimmed on the leg seams with lace, open shapes, or appliqué. Blouses worn with either shorts or slacks ranged from short-sleeved tailored shirts to fussy lace and eyelet-trimmed styles. Ski costumes were severely tailored, made of bonded stretch knit, and ski suits were composed of pants and matching jacket. During the late 1960s they were worn with turtleneck knit blouses. Car coats with attached hoods made in a wide range of materials ranging from fleece-lined wool to nylon were used extensively for winter sports events or sports car racing.

WRAPS
(1940-1969)
Women
coats
Chesterfield
shorty coat

"A" silhouette coat

Masculine cut in coats and the inclusion in nearly every coed's wardrobe of a black Chesterfield, with a flat velvet collar and wide lapels, carried out the broad-shouldered styling themes of the forties. The shorty coat, a boxy hip-length jacket with wide three-quarter or full-length sleeves, was designed with a cardigan neckline. This light-weight coat was often trimmed with nonfunctional buttons, though later styles were double-breasted. This style remained in fashion for several years. After 1947, long, full-backed coats with modestly puffed sleeves, bell sleeves, or straight sleeves with folded-back cuffs reflected the "A" silhouette of the New Look. Shoulders were made much narrower and sloping. Sleeves were inset, dolman, or raglan styles. The masculine type of coats,

Maxi-coat of boldly patterned wool (1969)

Chesterfields and heavy double-breasted greatcoats patterned after men's coats of the early nineteenth century, were replaced by more feminine wraps. Huge pyramidal coats with large, full sleeves and shawl, tuxedo, or tie-scarf collars, were made of handsome textured woolens. Three-quarter coats, so popular during the 1940s, with full bodices, tight waists, and flared skirts were discarded totally in the 1950s. Raincoats, chemically treated and made of colorful fabrics, replaced the reversible rain or casual wear coats of the previous decade. The reversible coat was designed with a tailored woolen side and a chemically treated gabardine side. They could be turned inside out and worn as protection against the rain, and yet retain the same design on the woolen side. The chemicals applied to these coats made them water-repellent.

During the 1950s coats ranged from cape shapes with modified batwing sleeves to wraparound cashmeres similar to the polo coat of the 1920s. Large head-hugging collars, shawl collars, and wide-standing circle collars (in the late 1960s) followed coat modifications from cape shape to bulky "barrel" shape. Coat hems rose with the dress hem, to mini-length. In 1966, a greatcoat with calf-length skirts was introduced and continued as a chic winter style for some years.

During the 1940s fur coats were designed with square shoulders, bell-shaped sleeves, and round or shawl collars. The "chubby" was the fur version of the shorty coat. It was made from fox fur with the pelts arranged with a dominant vertical line. During the 1950s and 1960s shoulder capes made of mink were patterned after the nineteenth century canezou. These were often called clutch capes. Mink capes, coats, and stoles were the most popular fur wraps for a number of years, but sable, leopard, and fox (with the pelts arranged in a horizontal pattern) were also worn. Cloth coats with dyed mink collars were styled with simple straight bodies and amply cut straight sleeves.

three-quarter coat

raincoat reversible coat

mini-coat greatcoat

fur coats

chubby coat

clutch cape stoles

Coat and felt helmet (1960s)

Coat (mini-length) and attached fur-lined hood (1960s)

imitation fur coat

Imitation furs were worn by both men and women during the late 1960s. Man-made furs had reached a high level of perfection, and their fakery, in the expensive versions, was difficult to detect. The imitation furs were often seal or beaver textures, designed with simple straight bodies and sleeves. They were worn either unbelted or girdled with thin leather belts or large link chain belts. They were thigh, knee, or calf length, warm but lightweight and quite elegant in appearance.

formal wraps

Formal wraps during the 1950s and 1960s were flamboyant or luxuriously sophisticated and made of rich velvet or silk fabrics for formal winter functions. Great tiered capes made with wide ruffles arranged horizontally from the neckline to the floor-length hem were made of vividly colored taffeta. Gossamer man-made fabrics were used for summer formal wraps. These were often styled with rows of bouffant puffs creating a billowing "A" silhouette from the shoulders to the ankle-length hem. Straight floor-length coats with severe lines, small standing collars, and side slit skirts were elegantly tailored evening wraps. They were made of velvet or brocaded silk. The evening wraps of these decades were more intricate than the broad-shouldered capes and three-quarter length wraps of the austere war years.

capes

coats

Formal evening wrap (late 1950s)

ACCESSORIES
(1940-1969)
Women
hats

During the first years of the 1940s hats were small and were worn cocked over one eye. Styles included: the turban; the tailored beret; small tipped-brim hats; turban and snood combinations; pillbox hats with ruffled falls or snoods in back; and small hats composed entirely of fabric flowers and trimmed with fine net puffs. Many of the hats of this period had coarse net face veils and were made of felt for winter wear and straw for spring and summer. During the mid-forties hats were much larger, with rolled brims and topless crowns. The gathered and draped fall trims of the previous years were replaced by more tailored decorations. The spring and summer hat fashions of the late forties included pancake and cartwheel straw sailors, while sequin or flower trimmed skull caps were worn for evening. During the 1950s hats for daytime wear were made of velour and trimmed with a variety of feathers and veils. Brims were asymmetric, tilted up on one side and hugging the cheek on the other. Pleated and draped pyramidal crowns with feather trims were worn well back on the head. From the mid-forties hats were set squarely on the head, a suitable position for the masculine derby forms with tall crowns and

rolled brims that were in vogue during the 1960s.
High crowned fedora styles; space age felt helmets;
leather caps with tall crowns and large bills; hair-
concealing tams; and fur hats made with dome-
shaped crowns and no brims, or imitative of the
fur hats worn by Russian men—these were some
of the winter hat fashions of the late 1960s.
Floppy-brimmed straw hats and cloth hats patterned after the 1930s beach hat were popular for
summer wear during this period. Hats, however,
were not the fashionable accessory they had once
been. Hats were worn primarily for warmth in the
winter, otherwise only the most chic or most conservative women continued to wear them. Even
the custom of women covering their heads when
attending church was discarded and small round
lace veils or large lace mantillas were worn instead. For tea or cocktail parties, net formed into
dome-shaped crowns and trimmed with velvet or
grosgrain ribbon bows and small artificial flowers
substituted for traditional hat forms. Frivolous
beehive-shaped feather and cloth flower hats that
completely covered the head were a casual style.
Mesh net bonnets with rows of ruffles, transparent
caps similar to the eighteenth century mob cap,
were worn about the house in a half-hearted effort
to hide hair curlers.

footwear

Shoes in the 1940s were heavy and clumsily designed. Leather was scarce during the war years
and shoes were designed to conform to the available materials. Toes and counters were often made
of leather while the area over the instep was made
from an elastic fabric. Shoe toes were round, heels
were thick, and soles were raised. These platform
soles were often made of cork and were quite

pumps
shanks
mare
baby dolls
wedgies

thick. Pumps, shanks mare, wedgies, and baby
doll ankle-strap sandals were among the more common shoe forms of the forties. During the 1950s,
shoes gradually became more pointed, with very
high, slender heels. During the 1960s heel shapes
changed each season, ranging from stiletto heels
set well back, to Louis heels placed toward the
instep, to large thick heels similar to those worn
during the seventeenth century. Shoe tops were
very shallow during the 1950s, growing increasingly heavy and foot-concealing as the end of the

boots

1960s approached. Boots, which appeared briefly
in 1947 as ankle-high, flared cuff forms, became
an important part of the total costume by the
1960s. With the advent of the mini-dress, suit
and coat, leg emphasis demanded rather startling
leg coverings. Women's boots ranged from ankle-
high duplicates of the nineteenth century male

boots to calf-high Hessian or riding boot styles to thigh-high boots with thick heels and square toes reminiscent of seventeenth century boots. These latter boot styles were made of man-made stretch leather and were tight and form-fitting.

sandals

Many sandal forms were worn for summer and casual wear. They ranged in design from the Japanese one-thong styles to Grecian thong sandals, with the thongs laced up the legs to the knees or thighs. The sandal designs available were almost limitless.

jewelry

Costume jewelry was generally accepted and necklaces, bracelets, and earrings were accessory items that changed each season. During the 1960s, plastic was used extensively for much of the costume jewelry, including huge rings, bracelets, and necklaces. Handcrafted, individually created silver jewelry in either rigidly geometric shapes or organic forms became the vogue during the same decade. There was a renewed interest in the small rings of the early nineteenth century which were worn on every finger in much the same way as they had been during the Renaissance. Charm bracelets, at first popular in the 1940s, were revived during the 1960s, but were usually gold rather than silver as the earlier versions had been. Band bracelets worn in multiples were either plastic, silver, or gold, thin or thick, and worn around the wrist or upper arm.

bracelets

watches

Women's watches, round and tiny during the 1940s, became small square shapes and finally, in the 1960s costume jewelry watches were made with huge faces, large numerals, and wide wrist bands. Pendant, pin, and ring watches were other forms popular in a period of great variety and availability of most jewelry items.

Elegant jewels were also worn, and diamond and precious gems were set in platinum or gold, designed in styles similar to those of the French Empire period.

body jewelry

Body jewelry was first introduced in the late 1960s. These exotic jewelry forms included: silver and gold bras; huge shoulder-to-breast collars; and large silver lorums, composed of wide circular silver collars and an ankle-length front panel of silver.

hand held accessories

The variety of hand held accessories was limited to purses, pocket books, "clutch purses," and umbrellas. Purses or bags ranged from soft, modestly proportioned cloth styles of the forties to envelope shapes to huge satchel forms or small clutch purses of the 1960s. They were made of leather, plastic, or straw. There were shoulder strap styles with ample pouches during the 1950s and minute purses with long chain straps during the 1960s.

umbrellas
Umbrellas were functional as well as decorative rainwear accessories. They were made of plain and patterned fabrics or transparent plastic. Some of the latter type were made of opaque plastic with transparent "portholes." There were styles with long handles, short handles, and collapsible telescoping handles. Many women carried the longer handled styles neatly furled, using them almost like walking sticks.

UNDERWEAR
Women
Most of the undergarments worn by women remained more or less constant from the late 1930s through the 1960s. Minor innovations were introduced in the 1950s, such as the half slip and refinements in brassiere design, including a thin padded interlining. Body stockings and panty hose (textured and plain) were two of the more significant innovations of the late 1960s. The former was a one-piece stretch knit garment of nylon or other man-made fiber fabrics. Panty hose were a combination of hose and pants. While hose were relatively subordinate to the rest of the costume, they remained smooth and were beige or brown in color. Nylon hose were introduced in the early 1940s, but were replaced during the war with stockings made of rayon. Silk totally disappeared as a fiber for making hose and was replaced, after the war, by nylon, stretch nylon and, during the 1960s, cantrece. When dresses, suits, and coats became very short, legs and leg coverings were considered part of the "total look" of the costume. Textured and patterned hose, of wide mesh stretch hose, and hose made in a broad range of colors were worn.

half slip

body stocking
panty hose

hose

corsets
foundation
garments
wasp waist
Merry
Widow
Corsets and foundation garments were worn to support hose and control the figures of more matronly women. The wasp-waist or Merry Widow corset was introduced at the time of the New Look to control the waist size. Panty girdles, garter belts and thigh-length elasticized underpants with detachable garters were also worn as hose supports and for minor figure control.

HAIR STYLES
(1940-1969)
During the first half of the 1940s hair was very long and worn pulled off of the forehead into a

**Women
pompadour**

feather cut

beehive

bubble

crop cut

**infant coif
Brutus cut
wigs**

falls

hair dyes

high pompadour. These pompadour arrangements were often divided into two sausage rolls that terminated in two facing curls in the center front. The hair in back was either allowed to fall free or was brushed up to the crown of the head and arranged into several curls behind the pompadour. More mature women wore modified versions of these two styles, but generally wore their hair somewhat shorter. A hair style dictated by the New Look was the short feather cut. This was a controlled version of the nineteenth century infanta coif. These styles were gently curled and remained in fashion from the late 1940s until the early 1950s when women's hair fashions changed radically. The gently curled skull-conforming feather bobs were abandoned, and huge beehive coifs, stiffly lacquered after much torturing and back-brushing, became the vogue. Straight hair was the fashion and women with naturally curly hair had it straightened. The bubble hair style, also large and bouffant, but without waves or curls, was followed by a closely cropped cut, combed from the crown over gently teased hair at the back, with forehead-concealing bangs and long pointed sideburnlike locks in front of the ears. Long straight hair, falling over the cheeks, was also worn with long bangs. There were towering coifs made up of huge round curls, fantastically arranged loop braids, straggling corkscrew curls worn for festive formal occasions, and severe styles with the hair pulled taut from the face and arranged into an inverted roll high on the back of the head. This type of coif was held in place by a broad flat bow placed beneath the roll at the base of the skull. Curls with a forehead-encircling bandeau, long braids, and waist-length falls of false hair were also popular. Infant and Brutus coifs were fashioned from the wearer's natural hair or carefully attended wigs. Wigs became the vogue in the early 1960s and were carefully matched to the natural hair or made of synthetic fibers in garish colors. False hairpieces or falls were also used extensively. Wig shops, similar to the shops of the seventeenth and eighteenth century perruquier, where wigs could be purchased, shampooed, and set, sprang up on streets, in shopping centers, and in major department stores. Another coif fad of the 1960s was changing the natural color by the use of dyes. Henna rinses and peroxide had been used throughout the three previous decades, and in the mid-forties a lavender rinse was used to give life to gray hair. During the late 1950s and on into the 1960s, every conceivable hair dye color was available, and many women, young and

frosting

old, used them. "Frosting," touching dark hair in random spots with bleach, was yet another coif fad.

SUITS
(1940-1969)
Men
business suit

zoot suit

Men's business suits of the 1940s had very broad shoulders, heavily padded to add breadth. The suit coats were long, single- or double-breasted, and buttoned at the waistline or slightly above. They were designed with flat collars and broad lapels. Trousers were full in the leg with rather deep pleats on either side at the waist extending into the center trouser crease. An exaggeration of the double-breasted business suit, called the zoot suit, was affected by some of the more eccentrically dressed young men. This suit consisted of a thigh-length double-breasted coat with huge pointed lapels and peg-top trousers, very full at the waist and tapered to a cuff so narrow that it was often difficult to get the foot through the opening. Zoot suits were usually made in rather garish colors, while the normal man's business costume was more conservative in coloring. While retaining the same general characteristics, men's suits during the 1950s and 1960s were modified in breadth of trouser legs, size and shape of lapels, and width of shoulders. The double-breasted coat style disappeared in the fifties, to be reintroduced during the late 1960s. Trouser legs became very slender, and an Edwardian or Italian cut was the fashion. During the individualistic period of the 1960s, flared cuffs, longer suit coats, Nehru suits (single breasted suits with small standing collars) and other innovative details were introduced into men's costumes. Waistcoats reappeared and were as decorative as their predecessors. They were single or double-breasted and designed with plain collarless V-necklines or trimmed with small collars and lapels. The revival of vests and waistcoats followed a decade when neither had been worn except by older men. During the 1950s men's suits were extremely conservative in styling and color. The grey flannel suit became a "uniform" of young executives for nearly a decade. However, color, which had originally been reserved for men's sports clothes, was introduced in the 1960s and ranged from rich subdued hues to brilliant and vibrant colors. Both business suits and sports or casual clothes were styled from colorful, man-made fabrics. The more flamboyant dandies (called the "In Group" or "The Beautiful People") of the latter years of the sixties affected velvet suit jackets and shirts with ruffled fronts, cuffs, and jabots. These were cut like either the eighteenth century justaucorps or the Nehru jacket. Trousers were worn low on the hips and trimmed with wide

Suit and vest (1969)

Nehru suits

waistcoat
vest

Turtle neck shirt and sack suit (1968)

sport coat
slacks

Double-breasted blazer (1968)

shirts

turtle neck
polo shirt

T-shirt
sport shirts
ties

Car coat (1960s)

leather belts with large decorative buckles. Striped, plain, or patterned materials in brilliant blues, dark wine reds, and burnt oranges were used in making these trousers. A jumpsuit with a sleeveless sack suit coat was proposed for airplane travel. The total effect of this costume was that of a conservative sack suit. The long-sleeved bodice section of the one-piece jumpsuit created a waistcoat when worn with the coat.

Beginning during the war when fabrics for suiting were in short supply, the sport coat or jacket and slacks were accepted as street apparel and for business. These garments continued in fashion after the war and were modified in cut and tailoring as the standard business suits' details changed. The jackets were usually tweed and the slacks gabardine or other smooth finish materials of natural or man made fibers. Slim trousers or sports slacks were worn low on the hips, creating a long-waisted appearance. Belts were slender or nonexistent accessories for these styles by the middle 1960s. The center trouser leg crease was eliminated during the period when very tight trousers were in fashion. Trouser cuffs, which had been discarded during the war, were reintroduced during the 1950s and again eliminated for a time during the 1960s.

Men's shirts were altered slightly in design, the long pointed fold-down collars being the details that changed most noticeably. During the fifties, collars were smaller and either rounded or pointed. These "Ivy League" shirts were made of a wide variety of fabrics from madras to drip-dry blends of acetate fabrics. They were styled with long or short sleeves, French or plain cuffs and button-down collars. The casual shirts were styled in a number of handsome and intricate designs, including: the conventional type fastened in front from collar to waist; turtle neck styles; polo or golf shirts made of knit material; deep yoke shirts with an unbuttoned diagonal neck opening; and colorful plain or horizontally striped T-shirts. Sport shirts were generally worn without ties, though the wide long ties of the 1940s were worn when the sport shirts were first introduced. Ties of the 1950s became quite slender and were elegant neckwear accessories. Other tie style variations included: the thong tie with sliding guide; the bow tie, which was very narrow until the late 1960s; the early nineteenth century string tie; the crossed and buttoned simplified version of the neckcloth; and the square or pointed-end knit or

Golf sweater and sports slacks (late 1950s)

figured tie, tied either in a large Windsor or four-in-hand knot. Soft, loosely tied scarfs and ascot cravats were also worn by some men.

formal suits

Formal clothes, tailored to meet the demands of current fashions (collar, lapel, and trouser size as well as coat length) included: the tuxedo, formal tail suit, lounge suit, and dinner jacket. The morning suit with cutaway, striped trousers, and grey waistcoat was used for formal morning functions. During the 1950s and 1960s, men's tuxedo jackets were made from a variety of dark decorative fabrics. Lapels were faced with watered taffeta or brocaded material and tuxedo coat sleeves were often styled with small cuffs that matched the lapel facings. Cummerbunds with matching ties and ruf-fled and tucked dress shirts were some of the evening wear innovations of the 1960s.

dress shirts

SPORT CLOTHES
Men
  swim trunks
  surfers
  bikini suits

Men's sport clothes were functional and decorative. The swim trunks of the late 1930s were modified in leg length and ranged from thigh-length boxer shorts swim trunks to calf-length surfers. Men also wore abbreviated bikini swim trunks. All of these styles were made of plain colored cotton fiber fabrics or man-made fiber materials in gay and bright patterns.

  slacks
  jackets
  golf sweaters
  ski suits
  Levi's
  jeans
  windbreakers

Sports costumes included: slacks and jackets; jumpsuits, one-piece cotton suits in a wide range of colors; ski suits; Levi's; jeans; golf sweaters; and windbreakers, intricately cut (with attached hoods) made of either nylon or woolen materials.

WRAPS
(1940-1969)
Men

During the 1940s men's overcoats were long, straight knee-length coats with raglan or inset, rather wide sleeves. They had flat collars and were usually single-breasted. As suit coat lengths were shortened, men's overcoats were also made with shorter skirts. During the late 1950s and 1960s, car coats, with or without attached hoods, became popular. These were often fleece-lined, thigh-length coats fastened with large buttons, brass hook devices, or heavy commercial zippers. Men's cold weather wraps for formal wear continued to include the Chesterfield with a velvet collar. During the 1960s, overcoats with beaver collars and fur coats made from skins of real animals or imitation furs became the fashion. The detail styling of these coats was similar to that of their cloth overcoat counterparts.

Fur overcoat

ACCESSORIES
Men
 jewelry
  watches

Wrist watches replaced the larger pocket watches by the 1930s and continued in fashion for the next two decades. They were stem-wound or self-winding, with calendars and alarm devices, and were generally made in thin oblong shapes. Stretch metal bracelets or leather strap watchbands were used to hold them about the wrists. Late in the 1960s, the watchbands increased in size and some were two inches or more wide. Identification bracelets made with a rectangular plate and large link chains were accessories for younger men. During the era of the "hippies" and "flower children," men affected "love beads," a single strand of small stone or glass beads, and pendant necklaces made either of a leather thong with a stone or metal pendant or a heavy chain with a metal pendant. The popular peace symbols or emblems of various ethnic religious movements were the design devices used for the pendant segments of these rather bold, masculine neckwear accessories.

  bracelets

  love beads
  necklaces

  rings
  earrings

Most men wore rings of conventional types. Small gold earrings, usually only one, were worn by some through a pierced ear.

 headwear
  fedora
  homburg
  straw
  boater

During the 1940s most men wore hats and these included the conventional styles: the felt fedora, the homburg, and the straw boater. These hats had smaller brims and shallower crowns than those of the previous decades. During the 1950s, the straw boater was replaced by a tall crowned, small brimmed straw hat made much like the felt fedora. The latter was worn during the winter as well as the Russian style of fur cap, the leather billed cap, and the ear-flap, billed cap. Most young men did not wear head coverings in the summer but during the winter months of the 1940s and 1950s, they wore the shallow flat-crowned porkpie hat. Later they wore brush-trimmed Tyrolean felt hats, caps, and Russian fur hats.

  Russian
  fur cap
  leather
  billed cap
  porkpie hat
  Tyrolean
  hat

 footwear

Men's shoes did not change much throughout the 1940s. They were either low-cut oxfords or variations of the saddle shoe. During the 1950s and 1960s, a wide variety of types were available, ranging from the casual moccasin type loafer to calf-high boots. Toes were round during the forties, gradually becoming more pointed and changing to squared-off toes during the latter years of the 1960s. Formal shoes were made of black patent leather with flat bows on the instep in low cut slipper styles. These formal shoes had leather soles, as did many of the other types, but rubber crepe soles, smooth rubber soles, and rubber soles with deep V-grooves were also used.

sandals

Men as well as women wore a variety of sandals including single-strap types, complex multistrap styles patterned after Mexican sandals or ancient Roman footwear, and woven (leather strips or straw) toed scuff sandals.

HAIR STYLES
(1940-1969)
Men

For the greater part of this three-decade period men worn their hair short, brushed from a part or in a slight pompadour. During the 1950s, younger men wore the closely shaven crew cut. However, at the end of the 1960s, men let their hair grow longer, grew long sideburns, and also affected beards. Many of the "hippies" or "flower children" let their hair grow to shoulder length, never cutting or shaping it and seldom washing or combing it. Younger more fastidious men, however, had their hair professionally groomed by hair stylists, who curled it, shaped it, and lacquered it with as much care as stylists did female coifs. Many of the longer hair styles for men were imitative of those worn during the romantic period of the nineteenth century, while others were reminiscent of the seventeenth century.

Additional pictorial resources

Visual resources may be found in bound copies or back issues of such fashion periodicals as *Vogue; Harper's Bazaar; Town and Country; Esquire; Gentleman's Quarterly; Playboy; Women's Wear Daily;* and *Men's Wear Daily.*

PART II   FASHION DESIGN

Gown design based on historic references (combination Renaissance and French Empire modes) presented in a finished illustration using mixed media, watercolor and pencil

Chapter 20

APPROACHES TO THE DESIGN OF COSTUMES

THROUGHOUT history, fashion has reflected the evolving social structure of civilization. During many periods, it has been an important factor in creating employment for many with specific skills and contributing to a country's economic stability. In the United States, fashion, including design, production, and reporting of trends, assumes a position as one of the largest industries in the country. An affluent society is an important consumer of the products of this industry, though the reasonableness of the interest in fashion is questionable. The economic impact of fashion cannot, however, be

279

overlooked. Consideration of the numbers of people dependent on the transient whims of fashion must include an awareness of the contribution they make to the gross national product. People directly or indirectly related to the fashion market include: designers, manufacturers, wholesalers, "jobbers," retail merchants, retail sales forces, employees of trade and metropolitan newspapers, dependent on retail advertising; and the sophisticated fashion periodicals and the artists and editorial staffs they employ. It also offers an outlet for the creative individual whose medium of expression is pliable fabric rather than paint or stone.

Designers from the time of Rose Bertin, fashioner of gowns for Marie Antoinette, to Mary Quant, the darling of Carnaby Street, have been accomplished drapers and molders of the materials of fashion—fabrics, laces, feathers, plastics, or materials made from man-made fibers. These designers and others, such as Worth, Doucet, Dior, Pucci, Lanvin, Galinos, and Balenciaga, were not only able to manipulate these materials in exciting and innovative ways but were sensitive to women's fashion whims. They, like Yves St. Laurents, Vionnet, Paquin, Schiaparelli, Norell, and Molyneux, were aware of the trends in the visual arts of their specific eras. They were also conscious of fashions of the past, costumes of ethnic groups, and exotic cultures.

Designers with talent and perception have combined their knowledge, experience, and awareness and have been guided by the aesthetic concepts of their times. The graceful garments seen in a Watteau painting or the classical styles depicted by David were representative of their age in the same way as the psychedelic patterns and mini-maxi fashions of our own time. Creative and sensitive designers willingly use new materials and have learned their potentials and limitations. Perceptive designers are also aware that costuming the human form is a design problem in three dimensions. They have

Quick pencil sketches drawn over figure templates visualizing three views of a gown concept

been conscious of the sculptural qualities of their creations. They have understood that the clothed human figure must also move in established activity patterns. These activity patterns are related to the actions required by the occasion, and the ball gown functions differently from the tennis dress. Different eras have prescribed differing activity patterns. Costumes of the Renaissance, the eighteenth century, and recent times were designed and structured according to the limitations or license allowed by society's mores. The successful designer melds all of these considerations when attacking the problem of creating attractive clothing.

The problems involved in designing for figure articulation combine with other factors that discipline the creativity of a costume designer. Basically functional, a costume must satisfy four demands: visual totality, action and movement possibility, personality classifications, and figure types. These demands act as controls which must be understood in their entirety. Properly used, they combine to allow movement, enhance the figure, and extend the personality of the wearer. Personality communication, by means of the superficial medium of costumes, is a difficult task in an age of mass-produced clothing. It is, however, one of the ways people clarify and identify themselves to others around them. The haut couturier has a less com-

The same gown illustrated in a technique suitable for representing costumes designed for the cinema. Note change in fabric texture from satin (page 279) to velvet (page 281)

plex task in creating identity-establishing costumes, for he often designs for a limited clientele which he knows well. The designer working for a wholesale manufacturer, however, creates for a cross section of the population. He must study people, become aware of the many personality traits, and create costumes that generalize these traits. He must evolve a list of traits, establish broad personality classifications, and combine them with a knowledge of figure types. It is important to him that he consider the existence of the many possible combinations. Through the use of line to establish the silhouette the designer commits his costume to the generalized needs of a wide range of figure types. He selectively uses linear proportion to refine his basic concepts of the final totality of his creation. With the selection of a limited range of colors, values, and textures he injects personality indicators into his design. Finally, by careful detailing, he creates a garment that incorporates subtle personality indicators. A costume thoughtfully planned will appeal to a broad range of prospective buyers.

The designer must make seasonal design changes because of the importance of fashion sales to the success of the business community in which he operates. Innovation is the essence of costume design and by it a demand is created in the fashion market place. This places a fifth control upon the creative activity of the designer. One of his most difficult tasks is to satisfy these five controls and remain faithful to his own creative sensitivity. New creative ideas emerge after the fashion artist has analyzed many significant factors. He weighs the foremost and rising concerns and the universal topical matters of the day. Next he must become familiar with the availability of new fabrics, their colors, textures, and patterns. He must determine if the figure emphasis area will be retained for another season, modified, or a totally new one established. He reviews the acceptance of the previous season's styling trends, specifically and in general. He attempts to determine if the buying public is bored with a silhouette or skirt length. He reflects on the sociological and philosophical concepts of the past that are fusing with the attitudes of his contemporaries. He does research in the areas of costume history, contemporary painting, and sculpture as well as in disciplines unrelated to his own. Consciously and subconsciously he organizes this information, combining it with his past experience. At last he is ready to translate this material into visual form, the designs for costumes he feels will meet the interests of the fickle fashion purchasers. This is but one approach, one means by which new styles are born. Many creative designers intuitively produce innovative and provocative costumes each season, driven by an inner motivation. Their perception is inherent and their designs spontaneously produced. Many select a theme derived from a specific culture with dominant characteristics. Others create for a specific personality, perhaps a model or a celebrity, whose type and appeal is unique and admired. Every successful designer, however, must have the ability to assess the future wants and needs of the public for which he designs. His skill in anticipating such demands also determines his success, for his work begins months before his creations are presented to the fashion editors and fashion buyers for their acceptance and then make their appearance in the marketplace.

The designer who is part of the motion picture industry has a number of controls and procedures that are totally unlike those imposed on the designer creating for the ready-to-wear field. The designer who creates for the cinema must extend the images of the characters involved by the costume designs he produces. In times past, the "star" demanded that the personality he had established must also be incorporated (in subtle or obvious ways) into the costume he wore as he played a specific role. The success or failure of a movie often depended on the "type casting" of certain "box office favorites." Designers for movies laid in the present had to anticipate fashion and be as aware of new trends as commercial designers, since movies took many months to produce. Currently films appear with less time lapse between "shooting" and "release" and therefore this is not now as important a factor. If the plot is laid in the past, the designer must have a complete knowledge of the history of costume and do exhaustive research in order to produce faithful copies of costumes of an exact period. The designer must also relate the clothing of minor players to the costumes of the stars, yet keep them subordinate. The mood of the film is projected to the audience through the hue (color), value (dark on light), and chroma (intensity of color) of the costume fabrics. The designer of costumes to be worn in black-and-white films must achieve characterization without the support of color symbolism to aid in the translation of the role to the viewer.

The theater designer has the same limitations as those placed on film designers and at the same time the opportunity for more creativity. In the presentation of legitimate drama the designer depends on illusion. Unlike the superrealism of the cinema, the stage performance communicates plot and characterization to the audience more directly in an intimate theater situation with live actors. Designers for the stage are in part responsible, through the color, line, and texture of the costumes, for the involvement of actor and audience. The theater costume artist has the added advantage of using the properties of colored lights. By changing the colored gel filters, both the mood of the set and the colors of the costumes of the actors on the stage can be altered. Another consideration often important to legitimate stage costuming involves quick costume changes. An actor's role may demand that in the scene sequence he appear within minutes in diametrically opposed situations. Costumes devised to "break away" or that can be totally revised by "snap-on" parts must be created to assist the players in presenting two differing illusions.

Theater, film, and television designers must be familiar with the design of the set before which the play is staged. Costumes must not contradict, compete with, or be subordinate to the sets. The illusion-making aspects of the dramatic presentations of stage or cinema are unobtrusively supported by the costumes. The inherent qualities of a play, a musical, an opera, or a ballet can be extended by the fanciful and personal visualizations of the costume artist who thoroughly understands the essence of the production. The total design of every scene depends on the visual interpretation of each character, the relation of one character to another, the scene mood established by the set, and the interrelation of these facets of the production. Ulti-

Quick color sketches for ballet costume designs

mately, the costumes and the sets are obligated to support the players, not surfeit their interpretations of their roles. The demands upon the designer working in the performing arts are exacting. He must have a knowledge of the history of costume, theater production techniques (including the potentials and limitations of lighting), and a sound background in dramatic interpretation. He must be creative, inventive, and sensitive so that he can properly present the necessary illusions ranging from scenes of poverty to elegant fantasies.

The designer working with a sketching technique as a means of presenting design concepts may proceed in a number of ways. Many working in the area of mass-produced garments develop a figure template. This usually includes three different figure poses, a frontal view, a side or three-quarter view, and a back or three-quarter back view. These templates may be drawn on heavy paper using a bold

Near cartoon style used in representing personalities of characters through costumes for the leads in "Roar of the Grease Paint, Smell of the Crowd"

line or may be made of thin cardboard and cut out. By tracing around the latter or over the former using vellum, quick figure indications can be established. Over these roughly indicated figures, the designer begins to "create" by establishing the general silhouette of the costume. Having determined the proportions and exterior character of a costume, he may then establish the position of construction details (darts, tucks, or pleats) necessary to make the fabric conform to the silhouette desired. These construction details must conform to the proportional relationships established by the silhouette. The designer next determines the size and shape of details such as collar, cuffs, neckline, pockets and fastening devices. He refines the shapes of these and perhaps alters the sleeve shape, waist width and height, skirt length, and shoulder breadth. He may also indicate intricate pattern details in the bodice, skirt, or sleeves. These details and the inventive shapes he creates for the collar, neckline, and cuffs, make a garment unique. At the termination of the initial steps of producing a new costume, the garment must function to clothe the human form and create a total unit of the figure and its articulating parts.

Many designers, of course, never sketch but rather drape a dummy or model. In either case, sketch or draped dress-dummy, the designer's visualized costume ideas become the "blueprint" from which the final garment is made. Pattern drafters take the sketches, determine the pattern shapes necessary, and make up a toile. Proficient designers are also able to do this. However, many make simple rough drawings while others carefully redraw each idea, continuing to refine the designs and paint them with a water-soluble medium. A quick and uncomplicated technique for painting fashion sketches includes the following procedures: the designer, using photographs rather than the figure template, and working on vellum over them, sets down his costume design concepts. When satisfied with these preliminary drawings, he transfers them to smooth finish illustration board. The simple steps in painting include: flat wash indicating skin tone, gradually lightening the color and drawing it into the areas covered by the garment; flat wash indicating basic garment color; addition of contrasting colors, if any, in collar, cuffs, belt, or other trimming; indication of hair color and coif; and, lastly, pencil or pen lines to indicate darts, tucks, pleats, or trimming details. The most easily mastered technique is the use of flat washes of color in an opaque medium. A more accurate impression of the designer's creative intentions is, of course, obtained through modeling, or limited indications of dark and light passages that occur because of the draping or pleating. The generalization of fabric textures by the use of mixed media, or the skillful handling of one medium, assists in establishing the designer's total creative concepts. However, the design intent must not be destroyed by over-manipulation. A clear, concise sketch will relate garment construction facts directly and convey more completely the unique details devised. Actual swatches of the fabric to be used, in the range of colors that are compatible to the silhouette and interior line design, are preferred to a poorly painted sketch.

Drawings and water color sketches prepared for theatrical costumes are often prepared in a free, flamboyant style. Many different media are used, and the attempt is more the visual illusion of the character than a photographic representation of the design in paint. The latter technique is, however, required for the preparation of sketches of costumes to be worn in a film. More exact sketches are needed because of the many people involved in approving the costumes' final form, including the stars, the director, the set designer, and the producer. These sketches are usually prepared by a sketch artist rather than the designer. They are painted with great attention to detail on figures that are miniature portraits (or nearly so) of the actors and actresses who will wear them.

Pressures upon the costume designer from exterior factors make his creative tasks exacting. In any of the fields of this applied art— haute couture, mass-produced ready-to-wear, theater, films, or television—the creative artist must meet the requirements of the industry while maintaining his identity as a creative individual. It is a demanding craft that requires of the artist talent, the intellectual capacity for research, an awareness of his period, and a sense of business.

PART III   **FASHION ILLUSTRATION**

Nineteenth century fashion sketch, meticulously detailed and full of innocent charm (from author's print collection)

Chapter 21

THE FASHION IMAGE, REPORT, AND RECORD

FASHION illustration and fashion photography report contemporary modes and function as a visual record for the future. These transient images of a changing facet of civilization are as necessary to the success of the fashion industry as the costume designs themselves. By the means of these drawings, the new, the different, and the chic are quickly communicated visually.

Fashion reporting is not a modern phenomenon, for during the eighteenth century means of communicating fashion news were

291

devised. The first fashion news medium was a pair of dolls, Big and Little Pandora. The former was dressed in miniature copies of court and ball gowns, while the latter was dressed in daytime costumes. These dolls were sent from Paris by courier to the royal courts throughout Europe, and their passage from country to country was given such high priority that battles were halted to insure their safe conduct through the lines. Bound fashion periodicals first appeared in the 1770s; one of them bore the masthead, *Galerie des Modes et Costumes Francais*. At the time of the introduction of the fashion magazine, Paris was the center of the fashion world, so it is understandable that the greatest number were published in that city. In addition to *Galerie des Modes, La Mode, Journal des Dames, Journals des Gens du Monde*, and the English version of *Galerie des Modes, Gallery of Fashion*, were published and edited exclusively for women interested in the current vogue. *Journal des Luxus der Moden*, edited by Bertuch in Weimar, Germany, was first introduced to the fashion-conscious public of that country in 1786. Nineteenth century fashion periodicals of English origin were *The Repository, The Lady*, and *The Queen*, while in the United States during the same century *Godey's Lady's Book* and *Peterson's Magazine* appeared. In most cosmopolitan centers, where fashion was important to the "ruling society," periodicals, topically oriented to the vogue of the day, were published. This was true of eighteenth century Vienna, where *Wiener Modes* was published for the edification of the fashion-conscious females of that romantic city. During the 1850s, *Harper's Magazine* devoted an extensive section, illustrated with fine line engravings, to fashion. Since the turn of the century the ranks of fashion publications have increased. They are also specialized, directing their editorial content to specific age and economic groupings. Most recently these publications have been dedicated to the young, whose rather exotic tastes offer editors, artists, and photographers more experimental potential. Unlike the earlier publications, modern mechanical reproduction processes assist the creative artists. These newer methods allow the artists and photographers the opportunity to explore new and unique ways of communicating visually. Early fashion periodicals were limited in reproducing full color illustrations, and many colored drawings were laboriously painted by hand. The skill with which these plates were drawn, reproduced, and then hand-tinted is remarkable. They remain an explicit record of the past, created by artists who were sensitive to the period in which they lived and worked.

The drawing style used by the artists making a visual report for the early fashion magazines showed little evidence of individuality or experimentation. The line was controlled, the poses were static, and the facial expressions were full of innocent charm. The docile nature of the eighteenth or nineteenth century female was explicitly conveyed by the fashion image. Attention was given to the depiction of femininity and coquetry. Generally, the techniques employed by nineteenth century fashion illustrators involved the massing of dark and grey areas by crosshatching or a series of small dot patterns. Contours of faces were defined by a rigid wire line. The representations of the garments were extremely realistic, with only a small amount of exaggeration or proportional adjustments to give emphasis

the illusion of demure linear attitude of women created in 1849 illustration from *Godey's Lady's Book* (from author's print collection)

to unique details. Laces, ruffles, bows, and other trimmings were carefully drawn. The figures of early illustrations were often placed in explicitly defined environments. The mood, activity, and wearing situation were thus carefully explained visually. In the 1849 sketch included in this text, the artist has slightly exaggerated the bell skirt to bring attention to the dominant silhouette of that year. The decolletage assumed a secondary role but remained a detail of the fashions of the day. After the costume news had been reported, the artist made the viewer aware of the environment. The low, pointed waistline was established as a central focus and from this point the artist developed a viewing sequence dependent on his use of line, value, and color. The power of the artist to "lead" his viewers through his illustration in sequence was achieved by developing points of tension. This is one of the means used in ordering space, composing the figure within that space and relating, visually, information concerning a specific costume. These tensions attract the eye in the desired order by establishing dominant and subordinate contrasting passages. The dominant areas retain interest, while the subordinate areas function as transitional passages.

In the evolutionary development of the fashion image, a number of different styles and techniques were employed. Many were directly related to the aesthetic concepts and techniques used by painters of the period in which the fashion drawings were made. During the early seventeenth century, when fashion plates were a means of distributing fashion news, the drawings were adapted to the techniques of woodcuts and engravings. In the eighteenth century, such renowned painters as Watteau created handsome fashion drawings that were characteristic of their own style of painting. The fashion folio, *Degli Habiti antichi e moderni* (1590), was illustrated by Titian's grandson, Cesare Vecellio, in a style typical of his age. The linear attitude (or

Environment subordinated to intricate garment detail (1835: from author's print collection)

pose) in every period of fashion illustration reflects the posturing attitudes of that age. Through the linear attitude, the viewer relates to the figure and costume in the drawing. The 1835 fashion sketch shown here establishes a pose that creates interest and specifically draws attention to the upper area of the illustration. A horizontal sight pattern, or viewing sequence, is developed through the area of the neckline of the central figure. This is reinforced by the contrasting diagonal movements of the coyly gesturing arms of the central figure. As the entire drawing is "read," the environmental situation is noted and attention given to costume and coif details. Tensions determined by repetition of skirt and coif shapes cause the focal interest to shift, creating a closure between these forms. Thus a total review of the illustration is demanded by the arrangement of the elements of the composition. The drawing style, figure, pose and compositional arrangement communicate the period as well as explicit fashion information.

A similar visual statement is made by the illustration from *Modes Parisiennes* of 1860, published by Herman T. Meyer. This illustration of afternoon gowns depends on its compositional order by interrelating the forms of the skirts and the forms of the furniture and the parasol. The sight pattern passes over the bodices of the gowns, their details, and finally to the gown skirts.

Sight pattern established by gown, gestures, and environmental detail (from author's print collection)

National attitudes were also apparent in the drawing styles used during the nineteenth century. Facial expression and feature differences are readily discernible by comparing the illustration from *Modes Parisiennes* and the drawing from *Allgemeine Modenzeitung* of the same decade. Nationalistic traits are also apparent in the illustrations from *Gazette de la Famille* (1890) of gay frivolous children at the seashore and the drawing of the stolid children's group that appeared in *Illustrirte Frauen-Zeitung* in 1893. There is an obvious difference in the attitude toward the French children, set in a carefree environment, and the dutiful German children shown performing the pedestrian task of putting on coats. Differences are apparent in the drawings of adults. These differences are visualized through the exterior contours of the faces and the definition of the eyes. In the reproduction from *Allgemeine Modenzeitung*, the expression is generally straightforward and direct, while the one from *Godey's Lady's Book* is demure, and that from the unknown French publication of 1835 depicts three coquettish ladies. The linear attitude supports the types represented by the differing expressions on the faces. The drawing technique is similar in that all three rely on crosshatching

Gay frivolous French children from *Gazette de la Famille* (from author's print collection)

Allgemeine Modenzeitung **sketch graphically illustrated nationalistic traits (1860: from author's print collection)**

to establish shadow areas. However, here the similarity ends. The drawing style of the French illustration is imaginative and sophisticated. The use of the crosshatch technique in the *Godey's Lady's Book* is blunt and the figures clumsily drawn. The German illustration appears to have been drawn by several different artists, with the central figure and the one on the extreme right showing the greatest dexterity in handling the problems of figure drawing and manipulation of the medium. The male figures in the *Godey's* illustration add to the mood of the scene and help to develop a charming compositional pattern. The aloof, stalwart German male functions to no compositional advantage but does reinforce the male attitude toward women in that country.

Stolid children as seen in an illustration from *Illustrirte Frauenzeitung* (1893: from author's print collection)

Photographic realism attempted (*Godey's Lady's Book*, 1869: from author's print collection)

By 1869, artists were attempting to achieve photographic realism in their fashion illustrations. In the reproduction taken from an unknown publication of that year, the gowns and faces are carefully modeled. The room setting is explicit, including the pattern in the carpet and the items in the cupboard. This interest in realistic representation continued for some time, as the drawing from an 1871 copy of *La Mode Illustrée* indicates. The forms were defined by gradually shaded areas of refined and controlled crosshatching. These shaded areas were important to the composition as well as to form definition. The eyes and mouth were carefully modeled and the expression that resulted was sad and sentimental.

During the 1880s, linear attitude and figure posturing became more brittle. The attempt at photographic realism continued, but was destroyed by the awkwardness of the poses. Frontal and side views were incongruously combined in one figure, as the illustration from the July 1884 issue of *Peterson's Magazine* indicates. Details were so distinct that they were no longer part of the figure but separate projecting decorations. The fashion artists of this period completely disregarded figure-ground relationships. Yet, for all the figure distortions

Forms carefully defined by shading in
La Mode Illustrée sketch of 1871 (from
author's print collection)

and lack of skill in composing the space, there is a charm in this group that defies the obvious errors. The mood is set, the era depicted, and the gown defined. The age and the costumes still communicate and lend credence to the necessity for deviation in figure indication in a fashion illustration. Exaggeration of figure distortion, to point up emphasis areas, continued into the twentieth century. The illustration from *La Mode Illustrée* emphasizes the pouter pigeon bosom by a sweeping curve and small waist. The figure is also elongated, adding grace to it and the slightly flared skirt. The unknown artist who created this sketch had a flair for selecting the areas of importance, the delicate detail, the silhouette, and the pose. Situation paraphernalia was eliminated and the single figure illustration was introduced.

Figure proportions and posture distorted to emphasize fashion in an illustration of Paris modes from an 1884 issue of *Peterson's Magazine* (from author's print collection)

Pose of *La Mode Illustrée* drawing exaggerates pouter pigeon bodice to enhance linear attitude (from author's print collection)

Charles Dana Gibson sketch of early 1900s (from author's print collection)

During the 1900s, while the drawing of faces retained an idealized realism, the figure was distorted to emphasize the exaggeration of the body form dictated by the design of the costume. Charles Dana Gibson injected into his drawing subtle, witty, and often satirical visual comments by the deft manipulation of his pen. The elegant ladies he sketched with their refined features and sweet expressions were at the same time haughty and aloof. He created the elegance of the Gibson Girl era by a changing linear weight, outlining the figure with a thin controlled line and defining shadows by adding pressure to the pen stroke, increasing the width of the line. He was perhaps the first to use this type of linear development in fashion sketches, though master artists had employed such expressive, flexible line for centuries.

Harsh brittle line used during the late 1920s (see Chapter 18 for sketching style of 1910s)

The slender hobble skirt that was introduced about 1913 did not lend itself to the drawing styles Gibson had developed. The effect of the change in costume design on drawing styles was dramatic. The simple straight silhouettes were better represented by a simplified drawing style. Printing techniques had also been refined and improved, and greater variety of pictorial representation of fashions was possible. Because of these new printing techniques, it was possible to reproduce costume news in color. The influence of Art Nouveau also directed the styles developed for fashion illustration. Stylized and simplified drawings using large flat areas of color and controlled curvilinear line were typical between the years 1910 and 1920. Figures in many of the fashion illustrations, such as those appearing

Figure elongation prevailed during the 1930s (see Chapter 18 for 1920s drawing style)

in *Journal des Dames et des Modes*, were posed in coy and mincing postures. Many were more like caricatures than drawings of fashion figures. However, some, like the drawings of Drian, were sensitive, the figures in action poses and thoughtfully placed within the space. When the rather startlingly new fashions of the flapper era were introduced, this style was modified. Sophistication was the theme of these drawings. They reflected the new social attitudes and costume styles and were stripped of romanticism and excessive decoration. During the 1920s, fashion illustrators showed tall, flat figures, using dark and light relationships copied from Japanese prints. Environmental details were often placed in the far distance. Others used the gradual shading of Rivera or the abstract shattering of background space characteristic of Marc or Feininger. Controlled fine line was introduced to indicate fabric draping, feature and contour delineation, or draw attention to costume details. Figure action was subordinate to the costume and hand gestures were stiff and placed in contrived positions.

By the end of this decade—and the tendency became more pronounced in the next—fashion illustrations were created with more flexible line and with dynamic fluid washes. Changes in dress design forced certain drawing technique adaptations, but the evolutionary development was slow. The tall, sleek designs created by Maggy Rouff were visualized by brisk lines, the figures extremely elongated and slenderized. The fashion artist Eric was perhaps the first to introduce this drawing style, developing a technique based on expressive line and fluid, changing washes. The fashion faces he depicted were softly feminine, in great contrast to the generally accepted style of 1929, when his drawings were first reproduced in *Vogue*. By the late 1930s, such fashion illustrators as Eric, R.B.W., and Grafstrom were creating fashion drawings with crisp lines and soft water color washes. The figures they drew had life, and there seemed to be a real body beneath the costumes. Nonfunctional linear treatment acted as transitional passages from figure to ground, the drawing surface.

Throughout the years of the Second World War, fashion illustrations began to show an artist's own style. This was in keeping with the bold, square-shouldered, masculine costumes of the period. The mood of the 1940s was a strange combination of sentimentality, conviction, and tenacity. The fashion artists reflected these moods in drawings that included a masculine silhouette, ridiculous hats, and long flowing hair or severely upswept coifs. The creative techniques explored during the previous years became the established style. There was more personal expression, and individual identifiable styles were developed. The new silhouette introduced by the Dior "New Look" and the creative designs of Fath, Givenchy, Coco Chanel, and Emilio Schubert during the 1950s added new possibilities. Fashion artists of this period were caught up in the art movements of Abstract Expressionism and the New York School of Painting. Dynamic, action-oriented statements created by bold lines with calligraphic characteristics were made by the perceptive and sensitive illustrators.

Fashion illustration was at its zenith between 1940 and 1953. It was during this time that artists created masterful figure representations

Soft sophisticated elegance of the 1950s

A.

B.

C.

through personally directed drawing styles. These visual fashion reports were reproduced in the important fashion magazines of America and Europe. The editorial pages of these periodicals were the primary visual outlet for the more imaginative and creative fashion drawings. Each artist was selected because of his ability and his sensitive interpretations of the current vogue. Freedom of creative expression was given impetus by astute fashion editors and art directors. These creative people of the leading fashion publications established a high standard of taste which was extended by the visual and verbal reports in their magazines. Drawings by Bouché, Eric, Vertés, and R.B.W. graphically extended the selective directions established in the editorial section. Painters also contributed to the zenith period of fashion art, designing creative and provocative cover illustrations. This roster of contributing artists included such prominent names as Dali, Berman, Bérard, and Beaton. In the case of the first three, the most successful covers they designed were based on modified concepts of Surrealism. Each artist interpreted the fashion face on his own terms. These terms were consistent with the social trends of the period and therefore communicated visually to the limited and sophisticated readership of the periodicals. In each of the covers the artist used the limitations of the magazine's format to advantage. Each element of the design was introduced to perform a specific space organizing function. The forms created were introduced after a careful evaluation of the proportions of the format and functioned in relation to them. The linear style of each artist served to further the organizational compatibility of the parts. Whether the motivation was intuitive or thoughtfully intellectual, unity of design existed in each.

The "time-taste" may be lasting or transient, depending on the cultural concepts of a period. The three *Vogue* covers, with a time lapse of nine years between the first and the last, illustrate that fashion is founded on a changing aesthetic base. The Bérard design for the March 1, 1938, issue, the Dali design for the April 1, 1944, issue, and the Berman design for the May 15, 1947, issue present vastly different images of the female face. Yet these same cover designs show that each artist had a concern for compositional order and an awareness of the attitudes current at the time he created his cover design. Berman composed his illustrations symmetrically, and Dali and Bérard employed an asymmetric order. They all capitalized on fantasy to extend the concepts of fashion, specifically defining the period by the treatment and character of the line.

Master artists who have contributed to the field of fashion (illustrations from *Vogue*)
A. Bérard—*Vogue* cover (March 1, 1938)
B. Dali—*Vogue* cover (April 1, 1944)
C. Berman—*Vogue* cover (May 15, 1947)

A Beaton illustration of Wallis Warfield Simpson done in 1936 was created with dynamic refinement. The planned, orderly use of personally expressive linear statement defines the central figure, her environment, and the artist's reaction to them both. This illustration was created during a period of fashion art when a refined selective visual statement of the costume, the personality of the individual represented, and the forceful inventive reactions of the artist were interrelated. Other artists whose work was based on this interrelation include: René Gruau, René Willaumez, Bouché, Vertés, and Eric. Gruau's style, derivative in part from Toulouse-Lautrec, was based on masterful draftsmanship visualized by strong exterior line. His illustrations were an elegant interpretation of ladies dressed in chic costumes, with little or no environmental reference, but with a conscious ordering of space. His figure-ground relationships were meticulously arranged by posing the figure in postures that were compatible to the proportions of the space. He specifically defined important details and generalized areas with little significance to the visual report he was making. He was a master of understatement.

In the evolution of visual fashion reporting, René Willaumez bridged the social changes that occurred between 1930 and 1950 by adjusting his personal drawing style. The fashion figures he sketched, however, retained a refined sophistication achieved by careful manipulation of wash and line. The moods of his drawings were established by the facial images he created, using slight and delicate lines and wash areas. The costumes being presented dominated the drawing and were defined by brisk confident strokes. An excellent draftsman, he introduced distortions of figure proportions which were complimentary to the totality of the illustration. All of the elements he used—brisk line, delicate line, and dynamically manipulated washes—united to communicate the desired visual messages. With line alone he was able to create the illusion of a moving figure and each stroke had a significant part in establishing that illusion. The linear style he used was modified throughout his career, changing from blunt short strokes of the brush to strokes that were more continuous, expanding and contrasting in weight.

Gruau establishes forms and details by lines with contrast and linear continuum (illustration from *Vogue*)

Mood and maturity of model established
by RBW (René Willaumez): (1950s, illustration from *Vogue*)

The fashion illustrations of Eric serve as a classic example of excellence in this field. He adapted his drawing style to meet the changing demands of the fashion silhouette and changing social attitudes. However, the manner in which he interpreted fashion, his basic fashion concepts, did not alter radically. The chief characteristics of his drawings were refinement of form and a sensitive fine line. The advent of boldness of linear statement did not force Eric to abandon his delicate yet purposefully undulating line as it carefully described specific facts of gown and face. Simplification, understatement, and functional linear value changes were employed to establish the illusion of elegance. Manipulation of line and mass convincingly suggested attitude and pose. Cut and garment styling were seldom sacrificed for unique poses.

Bouché achieved a dynamic linear statement reflecting the vigor of Abstract Impressionism (1948 illustration from *Vogue*)

Bouché, who was prominent in the fashion art field for many years, adjusted and altered his style of drawing most drastically. He created his early sketches in a soft romantic manner, then developed a bold vigorous linear style, and ultimately returned to his original linear approach, retaining the vitality of his middle period. His earliest drawings were based on the manipulation of fluid water-color washes and fused linear statements with crisp line accents. The total effect was rhythmic and delicate. He was able to capture personality classifications, whether he was sketching celebrities or nameless fashion models. His last works were painterly portraits created to meet his own high aesthetic standards and his personal art concepts. In every sketch or painting the line, color, and values established contrasts that dynamically functioned to produce a masterful work.

Bouché sketch for *Vogue* develops a dynamic linear quality (1955 illustration from *Vogue*)

Vertés, unlike the other fashion artist masters, created sketches that made visual comments as well as fashion reports. His main purpose in his drawings was to capture the spirit and zest he felt reflected by women. His drawings were elegantly caustic, mirroring the attitudes of his female contemporaries. Vertés's spontaneous style was slashed with wit and whimsy. It was dynamic, direct, and often cruelly perceptive. He figuratively stripped women bare while drawing them clothed in the most chic fashions. Vertés and the fashion illustrators working during the zenith period of this field appealed to the psychological responses of the readers of their visual reports. They communicated fashion trends, set taste patterns and recorded a segment of time through their sketches, drawings and paintings. Each of these artists responded to the contemporary costume vogue in an exciting personal manner. The portrayal of these personal versions represented a dynamic innovation and departure from many earlier stereotyped fashion reports.

With the advent of the 1960s and the many social changes that took place, fashion drawings no longer served to communicate costume news as dynamically as in the past. Fashion photography was used to create exciting images of the action generation. Steichen and Beaton had explored the creative potentials of fashion photography many years before. During the 1960s the avant garde expressionist photographers and creative perceptive editors captured the fast-paced mood of their individualistic period. The illustrators of the 1950s had established new directions, and the new fashion vision came into focus through the photographer's lens. The illustrations used were very decorative and stylized, incorporating the bold inventiveness typical of the other visual arts of the era. These colorful fashion images contrasted sharply with those created by photographers. Costume reporting by means of illustration, while limited in high style periodicals, was used extensively in newspaper reporting, however. In this mass communication medium and in magazine advertising, fashion illustrations maintained the quality standards established by the masters of fashion art. The dynamic linear statements introduced by these artists when combined with photographic techniques present new visual communication possibilities. The challenge of the expressive reporting and recording potentials of creatively conceived fashion images, perceptive to and compatible with the times, is always present.

The style of Vertés's caustic linear
comment

Chapter 22

LINE THE ESSENCE OF A FASHION DRAWING

AN ARTIST communicates his responsive reactions to his subject through the linear quality of his sketch. His style (his unique personal imagery by which he makes his perception concrete in his work) is refined by his exploration of the expressive potential of line. His capacity to search out a personal style of linear statement is limited only by his perceptual responses and his ability to capture those responses on the drawing board. His power as a communication medium lies in his ability to relate his past experiences to current attitudes. Notes on the importance of line were once set down by an unknown friend of Michaelangelo. In these notes he suggested, "The science of design, or line drawing, if you like to use this term, is the source and very essence of painting, sculpture, architecture—all the works of the human brain and hand are . . . design, that is line . . ." By using line, a series of varying ordered marks, shapes develop and a concept is visually established. In fashion illustration, it is the concept of the current mode of costume. The line used by the fashion artist is as flexible and expressive as the mind of the artist is perceptive and his talent is capable. The limits of linear expression are those imposed by the artist.

The creation of an excellent communicating fashion drawing is faithful to contemporary aesthetic concepts and based on an understanding of certain linear qualities. These qualities are varied but interrelated. The following definitions establish a specific nomenclature by which lines with individual characteristics can be recognized or identified. Most of these linear qualities exist in and are necessary to all drawings, and they are present in random sketches and detailed drawings. They are inherent in realistic or abstract images. An excellent drawing is the result of visual perception and manual dexterity. The most carefully organized drawing has a sense of brevity, while the most random sketch has a sense of order, both achieved by using a variety of lines. Each line, or mark, has a specific quality that contributes to the next. Together they create a unified drawing.

Linear Attitude is that quality of line which suggests the general attitude of the main figure and establishes the mood of the situation. It is usually a combination of several types of lines, each with a particular weight, length, texture, and value. These lines must function together to create the illusion of the figure's action, the environmental situation, and the costume's styling. Linear attitude is most successfully established when the lines used are compatible to

"Debauche," Toulouse-Lautrec

"Le Sommeil." Toulouse-Lautrec

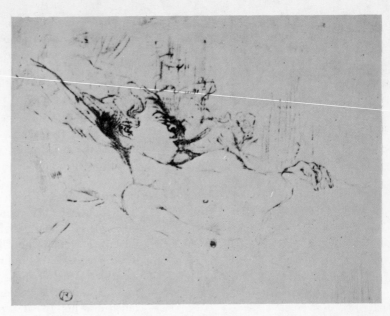

one another, consistently related, but not monotonous in their similarity. Consistency of linear attitude can be identified in the drawing by Toulouse-Lautrec, "Débauche." In this work the situation (linear attitude) is graphically communicated by a system of quickly drawn lines that have freedom and little order. Yet order exists, because of the repetition of similar lines, random urgent strokes, placed to speed the viewer's sight pattern over this sketch of a highly charged situation. The power of the line to reinforce the situation mood is apparent in another sketch by the same artist, "Le Sommeil." The complete relaxation of the figure, the total mood of the scene, is structured by the type, form, direction, and weight of the lines used. In Degas's "The Ballet Master" another mood is explored by a linear treatment that expands and communicates the character, mood, and attitude of the central figure. This figure is drawn with a combination of lines whose forms and directions seem to express the frustration of the ballet master toward the dancers in his charge. Many contemporary fashion artists also have the ability to create the mood and attitude of the figure by combining lines with expressive force that establishes a specific linear attitude. This is the result of intense observation of all types of figures in all types of situations and attitudes.

Implied Line, or *Negative Line*, is an "absent line" or "felt line," that develops between two areas of tension. These tensions are created by sharp contrasts of dark and light, bright and dull color, or angular shape against a flat or rounded shape. Basically, implied line capitalizes on the theory of closure, that optical phenomenon which forces the eye from one point of tension to another. Negative linear passages in fashion drawings function in several ways; they allow the figure-ground a close relationship; they create the illusion of sharp highlighting; and they permit the viewer to establish the line of closure of his choosing. Often the most vital passages in a fashion sketch are the result of the use of negative line. In Picasso's "Head of a Woman," implied line is used in the portion of the image that represents the forehead. No form definition is made, only a sight line

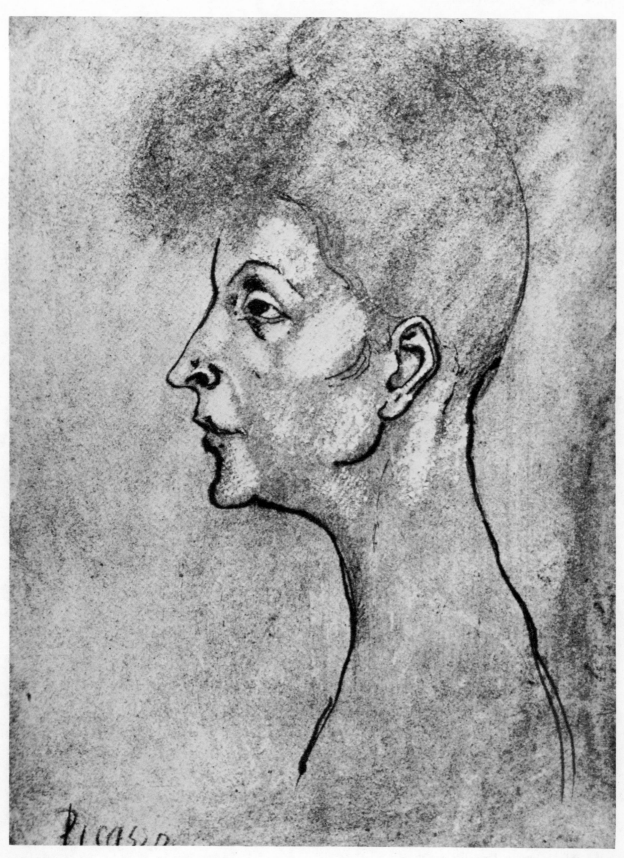

"Head of a Woman," Picasso (Thannhauser Collection, by courtesy
of Thannhauser Foundation, Inc., New York)

suggested. Form and drawing surface function as a total unit, not as an image applied to paper.

Multiple Line is a group or series of involved lines that simultaneously define form and establish value relationships within a drawing Because multiple line does not establish exactly defined shapes or forms, the selection of specific linear definition is left to the observer. In the Matisse drawing of Mme Manguin and in his sketch "Nude with Pipes," multiple line functions to establish the linear attitude as well as to define dark and light passages.

Linear Repetition involves the repeated use of lines with similar weight, length, and shape. The Matisse "Portrait of Mme Manguin" relies heavily on linear repetition to establish unity in the drawing. In addition to the unifying quality of linear repetition, expertly controlled, the use of the correct type of line can set a vivacious mood within a fashion illustration.

"Nude with Pipes," Matisse (permission S.P.A.D.E.M. 1969 by French Reproduction Rights, Inc.)

"Portrait of Mme Manguin," Matisse
(permission S.P.A.D.E.M. 1969 by
French Reproduction Rights, Inc.)

Linear Volume is established by a line whose outside contour represents a form contour and whose individual weight creates a volume or mass. The organization of the quick pen sketch, "Cock," by Bonnard is based on the use of linear volume. The bold linear structure creates a dual effect. Simultaneously the form of the cock represented is composed of lines that establish specific forms, and swell to create shadows, lines that define whole feathers (the tail) as well as one line that forms the cock's comb. Through the use of linear volume the spirit of the cock represented is created, not a photographic image of the cock.

Magnified Exaggeration is the combination of linear statements that distort the form's actual definition to emphasize its unique characteristics. This type of distortion depends on enlarging the form or magnifying its proportions. In the introduction of a new silhouette, attention can be concentrated on the fashion innovation by magnified exaggeration. Interest can also be directed to detailing features of a costume design in the same way, e.g., by enlarging the size of the collar, the width of the belt, or exaggerating the texture of the fabric.

Transitional Linear Movement is a series of lines whose weight, direction, and shape establish unified relationships between areas. Multiple line and linear repetition often combine to function as transitional linear movement. This quality of line also establishes the interrelationship between figure and ground. Transitional linear movement eliminates the conflicts that do develop between the illustration and the drawing surface.

Simplicity of Linear Statement is a quality which is developed by keen observation. Unnecessary features of costume, the figure and the environment, when recognized after careful study of the subject to be illustrated, may be discarded. This elimination of the unimportant factors creates simplicity of linear statement. Generalization of the visual facts described by simple and direct lines produces a simple and direct visual statement which communicates forcefully.

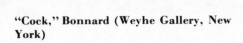

"Cock," Bonnard (Weyhe Gallery, New York)

Multiple line

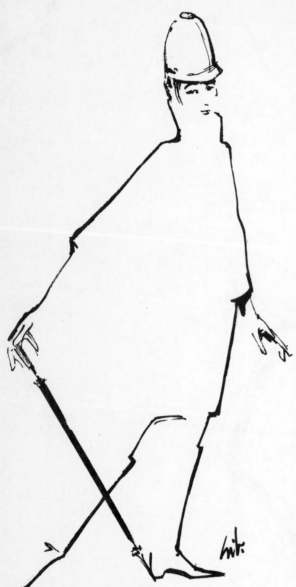

Linear simplicity and linear continuum describe form and mood.

Linear Elegance is that quality of line which depends on the artist's response to the costume. Linear elegance involves the subtle intangibles and refined aesthetic concepts that the artist has developed out of his personal experience. It results when the spontaneous reaction to a costume is set down on paper, and the personality classification, costume design, and situation are communicated. This visualization is most successful when the drawing is composed of lines that are selected for their ability to combine, for their differences, and their sameness.

The manipulation of the various media in creating fashion illustrations will produce lines with various qualities. Each artist from the time of primitive man to the present has explored the potentials of these media in his efforts to create communicating images. The sketches in da Vinci's notebooks, the confident random drawings of Picasso, or the vigorously executed images in the Altamira Caves dynamically illustrate the personality of the graphic communicators. Their drawings, in part, reflect their reactions as well as the limitations of their media. Their control over their media affects the final visualized images. Total mastery of the art of drawing depends on the design or composition of drawing areas. Composition of a drawing depends on the organization of lines with differing qualities. Degas has been called the "line impressionist." His compositional order depended on linear development that recorded gestures, environment, and social attitudes with plastic fluidity and an instantaneous quality. He was driven by an interest in capturing figures in chance action, but his design of the drawing was never by chance. Analysis of the design and linear statement in the drawing "Study of Nude" indicates Degas's sensitivity to the power of line to compose a drawing. The flexibility of line adds vitality to the design and to the mood of the drawing. Leonardo da Vinci and Matisse designed their drawings by using multiple line. Rodin, the sculptor, ordered the compositions of his sketches by combining linear repetition and multiple line. Picasso depended heavily on implied line, as did Latrouse-Lautrec and Degas, to create an organized unity in his drawings. Bonnard and Flannagan employed linear volume to create variation within their handsomely composed images. Artists and fashion artists consciously compose the lines of different qualities to create a unified image. In turn, they design the relationship of figure to ground to create a unified drawing.

An image is made more vital and a drawing more unified when the figure and ground are made one by letting the paper appear within a line. Both artist and fashion artist utilize the accidental happenings that occur as medium and drawing surface react to one another. In "Nude with Pipes" there is a casual order based on the interweaving of the form and ground because of the intrusion of the ground into the line. This drawing has a vital content and a vigorous linear vocabulary. The design is conceived by a thoughtful ordering of spaces and lines. A versatile linear vocabulary, thoughtfully ordered space, and a sensitive awareness of the potentials of the media used are essential in producing a successful fashion drawing.

Linear Variation is the most important quality of line, for it occurs in every drawing that is totally composed as a communicating image. The linear statement, if complete, full of vitality and dynamic, or languid and passive, relates these differing moods because varying lines have been used in its creation. Linear variation assisted in composing the many lithographs of Toulouse-Lautrec, the drawings of Rembrandt, and the sketches of Watteau. This quality eliminated the possibility of monotony in any drawing and particularly in a fashion illustration.

Subtle weight changes establish figure movement.

Linear Continuum is a line which may be either broad or narrow and defines a total form and its involved parts with one continuous, unbroken line. It may have the subtle delicacy which Klee used in "Child with Toy" to express the fragile character of the child. Linear continuum may also have the weight and subtle interweaving of the line and ground used by Lachaise in his drawing "Back of Nude Woman." Picasso's sketches done in his so-called classical period depend on linear continuum to establish their monumental quality. The fashion illustrator Gruau successfully used linear continuum in his sketches of chic women.

"Back of Nude Woman," Lachaise (in the Brooklyn Museum Collection, Brooklyn, New York)

Every artist's style has many phases as he explores all of these linear qualities that function as a communicating force through the medium he has selected. He uses these linear qualities in differing combinations to convey the intent of his visualized message. They serve to establish design and compositional order in his drawing. The linear vocabulary he develops depends on his creative capacity and innovative ability. Through dynamic linear order, fashion is vitalized and animated. An artist in the fashion field uses these means to record chic costumes on well-proportioned figure sketches that visualize the mood and attitude of the time. Drawings that have an air of vital conviction can establish an identity which the viewer can assimilate. Each drawing must contain the elements sought after by women interested in fashion. As Vertés said, "The meaning and spirit of contemporary fashion illustration is the subtle power that regulates the glow, sophistication, the elegance, the uniqueness, and the exquisiteness upon which feminine prestige is founded." The fashion artist gives attention, through exaggeration and linear comment, to the posturing gestures, the costume or "fluffy nothing" which women cannot do without, the illusive totality that is woman.

To capture these illusive qualities, the involved fashion illustrator develops a linear vocabulary which he adapts to the changing fashion silhouette. The fashion artist must be multifaceted so that he can communicate the vogue of his time through the images he creates. These images are abstractions of the human form which adapt with every silhouette change and become the embodiment of all the parts of the human form, designed to enhance the styling of the garment visualized. A well-designed fashion figure depends on an ability to translate the human form by adjusting the proportional relationships and by positioning of the parts of the figure. The positions of the figure parts in any given pose must be convincing. Accurate reference to the human form, with proportional distortions to meet the demands of the garment design, is made when the human figure is understood. An accurate reference may be either "suggestive," "academic," or "abstracted." The "suggestive," "academic," or "abstracted" fashion figure must always be consistent with the costume designer's concepts revealed in the design of the garment. The highly skilled fashion illustrator is able to control his innovative creativity to communicate the essence of the costume he is reporting.

When the first mark is made on the drawing surface, proportional relationships have been tentatively established. The artist adjusts the rest of the visualization of the image to that first mark, made after careful evaluation of the subject he is to draw. In the case of a fashion sketch he evaluates the silhouette, for this determines the proportions of the figure, the mood of the sketch, and the environmental detail needed to expand the mood. Different parts of the figure are emphasized as the silhouette changes. Though figure proportions vary with style change, general figure relationships are (using the head as a unit of measure): two head lengths from the top of the head to the bust; one from bust to waist; one from waist to hip socket; three from hip socket to knee; and three from knee to foot. Adjustments, because of costume design, are made in the length of the neck, feet, and the distance between the knee and the foot.

Drawing styles must adapt

As hems rise and fall, the leg length must be varied to give the figure more grace. The fashion figures created in the 1890s and those sketched in the 1940s graphically illustrate this point. During the era of the "New Look" (1947) and the "wafer silhouette" (1930), the height of the figure was extremely elongated, abstractly creating the illusion of feminine elegance. When skirts have higher hemlines, more conservative proportioning of the fashion figures is used.

The facial expression and its visual interpretation establish the linear attitude and the situation mood of a fashion sketch. The angle of the eyes, their expression and size, governs the size and proportions of the rest of the features. These, in turn, establish the proportional relationships of the rest of the figure, for the head size is a convenient unit of measure. The fashion illustrator must be concerned

Linear volume creates hand, hat, coat texture, and environment mood.

As head is turned, linear attitude as well as figure proportions are established.

with his visual statement that reads "eye" and the anatomical characteristics of this important expressive feature. There are a number of eye forms that can establish the mood and expand the functional concepts of the garment. Wide open, round eyes create the innocent illusion of youth, while hooded eyes with a side glance project an air of sophistication. In either case the definition of the eyes must be compatible with the indication of the brow. The eyebrow delineation functions as transitional linear movement from the eye to the hair and from the eye to the line marking the nose and to the mouth. Indication of eyes and mouths must also adjust to the current cosmetic fashions. As within the costume, so within the face, different features are emphasized during different fashion periods. Eyebrows of the 1930s were pencil thin and arched, during the 1940s they were arched and heavy. During the 1960s eye makeup was theatrical, colorful, and heavy false eyelashes were worn. Attention must be given to changing fashions in cosmetics and to the changing styles of coifs, for they are important in setting the linear attitude of the fashion sketch. Coiffures also function in the design of the drawing as transitional linear movement, relating the figure to the ground. The indication of hair and features must have linear consistency and simultaneously communicate visually the textural difference between them. The face as a unit is significant in gaining interest. The eyes function by giving impetus to the flow of the sight pattern over the costume. Individual or interestingly provocative features—but not grotesque, pedantic, or contrived expressions—can create the necessary interest and establish the desired sight pattern.

Facial contours are also important in creating the image of the selectively unique female with which women wish to be identified. There are many contour variables but generally they are: oval, round, heart, egg, or rectangular. During each style epoch there have been those face shapes which were fashionable or desirable. The tilt of the head and the contour definition of the cheek assist in confirming the mood established by the linear attitude. The complexity of the contour of the face, made up of concave and convex curves, can be described by linear variation and implied line. Variation of line conveys a vibrant and alert personality, implied line functions to inject the ground into the figure, and transitional linear movement acts to relate the head to the rest of the figure. The features, coiffure, and face contour must relate in line and proportion to the total figure. Linear qualities must visualize surface and textural differences, but must also be compatible with one another. Each part of the fashion sketch must communicate its inherent differences, but be coordinated to create a unified drawing. All of this must be done with flair, personally developed line, and wash techniques, and at the same time be conceptually faithful to the garment represented. An excellent fashion drawing establishes (through dynamically posed figures with facial expression, hands, feet and tilt of head deftly indicated), the current vogue. Fashion illustrations are a commentary on their times as they report and merchandise costume designs. A fashion drawing cannot be an excellent one unless it functions adequately for the purpose for which it was created, selling and reporting fashion trends. A fashion sketch cannot attain the function of a recording image unless it is created with the intent of being a fine visual art form.

BIBLIOGRAPHY

Amrams, Barney. *The Technique of Fashion Layout.* New York: Harper Brothers Publishers, 1949.

Ackermann, Rudolph. *Changeable Ladies; being an assemblage of moveable human features.* London: R. Ackermann, 1819.

Anspach, Karlyne. *The Why of Fashion.* Ames, Iowa: The Iowa State University Press, 1960.

Adams, James D. *Naked We Came: a more or less lighthearted look at the past, present, and future of clothes.* New York: Holt, Rinehart and Winston, Inc., 1967.

Adhélmar, Jean. *Toulouse-Lautrec, His Complete Lithographs and Drypoints.* New York: Harry W. Abrams, Inc., Publishers, 1965.

Allemagne, Henri René d'. *Les Accessoires du Costume et du Mobilier depuis le treizième siècle jusqu'au milieu du dixneuvième siècle.* Paris: Schmit, 1928.

Aretz, Gertrude. *The Elegant Woman from the Rococo Period to Modern Times,* with a preface by James Laver. London: G. G. Harrap & Co., Ltd., 1932.

Baker, Mrs. Blanch (Merrit). *Dramatic Costume Bibliography.* New York: The H. W. Wilson Company, 1933.

Ballard, Betina. *In My Fashion.* New York: Davis McKay Co., Inc., 1960.

Barfield, T. C. *Longman's Historical Illustrations: England in the Middle Ages; drawn and described.* 6 portfolios. New York: Longmans, Green & Co., Inc., 1915.

Beaton, Cecil Walter Hardy. *The Glass of Fashion.* Garden City, New York: Doubleday & Company, Inc., 1954.

Benet, William Rose. *The Reader's Encyclopedia.* New York: Thomas Y. Crowell Company, 1948.

Bertin, Celia, *Paris à la Mode,* trans. Marjorie Deans. New York: Harper & Brothers, 1957.

Blanc, Charles, *Art in Ornament and Dress,* trans. from the French. New York: Scribner, Wilford and Armstrong, 1877.

Bonney, M. Therese. *Remember When; a pictorial chronicle of the turn of the century and of the days known as Edwardian.* New York: Coward McCann, Inc., 1933.

Boucher, Francois. *20,000 Years of Fashion; the history of costume and personal adornment.* New York: Harry N. Abrams, Inc., 1966.

Braun-Ronsdorf, Margarete. *The Wheel of Fashion.* London: Thames and Hudson, Ltd., 1964.

Bridgwater, William, ed. *The Columbia-Viking Desk Encyclopedia.* New York: The Viking Press, Inc., 1953.

Carco, Francis. *Vertes.* New York: Atheneum Publishing Co., Inc., 1946.

Chase, Edna Wollman and Ilka. *Always in Vogue.* Garden City, New York: Doubleday & Company, Inc., 1954.

Chastel, Andre. *The Flowering of the Italian Renaissance,* trans. Jonathan Griffin, New York: The Odyssey Press, 1965.

Contini, Mila. *Fashion, from ancient Egypt to the present day,* ed. James Laver. New York: The Odyssey Press, 1965.

Corson, Richard. *Fashions in Hair, the first five thousand years.* London: Peter Owen, 1965.

Coughlan, Robert, and the editors of Time-Life Books. *The World of Michelangelo.* New York: Time Inc., 1966.

Craven, Thomas. *The Story of Painting; from cave pictures to modern art.* New York: Simon & Schuster, Inc., 1943.

Crawford, Morris De Camp. *The Philosophy of Dress.* New York: Bonwit-Teller Co., 1925.

_____ . *The Ways of Fashion.* New York: G. P. Putnam's Sons, 1941.

Cross, Milton. *Encyclopedia of the Great Composers and Their Music,* Vol. II. New York: Doubleday & Company, Inc., 1962.

Cunningham, Cecil Willet. *Why Women Wear Clothes.* London: Faber & Faber, Ltd., 1941.

_____ and Phyllis. *The History of Underclothing.* London: Michael Joseph Ltd., 1957.

Davenport, Millia. *The Book of Costume.* New York: Crown Publishers, 1966.

Dobkin, Alexander. *Principles of Figure Drawing.* New York: The World Publishing Company, 1966.

Doten, Hazel, and Counstance Boulard. *Fashion Drawing, How to Do It.* New York: Harper & Brothers, 1953.

Dubouchet, engr. Sigmund Freudenberger. *Estampes de Freudenberg pour le Monument du Costume.* Paris: L. Conquet, 1885.

Eimerl, Sarel, and the editors of Time-Life Books. *The World of Giotto.* New York: Time Inc., 1967.

Foote, Timothy, and the editors of Time-Life Books. *The World of Bruegel.* New York: Time Inc., 1968.

Frost, Rosamund, and Aimée Crane. *Contemporary Art, the March of Art from Cézanne until Now.* New York: Crown Publishers, 1942.

Forgarity, Ann. *Wife Dressing.* New York: Julian Messner, Inc., 1959.

Galvel, Wencealea. *Costtumbres Sateras Observacioneis.* N.d.

Gardner, Helen. *Art Through the Ages,* 3d ed. New York: Harcourt, Brace & Co., 1948.

Garland, Madge. *The Changing Face of Beauty, four thousand years of beautiful homes.* New York: M. Barrows and Company, 1959.

Grunwald, Henry A., and the editors of Time-Life Books. *The Age of Elegance.* New York: Time Inc., 1968.

Hawes, Elizabeth. *Fashion is Spinach.* New York: Random House Inc., 1938.

Head, Edith. *The Dress Doctor.* Boston: Little, Brown & Co., Inc., 1959.

Huer, Phillip. *Great Masters in Art.* New York: Crown Publishers, 1960.

Janson, H. W. *History of Art.* New York: Harry N. Abrams Inc., 1962.

Jarnow, Jeannette A., ed. *Inside the Fashion Business.* New York: John Wiley & Sons, Inc., 1965.

Kaufmann, Edgar, Jr. *What Is Modern Design?* New York: The Museum of Modern Art, 1950.

Kelly, Francis M., and Randolph Schwabe. *Historic Costume, 1490-1790.* London: B. T. Batsford, Ltd., 1925.

Köhler, Carl. *A History of Costume,* ed. and augmented by Emma von Sichart, tr. A. K. Dallas. New York: G. Howard Watt, 1928.

Koningsberger, Hans, and the editors of Time-Life Books. *The World of Vermeer.* New York: Time Inc., 1967.

Labovitch, Mark. *Clothes Through the Ages.* London: Quality Press, Ltd., 1944.

Leepa, Allen. *The Challenge of Modern Art*. New York: Beechhurst Press, 1957.

Leloir, Maurice. *Dictionnaire du Costume*. Paris: Librairie Grund, 1951.

Lester, Katherine, and Bess Oerke. *Accessories of Dress*. Peoria, Illinois: Charles A. Bannett Co., Inc., 1940.

Levin, Phyllis Lee. *The Wheels of Fashion*. Garden City, New York: Doubleday & Company, Inc., 1965.

Levy, Emile, ed. *M. Paul Cerau*. Paris: Librairie Centrale des Beaux Arts, 1882-1887.

Lewison, Sam Adolph. *Painters and Personality, a collector's view of modern art*. New York: Harper Brothers Publishers, 1948.

Leymarie, Jean. *The Drawings of Degas*. New York: Continental Book Center, 1948.

London, Adelaide Bolton. *Historic Costume Through the Ages*. Philadelphia: H. C. Perleberg, 1936.

Lucas, E. V. *The Wanderer in Florence*. New York: The Macmillan Company, 1912.

Marshall, Francis. *Fashion Drawing*. London, New York: The Studio Publications, 1948.

McJimsey, Harriet T. *Art in Clothing Selection*. New York: Harper & Row, 1963.

Monro, Isabel Stevenson, and Dorothy Elizabeth Cook. *The Costume Index*. New York: The H. H. Wilson Company, 1937.

Morse, Mrs. Harriet (Klamroth). *Elizabethan Pageantry; a pictorial survey of costume and its commentators from c. 1560-1620*. London: The Studio Ltd., 1934.

Payne, Blanche. *History of Costume*. New York: Harper & Row, Publishers, 1965.

Picken, Mary Brooks. *The Language of Fashion*. New York: Funk & Wagnalls, 1929.

Planché, James Robinson. *A Cyclopedia of Costume or Dictionary of Dress*, including notices of contemporaneous fashions on the continent, a general chronological history of the costumes of the principal countries of Europe, from the commencement of the Christian era to the accession of George the Third. London: Chatto & Windus, 1876-1879.

Pope-Hennessy, John. *The Portrait in the Renaissance*. New York: Pantheon Books, 1966.

Praz, Mario, tr. William Weaver. *An Illustrated History of Furnishing from the Renaissance to the 20th Century*. New York: George Braziller, Inc., 1964.

Prideaux, Tom, and the editors of Time-Life Books. *The World of Delacroix*. New York: Time Inc., 1966.

Rand, Paul. *Thoughts on Design*. New York: Wittenborn, Schultz, Inc., 1951.

Rashco, Bernard. *The Rag Race*. New York: Funk & Wagnalls, 1963.

Richardson, Herbert. *Costume in History*. London: Royal Society of Arts, 1934.

Rogers-Marz, Claude. *The Lithographs of Toulouse-Lautrec*. New York: The Continental Book Center.

Rosenberg, Adolph. *The Design and Development of Costume from Prehistoric Times up to the Twentieth Century*. London: W. & G. Foyle, Ltd., 1925.

Rudofsky, Bernard. *Are Clothes Modern?* Chicago: Paul Theobald & Company, 1947.

Ruhemann, H. and E. M. Kemp. *The Artist at Work*. London: Penguin Books, Ltd., George Putnam & Sons., Ltd., 1951.

Russell, Francis, and the editors of Time-Life Books. *The World of Dürer*. New York: Time Inc., 1967.

Schneider, Pierre, and the editors of Time-Life Books. *The World of Watteau*. New York: Time Inc., 1967.

Simon, Howard. *500 Years of Art and Illustration, from Albrecht Dürer to Rockwell*. New York: Garden City Publishing Co., 1948.

Stites, Raymond Somers. *The Arts and Man*. London and New York: McGraw-Hill Book Company, 1940.

Tenner, Edmond. *Tableau de Paris*. Paris: Lechevalier (Editions Paul), 1853.

Wallace, Robert, and the editors of Time-Life Books. *The World of Leonardo*. New York: Time Inc., 1966.

———————. *The World of Rembrandt*. New York: Time Inc., 1968.

Wedgewood, C. V., and the editors of Time-Life Books. *The World of Rubens*. New York: Time Inc., 1967.

West, Willis Mason. *Modern History*. Boston and Chicago: Allyn & Bacon, 1907.

Wheeler, Monroe. *Modern Drawing*. New York: Museum of Modern Art, 1946.

Wilcox, R. Turner. *The Mode in Costume*. London, New York: Charles Scribner's Sons, 1942, 1948, 1958.

Williams, Jay, and the editors of Time-Life Books. *The World of Titian*. New York: Time Inc., 1968.

Worth, Jean Philippe. *A Century of Fashion*, trans. Ruth Scott Miller. Boston: Little, Brown & Co., 1928.

Viking Press and VOGUE (compilers). *The World in Vogue*. New York: Viking Press, 1963.

IN PRINT PERIODICALS

Elle, 133 Champs Elysées, Paris, France

Femina, published by Societé d'Etudes et des Publications Economiques, 13 rue St. George, Paris, France (currently published as *Réalités*)

Harper's Bazaar, published by Hearst Magazines, Inc., 717 Fifth Avenue, New York 10022

Horizon, A Magazine of the Arts, published by American Heritage Publishing Co., Inc., 554 Fifth Avenue, New York 10017

Time, published by Time Inc., Time-Life Building, Rockefeller Center, New York 10020

Town and Country, published by Hearst Magazines, Inc., 717 Fifth Avenue, New York 10022

Vogue, published by Condé Nast Publications, Inc., 420 Lexington Avenue, New York 10017

Women's Wear Daily, published by Fairchild Publications, Inc., 7 E. 12 Street, New York 10003.

OUT OF PRINT PERIODICALS

Allgemeine Modenzeitung
Arbiter
Ars Suteria
Belle Assembles
Cahiers Bleus
Der Bazar
Flair
Galerie des Modes et Costumes Francais
Gazette de Bon Ton
Gazette de la Famille
Godey's Lady's Book
Journal des Dames
Journal des Dames et des Modes
La Femme Chic
La Mode
La Mode Illustrée
Modes Parisiennes
Peterson's Magazine
Vanity Fair

INDEX